Advancing Democracy Abroad

HOOVER STUDIES IN POLITICS, ECONOMICS, AND SOCIETY

General Editors
Peter Berkowitz and Tod Lindberg

Advancing Democracy Abroad

Why We Should and How We Can

Michael McFaul

HOOVER STUDIES
IN POLITICS, ECONOMICS,
AND SOCIETY

Published in cooperation with
HOOVER INSTITUTION
Stanford University • Stanford, California

ROWMAN & LITTLEFIELD PUBLISHERS, INC.
Lanham • Boulder • New York • Toronto • Plymouth, UK

ROWMAN & LITTLEFIELD PUBLISHERS, INC.

THE HOOVER INSTITUTION ON WAR, REVOLUTION AND PEACE, founded at Stanford University in 1919 by Herbert Hoover, who went on to become the thirty-first president of the United States, is an interdisciplinary research center for advanced study on domestic and international affairs. The views expressed in its publications are entirely those of the authors and do not necessarily reflect the views of the staff, officers, or Board of Overseers of the Hoover Institution.

www.hoover.org

Published in the United States of America by Rowman & Littlefield Publishers, Inc.
A wholly owned subsidiary of The Rowman & Littlefield Publishing Group, Inc.
4501 Forbes Boulevard, Suite 200, Lanham, Maryland 20706
www.rowmanlittlefield.com
Estover Road
Plymouth PL6 7PY
United Kingdom
Distributed by National Book Network

Published in cooperation with the Hoover Institution at Stanford University.

First printing, 2010
16 15 14 13 12 11 10 09   9 8 7 6 5 4 3 2 1
Manufactured in the United States of America

British Library Cataloguing in Publication Information Available

Library of Congress Cataloging-in-Publication Data Available

ISBN: 978-1-4422-0111-8 (cloth : alk. paper)
ISBN: 978-1-4422-0113-2 (electronic)

∞ The paper used in this publication meets the minimum requirements of American National Standard for Information Sciences—Permanence of Paper for Printed Library Materials, ANSI/NISO Z39.48-1992.

for Cole and Luke

Contents

Preface

After eight years of the George W. Bush Administration, most Americans, as well as many people around the world, had grown tired of the United States' efforts to promote democracy in other countries. During the Bush era, the methods for advancing freedom seemed blunt and the results appeared few. With the United States and the rest of the world facing a financial crisis by the end of 2008, supporting democracy or defending human rights seemed to many to be a secondary or peripheral concern.

By taking a longer historical perspective, this book seeks to make the opposite case. Under democracy, people around the world enjoy better government, more security, and economic development. In parallel, the advance of democracy abroad has made Americans safer and richer. Despite the limited results of the Bush Administration's attempts at democracy promotion, the United States and our allies also have developed a wide range of instruments that can facilitate democratic development. We should and we can still foster the advance of democracy around the world.

Given the popular backlash against democracy promotion, this book primarily focuses on answering the "should we" question. The last two chapters address the "can we" question, offering examples of successful strategies for democracy promotion in the past and outlining suggestions for how to support democratic development more effectively in the future.[1] The book is intended to be accessible to people with varying levels of expertise: the general reader, the American foreign policymaker, and the specialist on democracy promotion. In seeking to reach all three audiences, I have tried to keep jargon and technical language either out of the book altogether or hidden in the footnotes.

As an occasional political activist, I am not a dispassionate observer of democratic developments around the world. I admit it. The formative experience of my undergraduate days at Stanford University a quarter century ago was participating in the anti-apartheid movement. In the mid-1980s, I lived for two summers in Poland, where I drew inspiration from the then-struggling and underground Solidarity movement. I then lived in the Soviet Union during its waning years, eventually becoming an honorary member of the Democratic Russia movement. To this day, I remain connected to and in awe of democratic activists all over the world—in Afghanistan, Bahrain, Belarus, Burma, China, Egypt, Malaysia, Morocco, Uganda, Iran, Russia, Syria, and Zimbabwe——who risk their lives and well-being every day for the cause of democracy and human rights. But I am also a card-carrying member of the American Political Science Association. Although sometimes meandering into policy work, I always have

[1] My next book will extend the preliminary finding in chapters 5 and 6. It will be aimed primarily at the expert community in the field of democracy promotion.

gravitated to academia, where facts usually trump opinion, logical arguments generally prevail over convictions, and our peers exercise some degree of quality control over what we publish as scientific scholarship.

This book represents my attempt to square my deep convictions with my parallel commitment to rigorous social science standards.

1

The Backlash Against Democracy Promotion

In response to the terrorist attacks on September 11, 2001, President George W. Bush embraced the promotion of freedom around the world as a major foreign policy goal of his administration. Bush had not come to Washington to spread democracy around the world. On the contrary, before September 11, he championed modest foreign policy goals: building a national missile defense system, managing relations with China and Russia, and getting the United States out of the nation-building business. The September 11 attack, however, fundamentally altered Bush's perception of the threats to American national security, as well as his strategy for addressing them. Over time, promoting democracy abroad, or what Bush called his Freedom Agenda, emerged as a major component of his new grand strategy for fighting what he described as a global war on terror.[1] As he explained in May 2003,

The advance of freedom is the surest strategy to undermine the appeal of terror in the world. Where freedom takes hold, hatred gives way to hope. When freedom takes hold, men and women turn to the peaceful pursuit of a better life. American values and American interests lead in the same direction. We stand for human liberty.[2]

Bush devoted nearly his entire second inaugural address to explaining the mission. He first described why Americans should care about democracy abroad: "The survival of liberty in our land increasingly depends on the success of liberty in other lands. The best hope for peace in our world is the expansion of freedom in all the world."[3] Therefore, he argued, American foreign policy must "seek and support the growth of democratic movements and institutions in every nation and every culture, with the goal of ending tyranny around the world." In this speech, Bush used the word "freedom" twenty-five times, "liberty" twelve times, and "democracy'" or "democratic" three times. The following year, The National Security Strategy of the United States, issued by the White House in March 2006, opened with the following:

It is the policy of the United States to seek and support democratic movements and institutions in every nation and culture, with the ultimate goal of ending tyranny in our world. In the world today, the fundamental character of regimes matters as much as the distribution of power among them. The goal of our statecraft is to help create a world of democratic, well-governed states that can meet the needs of their citizens and conduct themselves responsibly in the international system.[4]

By the end of Bush's second term, political support for the president's focus on freedom had waned. In the last year of his administration, the U.S. Congress cut budgets to several democracy assistance programs.[5] Some presidential candidates and leaders from both parties either rejected or downplayed the importance of democracy promotion. Academia and the think-tank world produced a series of books and reports explaining why the Freedom Agenda had to end.[6] Perhaps most importantly, American popular support for the mission faded dramatically. In 2002, a Pew Global Attitudes Survey revealed that 70 percent of Americans agreed that the "US should be promoting democracy around the world." In a 2007 survey, only 23 percent of respondents believed the "US can effectively help other countries become democratic," while 64 percent thought "democracy is something that countries only come to on their own."[7] Only 26 percent of respondents in a 2005 national poll agreed with the statement, "When there are more democracies the world is a safer place," while 68 percent believed that "democracy may make life better within a country, but it does not make the world a safer place."[8] Americans also gave Bush poor marks as a democracy promoter. In a July 2006 poll conducted by NBC News and the Wall Street Journal, only 2 percent of respondents thought the Bush administration's efforts to promote democracy had been very successful; 37 percent thought his policies had been somewhat successful, 26 percent found them somewhat unsuccessful and 32 percent declared them to be very unsuccessful.[9]

Many factors and arguments produced this diminished support for democracy promotion. One line of criticism focused on the meager results of Bush policies. Seven years after President Bush made the Freedom Agenda a central issue of his foreign policy, it was not clear that more people were living in freedom than were a decade before.[10] Beginning in 2001, Freedom House counted 121 electoral democracies in the world. Between 2001 and 2008, some new electoral democracies emerged and others collapsed, resulting in the same number, 121, in 2008. Similarly, over the course of the Bush administration, the portion of countries classified as "free" by Freedom House increased only marginally, from 45 percent to 47 percent. Trends at the end of Bush's term were much worse than in his earlier years. According to Freedom House,

> The year 2007 was marked by a notable setback for global freedom . . . [R]esults of 2007 marked the second consecutive year in which the [Freedom House] survey registered a decline in freedom, representing the first two-year setback in the past 15 years. In all, nearly four times as many countries registered declines during the year as improvements.[11]

Where it mattered most, progress looked most minimal. In Afghanistan and Iraq, the regimes in place today are more democratic than the autocracies in both countries before American-led military interventions. Before their elimination, Taliban totalitarianism and Saddam Hussein's dictatorship ranked as two of the most ruthless regimes in the world. Yet, by the end of Bush's second term, democracy had not taken root in either country. In 2008, Freedom House rated Afghanistan a five and Iraq a six on a scale of one to seven, with one being the highest "free" ranking and seven being the lowest "not free" ranking.[12] Others assessed the situation in both countries in more dire terms.[13]

The use of military of force to advance freedom not only produced limited results in Afghanistan and Iraq, but also tainted all other American efforts to promote democracy. Bush's soaring rhetoric about liberty was juxtaposed with the instability in Iraq and Afghanistan, making it easy for autocrats and anti-Americans to argue that democratization was bad for individual countries and that this American "crusade" undermined world order. President Bush exacerbated the problem by trying to hold up Iraqi democracy as a model for other countries to follow. During a visit to St. Petersburg, Russia, in July 2006, Bush told a reporter he had talked to Russian President Vladimir Putin "about my desire to promote institutional change in parts of the world like Iraq where there's a free press and free religion, and I told him that a lot of people in our country would hope that Russia would do the same thing."[14] Putin responded, "We certainly would not want to have the same kind of democracy as they have in Iraq."[15] In other countries such as Egypt and Iran, democratic activists eventually considered it a liability to be seen or identified with the Bush administration or Americans more generally.[16]

During Bush's tenure, the Rose Revolution in Georgia in 2003 and the Orange Revolution in Ukraine in 2004 catapulted democracy forward in these former Soviet republics and inspired other challengers to autocracy in Lebanon, Kyrgyzstan, and Egypt the following year. However, the regimes in Ukraine and Georgia continue to struggle to consolidate democracy (in part because of a powerful autocratic neighbor, Russia) while the temporary advances in Egypt, Lebanon, and Kyrgyzstan were completely wiped out by subsequent anti-democratic developments.[17]

In this same time period, a budding renaissance of political thought began in the Middle East, which liberals in the region attributed in part to Bush's statements about freedom. Some autocratic leaders in the Middle East, including President Hosni Mubarak in Egypt, the kings in Morocco and Jordan, and the sheiks in the United Arab Emirates, Kuwait, and even Saudi Arabia, introduced marginal political reforms in the early years of

Bush's second term. By the end of Bush's time in office, however, trends in the region were moving against political liberalization, as Middle East authoritarians learned how to suppress political pluralism more effectively.[18] Most blatantly, Mubarak reversed his incremental political reforms entirely and jailed Ayman Nour, the Egyptian leader he had allowed to participate in the 2005 presidential election.

Elsewhere in the world, democracy made some hopeful advances, including most importantly in Pakistan in 2008, but also in Nepal, Bhutan, and Liberia. Malaysia also appears ripe for a genuine democratic transition. Bush's contributions to these gains, however, were hard to trace. In some cases, Pakistan in particular, Bush's support for the autocratic government delayed rather than fostered democratization. These marginal gains towards greater democracy in the world were more than offset by more serious democratic reversals in Russia, Zimbabwe, Iran, Bolivia, Kenya, Venezuela, and the Philippines during Bush's tenure.

In addition, the world's anti-democratic forces started to fight back during the Bush era.[19] Governments in Russia, Iran, and Venezuela did not simply defend their own autocratic systems, but provided ideas and resources to other anti-democratic governments and social movements.[20] China, by the power of example, offered a potent alternative for those in the developing world seeking economic growth above all else. This struggle between autocratic and democratic models is qualitatively different from the 1990s, when democracy seemed to have no rivals.

Just as crediting Bush with all democratic gains around the world would be wrong, holding Bush responsible for these anti-democratic trends is equally unfair. On balance, though, democracy did not advance and may have slightly receded from 2001 through 2009. This flat or negative trend is especially striking when compared to the dramatic advance of democratic government around the world in the 1980s and 1990s.[21]

A second attack on the Freedom Agenda focused on Bush's use of military force as an instrument for democracy promotion. For many Americans, the close association between the American-led invasion of Iraq and the Freedom Agenda—an association Bush promoted after the war began—dampened their support for democracy promotion. This correlation also had a partisan pattern. Polls show that while support for democracy promotion decreased among all Americans, it decreased more among Democrats than among Republicans.[22]

Even supporters of the general idea of democracy promotion criticized the Bush strategy.[23] The term "regime change," once an innocuous piece of jargon from American political science, became especially polarizing when used in the context of U.S. foreign policy because most American non-governmental organizations (NGOs) in the democracy promotion business reject it as an objective of their work. The very fact that American democracy promoters were debating whether they favor regime change in countries with dictatorships reflects the deep rift that Bush policies helped generate.[24]

A third argument rejects the very mission of democracy promotion, whether by Bush or any other American president. Self-described "realists" contend that the United States should not promote democracy because such a foreign policy objective does not serve American interests.[25] As Johanna Gowa has argued, "However desirable it might be on other grounds, an expansion of democracy abroad does not seem likely to enhance U.S. security."[26] Others in this camp contend that promoting democracy can trigger conflict between and within states. "Pushing countries too soon into competitive electoral politics," Edward Mansfield and Jack Snyder argue, "not only risks stoking war, sectarianism and terrorism, but it also makes the future consolidation of democracy more difficult."[27] Those who embrace realist ideology see a trade-off between stability and democracy, and therefore favor stability over democracy.[28] In their view, the U.S. should stop trying to change the world and instead focus on nurturing stability, courting allies to fight the war on terror, developing partners for mutual economic benefit, and pursuing "off shore" balancing of other great powers that might potentially threaten the United States.[29] Bush's soaring rhetoric and limited achievements regarding democracy promotion ushered in a renaissance in realism, not only in academia but on both sides of the partisan divide, and, by the middle of Bush's second term, within the Bush administration itself.[30] By the end of his term, even Bush's valedictory speeches downplayed the significance of democracy promotion among his goals or achievements.[31]

A fourth school of thought, closely related to the third, recognizes democracy promotion as a noble mission, but asserts that other foreign policy objectives must take precedence. As Richard Haass has argued,

> It is, however, neither desirable nor practical to make democracy promotion a foreign policy doctrine. Too many pressing threats in which the lives of millions hang in the balance—from dealing with today's terrorists and managing Iranian and North Korean nuclear capabilities to coping with protectionism and genocide—will not be solved by the emergence of democracy. Promoting democracy is and should be one foreign policy goal, but it cannot be the only or dominant objective. When it comes to relations with Russia or China, other national security interests must normally take precedence over con-

cerns about how they choose to govern themselves. The fact that promoting democracy can be difficult and expensive also reduces its attraction as a foreign policy compass.[32]

The analysts in this camp differ over what the priority should be. For some, the paramount goal of defeating jihadists pushes democracy promotion down to the sidelines. David Brooks, for instance, posited that the "next [American] leader will have to build a coalition of autocrats against the extremists, not grow apoplectically rigid in the face of their barbarism."[33] In making recommendations for how to recover from Bush's mistakes in the Middle East, Robert Kaplan suggested, "The [next] president may need to pull closer to the Saudi royals, Egypt's Hosni Mubarak and Jordan's King Abdullah."[34] For others, building effective states is the imperative.[35] Another camp stresses economic development and the elimination of poverty as the more pressing foreign policy issues, advocating a shift from the freedom agenda to a "prosperity agenda."[36] All of these critics agree, however, that President Barack Obama must move democracy promotion down on the list of priorities.

A fifth attack on democracy promotion comes from those who reject American involvement in foreign affairs altogether and call for greater attention to problems at home. Even previously forward-leaning engagement advocates such as Thomas Friedman have espoused nation-building at home instead of abroad, claiming that the United States is the "one who needs a better-functioning democracy—more than the Iraqis and Afghans. We are the ones in need of nation-building. It is our political system that is not working."[37] As the American economic crisis took deeper root in the fall of 2008, this lament grew wider. Isolationists from the left and right called for a major withdrawal of American engagement in the affairs of the outside world, especially the internal affairs of other countries.[38] Some in this camp even contended that the rhetorical emphasis on democracy promotion camouflaged a more sinister project to broaden America's empire.[39]

American Schizophrenia about Democracy Promotion

This policy debate about democracy promotion is not new. President Bush did not invent the notion of encouraging democracy abroad, and critics of that objective first surfaced at the very beginning of the American republic, not just in recent years.

Throughout American history, democracy promotion has competed with other U.S. objectives. No American president would disagree that the paramount objective of American foreign policy must always be to defend the security of the American people. Few presidents have made democracy promotion their primary strategy for achieving this goal. Other priorities—deterring military foes, forging alliances, securing access to stable flows of natural resources, creating and maintaining U.S. military bases, and expanding trade and investment opportunities for American corporations—took precedence. As the United States emerged as a global power, the desire for regional stability frequently trumped the call for democracy.

At the same time, and from the very beginning of the republic, U.S. leaders have consistently defined a special, ethical role for the United States in world affairs. Unlike the power-hungry European nations of the time, many American leaders championed the United States as a new moral force in international politics.[40] In the eighteenth and nineteenth centuries, advocates of America's special purpose had limited means and limited horizons; the state-led American impulse to promote democracy rarely extended outside the American hemisphere. Only after the United States entered World War I did President Woodrow Wilson attempt to introduce values onto the global stage.[41] Outlining his fourteen points for a new world order, he explained to a joint session of Congress in January 1918,

> What we demand in this war . . . is nothing peculiar to ourselves. It is that the world be made fit and safe to live in; and particularly that it be made safe for every peace-loving nation.[42]

In Wilson's view, the best way to achieve American security was not to defend the United States against the outside world but to change the outside world fundamentally. In policy circles, this tradition became known as Wilsonianism or Wilsonian liberalism.

Wilson's attempt to make the world safe for democracy failed. The Republican-controlled Senate even blocked American membership in his League of Nations. The Great Depression in the 1930s turned Americans inward again, affirming for a while another long-standing tradition in American foreign policy—isolationism. The rise of Nazi Germany and Communist Russia in Europe and the onset of World War II stimulated the emergence of another philosophy about American foreign policy—realism.[43] In response to Wilson's "naive idealism," realists countered that the United States had to pay greater attention to the capabilities of states and the balance of power between them. How states were organized internally—whether they were democratic or autocratic—mattered much less. This school rose to prominence during the Cold War, when the chief imperative for American foreign policymakers became containing Soviet power. During the

Cold War period, this theory of international affairs also dominated American academic thinking.

During the Cold War, however, the impulse to promote
democracy abroad did not disappear. On the contrary, American
politicians invented an assortment of new foreign policy tools—
including the United States Agency for International Development (AID), the Peace Corps, the Alliance for Progress, Radio
Free Europe, and the National Endowment for Democracy
(NED)—to encourage democratic change in other countries.

Liberal and realist tendencies in American foreign policy
were not tied to the president's political party. Republican President Richard Nixon and his chief foreign policy adviser, Henry
Kissinger, spoke and acted like classic realists who, for example,
sought to preserve America's position in the world by reaching
out to China to balance against rising Soviet power. While in office, Nixon and Kissinger cared little about the internal politics
of the USSR or China. As Nixon once told Chinese leader Mao
Zedong, "What is important is not a nation's internal political
philosophy. What is important is its policy toward the rest of the
world and toward us."[44] In contrast, fellow Republican President
Ronald Reagan devoted more attention to domestic regimes,
crafting policies that sought to undermine anti-democratic governments.[45] Reagan worried more about communist dictatorships
in Eastern Europe than about capitalist dictatorships in Africa or
Latin America. Nonetheless, Reagan's approach to international
politics had more in common with that of Democratic presidents
Wilson and Harry Truman than with Nixon's. At critical moments, Reagan was even prepared to help ease old autocratic allies out of power in favor of new democratic challengers.[46]

The Cold War's end did not resolve this debate between realists and liberals. Soviet democratization and then dissolution—
not arms control or Soviet military decline—eventually reduced

Cold War tensions, an outcome that seemed to confirm the liberal view of world politics. Yet, even as the Soviet Union democratized and then imploded, President George H.W. Bush and most of his senior foreign policy advisors supported Soviet leader Mikhail Gorbachev, placing territorial preservation of the Soviet Union ahead of democratization as an American national interest.[47] Under President Bill Clinton, the pendulum swung back toward liberalism. The idea of a democratic peace in which democracies do not go to war against each other became a mantra of U.S. rhetoric in the 1990s.[48] Clinton and his senior foreign policy advisors made democratic enlargement a principal foreign policy objective.[49] On the eve of his first presidential trip abroad to meet Russian President Boris Yeltsin in April 1993, Clinton described his strategy for dealing with Russia in the following manner:

> Think of it—land wars in Europe cost hundreds of thousands of American lives in the twentieth century. The rise of a democratic Russia, satisfied within its own boundaries, bordered by other peaceful democracies, could ensure that our nation never needs to pay that kind of price again. I know and you know that, ultimately, the history of Russia will be written by Russians and the future of Russia must be charted by Russians. But I would argue that we must do what we can and we must act now. Not out of charity but because it is a wise investment. . . . While our efforts will entail new costs, we can reap even larger dividends for our safety and our prosperity if we act now.[50]

In his State of the Union address the following year, Clinton explained very explicitly why the United States had an interest in promoting democracy abroad: "Ultimately the best strategy to ensure our security and to build a durable peace is to support the advance of democracy elsewhere. Democracies don't attack each other, they make better trading partners and partners in diplomacy."[51] The Clinton administration also saw enlargement of the North Atlantic Treaty Organization (NATO) as a way to expand the democratic community of European states.[52] At times, including most dramatically in the 1999 war against Serbia, Clinton was even prepared to use military force for moral purposes.

Throughout the twentieth century, even when realists were the principal architects of American foreign policy, democracy and human rights promotion was never completely abandoned. At the height of Nixonian realism, Senator Henry "Scoop" Jackson (D-WA) and Representative Charles Vanik (D-OH) added an amendment to the Trade Act of 1974, linking "most favored nation" trade status for the Soviet Union to Jewish emigration levels. Although Nixon did not believe in promoting American values abroad, several congressmen remained committed to defending human rights.[53] Conversely, during the height of Reagan's liberalism, building up American armed forces to balance Soviet power also was a top priority.[54] Rarely have the members of American administrations been unanimous in their views. Instead, internal divides on this central foreign policy issue often provide major drama between fighting factions within the bureaucracy.[55] Whether to engage in democracy promotion has always been an American debate.

Do We Know How to Promote Democracy?

Even when there is the will to promote democracy, there is not always the way. Democracy promotion is neither a science nor an engineering problem, and theoretical disagreements persist about how democracies emerge and how they endure.[56] Is democratization nurtured by economic growth and modernization more generally or do economic crises trigger abrupt democratic change?[57] Is the process driven by structural conditions or by individual actions? Are elite leaders more important than mass movements? Does democracy come from conflict or compromise?[58] Are some cultures more prone to democracy than others? To date, scholars have has no clear answers to these fundamental questions.

Big debates also continue over institutional design. Are parliamentary systems more stable and more democratic than presidential systems or is semi-presidentialism the best design? Is proportional representation a better electoral system than first-past-the-post electoral laws? When are unitary states preferable to federal systems? There is also disagreement on the best sequence for democratic reforms. Which should come first: elections or a constitution? Should regional elections be held before national elections? Is the rule of law a necessary precondition for effective elections? If so, how can we postpone elections while legal institutions develop? A similar debate has gained steam about whether capable states or democratic regimes come first. Among democratic theorists, no consensus exists on the relative importance of political parties, civil society, and courts.

Not surprisingly, therefore, our understanding of how international instruments impact domestic outcomes remains underdeveloped.[59] From the late 1960s through the 1990s, scholars portrayed the democratic transition process essentially as a domestic drama.[60] As late as the early 1990s, the role of international actors was correctly described as the "forgotten dimension" in the study of democratization.[61] Since then, academia and the think tank world have devoted much greater attention to understanding the international dimensions of democratization, but the subject still remains strikingly understudied.[62]

This lack of understanding about democratization in turn has produced inconsistent U.S. policies regarding democracy promotion, even when presidents and their advisors were committed to the cause. For instance, advocates of modernization theory push for increased trade with autocratic regimes to promote democracy, as in American policy toward China. Conversely, those convinced that economic crisis triggers democratic change advocate economic sanctions to precipitate democratization. American policy toward Iran and Cuba in recent decades reflects this strategy.

Similarly, U.S. democracy promoters have advocated a variety of approaches to institutional design, oftentimes espousing conflicting models in the same country. For instance, some American officials favored a strong presidential system in Russia in the early 1990s to best implement radical economic reforms, while other U.S. advisors pushed for a parliamentary democracy and proportional representation to stimulate party development and, in their view, create a more democratic regime.[63] After the invasion of Afghanistan, U.S. institutional designers recommended a presidential system, whereas after the invasion of Iraq, U.S. advisors pushed for a parliamentary system. The divergence had less to do with optimizing democracy and more to do with short-term calculations about U.S. allies on the ground. In Afghanistan, American officials saw Hamid Karzai as a strong American ally and pressed for a system that would give him the most power. In Iraq, they were unable to identify a similar individual, so U.S. institutional designers pressed for a parliamentary system there.[64] American officials demonstrated similar inconsistency in advocating different electoral laws in Afghanistan and Iraq.

Given the analytic confusion about how democracies emerge and consolidate, American government agencies and NGOs that assist new democracies have resorted to checklists.[65] Liberal democracies in the West have constitutions, parliaments, supreme courts, ombudsmen, political parties, independent media, bar associations, trade unions, women's organization, and human rights monitoring groups; new democracies, presumably, required a similar set of institutions and organizations. Especially in the former communist world, where very few of these institutions existed at the time of communism's collapse, the initial strategy for democracy promotion (and everything else) was simply to try everything and see what worked.

Resources for Democracy Promotion

If American officials rarely make democracy promotion a top priority, and if academics and practitioners remain uncertain about how best to support democratic development, it should be no surprise that the resources devoted to this endeavor have remained minuscule for most of American history.

Since the Spanish-American War in 1898 and the subsequent occupation of the Philippines, American presidents have deployed economic and military resources intermittently to foster democratic change following the use of American force, and especially after American occupation. However, these efforts at regime transformation after war have always been episodic and never the product of a deliberate strategy to foster democratic change. The absence of a consistent effort is explained in part by the fact that the United States' use of military force has always been driven by immediate national security objectives. Only after American military forces have engaged in combat has the mission expanded to include fostering democratic development (albeit often in a haphazard way). Strikingly, a bureaucracy to foster post-war democratic governance does not exist in the U.S. government. After the wars began in Afghanistan and Iraq, the Bush administration recognized this void and created in 2004 the Office of the Coordinator for Reconstruction and Stabilization (S/CRS) within the State Department "to enhance our nation's institutional capacity to respond to crises involving failing, failed, and post-conflict states and complex emergencies."[66] Yet the paltry budget for this office underscores the American uneasiness with institutionalizing state-building, and especially democratic state-building, as a function of the U.S. government.

For the first one hundred years of American history, the United States government devoted very few resources to fostering democratic change abroad. The United States devoted major resources to democracy building and state building more generally to the Philippines after the Spanish-American War, but that project's failure produced a major retreat from democracy promotion thereafter. Not until the Cold War, when the United States faced a foe that sought to export its system of government, did the nation become directly involved in this effort again. In 1942, Voice of America (VOA) began broadcasting with the indirect aim of propagating the American system of government. The United States waged an information campaign against Soviet communism with the creation of the CIA-sponsored Radio Free Europe in 1949 and Radio Liberty in 1951. Their missions were to broadcast independent news analysis into Eastern Europe and the Soviet Union respectively.[67] Over time, the U.S. came to use this method of promoting democratic change by circulating independent news and propagating democratic ideas in most of the autocratic world. VOA eventually reached nearly the entire world, and later expanded to include satellite and local television programming. Radio Free Asia provided an avenue of communication into China and other Asian autocracies, and Radio Marti provided a similar vehicle in Cuba. In 1998, Radio Free Europe/Radio Liberty started Radio Free Iraq, which eventually became Radio Sawa, and a Persian radio service for Iran, which became Radio Farda.

Broadcasting news and championing the American model of governance through the media represented an indirect approach to fostering democratic development. President John F. Kennedy launched a more direct program. Because senior officials on his foreign policy team believed that economic development and democratic change were intertwined, they began a series of new initiatives—including, most importantly, the Alliance for Progress with Latin America, AID, and the Peace Corps. All were designed to encourage economic development as a means of fostering democratization. The Alliance for Progress Charter defined the strengthening and improvement of democratic institutions as a goal, but focused programmatically on land reform, improved health care, more affordable housing, and better education. Likewise, for the first three decades of AID's existence, its principal focus remained social and economic development, not democracy promotion.

American democracy promotion efforts marked an important milestone in 1983 with the creation of the National Endowment for Democracy (NED). Although funded by the U.S. Congress, NED was an independent NGO focused exclusively on democracy promotion. To insulate the organization from day-to-day policy concerns of the U.S. government, NED established a bipartisan board. Rather than provide direct aid to government institutions or technical assistance to civil society organizations, NED provided direct grants to democratic organizations, a radical innovation at the time. In stark contrast with the CIA, NED also provided only overt aid and no military assistance. At the same time NED was established, four other independent organizations were created with NED funding: the

International Republican Institute, or IRI (formerly the National Republican Institute), affiliated with the Republican Party of the United States; the National Democratic Institute for International Affairs, or NDI, affiliated with the Democratic Party of the United States; the American Center for International Labor Solidarity (ACILS, formerly the Free Trade Union Institute, FTUI), created and run by the AFL-CIO; and the Center for International Private Enterprise (CIPE), affiliated with the U.S. Chamber of Commerce.[68]

Funding for NED and its affiliated organizations remained paltry for much of the 1980s and early 1990s, reaching roughly $30 million a year by 1993 and facing constant threats of cuts from Congress.[69] The scope of NED and its affiliates expanded dramatically over the next two decades, however, especially after NDI and IRI began to obtain funding directly from AID after the collapse of communism. Congress also encouraged a greater focus on democracy promotion by passing the Support for Eastern Europe Democracy (SEED) Act and the Freedom for Russian and Emerging Eurasian Democracies and Open Markets (FREEDOM) Support Act (FSA) for the former Soviet Union, both of which provided new funds for economic and democratic assistance for the post-communist region.[70] In 1994, the Clinton administration also created a new bureau on Democracy, Human Rights, and Labor (DRL) within the State Department, which also developed a small grants program for democracy assistance. With the announcement of its "Democracy Initiative" in December 1990, AID established democracy promotion as a central objective and soon became the main funder of U.S. democracy assistance programs, with a budget dwarfing that of NED. With this expansion, the list of AID partners for democracy and governance programs extended well beyond the NED family.

Several very old organizations are more recent recipients of AID funding, including Freedom House, the International Research & Exchanges Board (IREX), the African-American Institute, and the Asia Foundation. Newer democracy promotion NGOs have also received AID support, including the International Foundation for Electoral Systems (IFES), which monitors, supports, and strengthens the mechanics of the election process in emerging democracies; the American Bar Association's Central and East European Law Initiative (ABA/CEELI), which promotes rule of law; and Internews, an organization focused on promoting independent media. In addition to these non-profit NGOS, many for-profit companies have developed democracy and governance divisions since the mid 1990s. Both the NGOs and the for-profit companies, which had originally focused on economic development, expanded their operations to include democracy and governance.[71]

After September 11, 2001, President Bush offered all these organizations greater funding. Promoting democracy had become a principle objective of American foreign aid.[72] In 2008, NED's budget grew from $40 million in 2001 to $100 million.[73] DRL's budget expanded dramatically, from $7.82 million in FY 1998 to more than $126.55 million in FY 2006, before dropping back down to $64 million in FY 2008.[74] Within the State Department, the Bush administration also created the Middle East Partnership Initiative (MEPI) in 2002. Its mission was to implement Bush's "forward strategy of freedom" by providing small grants to civil society actors in the region.[75] MEPI's budget grew from $29 million in FY 2002, to $100 million in FY 2003, before decreasing to roughly $150 million in FY 2005. The Bush administration also helped to launch the Foundation for the Future, an organization whose mission is "to support civil society organizations (CSOs) in their efforts to foster democracy and freedom in the Broader

Middle East and North Africa while recognizing and respecting the uniqueness of the heritage and culture of each country."[76] By FY 2009, the United States government was spending $1.72 billion on what the Bush administration called "Governing Justly and Democratically," up from $600 million in FY 2001.[77]

Through the Millennium Challenge Corporation (MCC), another new organization created by the Bush administration, some economic assistance also became explicitly tied to democratic change.[78] Although most of its sixteen indicators for judging performance are economic, the MCC has incorporated three indicators under the category of "ruling justly" into its criteria for lending, giving countries that seek economic assistance a clear incentive to meet certain democratic standards. Creators of the MCC also hoped that the transparent articulation of threshold indicators would insulate MCC decision-making from American strategic considerations.[79] As Bush stated very explicitly, the MCC was supposed to "reward nations that root out corruption, respect human rights, and adhere to the rule of law."[80]

These institutional innovations and expanded budgets underscored a real shift in attention towards democracy assistance, especially in the Middle East, during the Bush administration. Compared with spending on defense or even as a fraction of total foreign assistance, however, resources for supporting democratic development remained minuscule even at the height of the Bush administration's focus on these efforts. In FY 2008, Bush requested $481.4 billion for the Department of Defense's base budget and an additional $141.7 billion in supplemental funds for the "Global War on Terror."[81] In other words, the United States planned to spend 479 times more on defense than on democracy promotion in the final year of Bush's term. No one could cite this ratio as evidence to suggest that the United States assigns serious priority to democracy promotion.

A Roadmap

Despite the relatively few American successes in promoting democracy recently, our rather underdeveloped understanding for how democratization occurs, and the limited resources available for supporting democratic development abroad, this book still aims to make the case that the United States should promote democracy and that, under the right circumstances and with the right policies, the United States can promote democracy. Many of the recent assessments of Bush policy limitations have merit. But the policy response to these diagnoses should not be isolation, a return to realism, or a rejection of the objective of democracy promotion. Short term, knee-jerk reactions against Bush could produce long-term negative strategic consequences for American national interests. Those fighting tyranny and seeking to advance democracy around the world also would suffer. Instead, the leaders responsible for pursuing American national security interests after the Bush administration must remember the moral, security, and economic interests the United States has in promoting democracy, and then look for ways to pursue this policy objective more effectively.

The next three chapters make the case for why the United States should promote democracy. Chapter 2 discusses the advantages of a democratic system of government, outlining why democracies provide more accountable government and a better guarantee of basic human rights, why democracies tend to provide more prosperity, and why democracies produce more security for their citizens and neighbors compared with other forms of government. Chapter 3 makes the case that the advance of democracy abroad serves American security and economic interests at home. Chapter 4 explores more speculatively how increasing democracy around the world in the future might serve American national interests.

To posit that the United States should promote democracy is not an endorsement of the Bush policies. We must develop a new course to rebuild the international legitimacy and domestic support needed to sustain democracy promotion for the long haul. Chapters 5 and 6 offer a set of recommendations for charting this new course. Chapter 5 examines the changes needed in U.S. policy and Chapter 6 outlines actions that American leaders should take to further internationalize democracy promotion efforts.

2

The Value of Democracy

"No one pretends that democracy is perfect or all-wise. Indeed, it has been said that democracy is the worst form of Government except all those others that have been tried from time to time."

Winston Churchill

If Churchill was right, it has taken the world a long time to appreciate his wisdom. For millennia, monarchs, emperors, and kings ruled on supposed authority from God. In the name of the Almighty, they claimed legitimacy over alternative methods of government, including democracy. In the twentieth century, communist and fascist thinkers crafted alternative political models to both monarchy and democracy. When these ideologues seized control of powerful states such as Germany and Russia, a normative debate about democracy and its alternatives accompanied the power struggle between the world's superpowers. As late as 1942, only twelve democratic regimes existed in the world.[1] The ideological contest between communism and democracy was particularly competitive, since communist doctrine championed normatively appealing goals, including modernization and equality. For a while, the Soviet economic model of state ownership and fixed prices produced growth rates on par with or higher than those of capitalist economies.

Eventually, command economies faltered, opponents to communist dictatorship strengthened, the Soviet empire collapsed, and this challenger to democracy as a system of government all but vanished, except for a few isolated pockets of true believers left in Havana, Moscow, and Berkeley. However, the idea that autocracies are better than democracies at producing such valued public goods as economic growth, stability, and order is alive and well throughout the world. The Chinese economic miracle, stewarded by a Communist Party dictatorship, provides a powerful contemporary challenge to Churchill's claim. Stability is another highly valued condition that some think autocracies are better at providing than democracies. The calm and predictability of monarchies in Morocco and Saudi Arabia look rather attractive when compared to the chaos of Afghanistan or Iraq.

Some democracy critics also claim that autocracies are better at providing order and rule of law. Others contend that democratizing states are more likely to initiate war than other kinds of regimes.[2] Still others believe democratization weakens state power and therefore the ability of these states to fight terrorism or other nasty authoritarian regimes. More subtly, some argue that democracy is a good system of government, but only for some peoples and at the appropriate time. In addition, the close association of the idea of democracy with the United States has compelled some critics of American power to become opponents of democracy. Osama bin Laden and his lieutenants have been most adept in using this line of thought to develop an ideological movement, which not only rejects democracy as the best system of government, but offers an alternative values-based polity. Few people in the world actually subscribe to Osama bin Ladenism and its ideological soul mates, but anti-Americanism around the world has generated increased antipathy towards liberal and democratic values.

These critics are wrong. Democracy is a difficult form of government. As a construct for making governing decisions, democracy cannot solve all problems immediately. But compared to other regimes, democracy is a better system of government— one that can produce economic development just as well as autocracies do and one that does not produce or encourage greater conflict than other forms of government.

To understand the virtues of democracy, we need first to have a working definition of the term, recognizing that this system of government takes many forms, some of which bear little resemblance to American democracy. That will be the assignment for the first part of this chapter. Section two makes the case for why democracy is the best system of government. Section three provides evidence to support the claim that most people around the world have come to accept democracy as the best system of government. Section four explores the relationship between democracy and development, demonstrating that democracies on average do not grow at a slower rate than autocracies and that under certain circumstances, democratic transitions can spur increased growth. Section five examines the relationship between democracy and security, making the case that democracy is a more peaceful and stable form of government than others. Section six reexamines arguments about sequencing, addressing hypotheses about the need for modernization, state-building, and liberalism before democracy.

Defining Democracy

There is no universally accepted definition of democracy. Analysts and leaders have stretched the concept to describe so many different varieties of political systems that the term has lost some of its descriptive meaning. As Seymour Martin Lipset and Jason Lakin have remarked, "There are almost as many theoretical definitions of democracy as there are scholars who study democratic politics."[3]

This book follows Joseph Schumpeter in defining democracy most minimally as "the institutional arrangement for arriving at political decisions in which individuals acquire the power to decide by means of a competitive struggle."[4] The method of selection almost always now must come through elections of some sort, in which all citizens of a certain age can participate. Universal franchise is now a necessary component of democracy. Elections also must be conducted according to fixed or certain rules, but with some uncertainty about the outcomes—that is, some competition. As Adam Przeworski pithily stated, "Democracy is a system in which parties lose elections."[5] Once an election occurs, those who lost or who oppose the outcome may not reverse the results, be they incumbents, the military, or a religious authority. Elections also must be held for offices that actually govern, not for decorative bodies with little or no power. This minimal definition of democracy is often called *electoral democracy*.

Electoral democracy is qualitatively different from autocracy. Autocracy also comes in many forms, but its essence consists of one distinctive feature: a subset of the population, not all citizens, selects the government.[6] This subset can consist of a royal family, the landed aristocracy, a hegemonic party, a military junta, or religious leaders.[7] In democracies, citizens elect the leaders. In autocracies, a group of elites selects the leaders.

The distinction between democracy and autocracy is not always easy to discern, both because many autocracies contain some democratic elements, and because some autocracies have learned how to disguise their system of rule by mimicking democratic procedures. For instance, almost all countries in the world today hold elections in which most people can participate. Nonetheless, elections do not guarantee democracy because autocratic leaders can hold formal elections without allowing voters truly to have a say in who governs. Autocrats may manipulate the electoral process by limiting who can appear on the ballot, constraining the campaign arena by denying some candidates access to financial resources or national media outlets, or falsifying the actual election results.[8] Clever autocrats also allow some degree of independent media, organized civil society, and even opposition political parties to give the regime a democratic veneer. This kind of autocracy has become especially prevalent since the 1990s.[9]

A competitive and meaningful election is the pivotal feature of a democratic political system—the one attribute that distinguishes democracy from autocracy. More developed or what some refer to as liberal, democracies have many other features beyond elections.[10] Terry Karl and others have warned rightly about the "fallacy of electoralism," cautioning against an overemphasis on elections accompanied by a neglect of other institutions that make democracies work.[11] Many agree with this observation, but arguments quickly emerge over what else needs to be included in the definition of liberal democracy. More expansive def-

initions, for instance, add themes of equality, justice, private property, and "economic democracy." Liberal democracy as defined in
this book is more restrictive, and includes only political components, as outlined most comprehensively by Larry Diamond:

1. Control of the state and its key decisions and alloca-
   tions lies, in fact as well as in constitutional theory,
   with elected officials (and not democratically unaccountable actors or foreign powers); in particular, the
   military is subordinate to the authority of elected
   civilian officials.

2. Executive power is constrained, constitutionally and
   in fact, by the autonomous power of other government institutions (such as an independent judiciary,
   parliament, and other mechanisms of horizontal accountability).

3. Not only are electoral outcomes uncertain, with a significant opposition vote and the presumption of party
   alteration in government, but no group that adheres
   to constitutional principles is denied the right to form
   a party and contest elections (even if electoral thresholds and other rules exclude small parties from winning representations in parliament).

4. Cultural, ethnic, religious, and other minority groups
   (as well as historically disadvantaged majorities) are
   not prohibited (legally or in practice) from expressing
   their interests in the political process or from speaking
   their language or practicing their culture.

5. Beyond parties and elections, citizens have multiple, ongoing channels for expression and representation of their interests and values, including diverse, independent associations and movements, which they have the freedom to form and join.

6. There are alternative sources of information (including independent media) to which citizens have politically unfettered access.

7. Individuals also have substantial freedom of belief, opinion, discussion, speech, publication, assembly, demonstration, and petition.

8. Citizens are politically equal under law (even though they are invariably unequal in their political resources).

9. Individual and group liberties are effectively protected by an independent, nondiscriminatory judiciary, whose decisions are enforced and respected by other centers of power.

10. The rule of law protects citizens from unjustified detention, exile, terror, torture, and undue interference in their personal lives not only by the state but also by organized non-state or anti-state forces.[12]

No regime in the world meets Diamond's high standards. As Robert Dahl has observed, "In every democratic country a substantial gap exists between actual and ideal democracy."[13] Every democracy can be improved. Nonetheless, Diamond's list does help us establish a benchmark for measuring different kinds of democracies and making judgments about why some democracies should be considered of higher quality than others. Scholars and politicians do not recognize a universal set of metrics for measuring democracy. In the United States, the non-partisan, nongovernmental organization Freedom House has the longest tenure in measuring freedom, but several new indices, including the Polity index, have begun to challenge its monopoly on judging the extent of democracy in other countries.[14] Broad agreement in academia and the policy community has emerged on both a minimalist definition of democracy and the kinds of institutions and attributes needed to transform electoral democracies into more robust democratic systems of government.

Varieties of Democracy

The adjective "American" does not appear on Diamond's list of ideal characteristics for liberal democracy. The American political system is a liberal democracy, but many other different designs work equally well if not better. In fact, many institutional features of the American political system work less effectively and less democratically in other countries. For instance, the creation of the office of the president and the separation between the executive and legislative branches of government—a constitutional feature Americans celebrate for guaranteeing checks and balances—has helped to undermine democracy in other regions of the world.[15] According to Przeworski, Michael Alvarez, Jose Antonio Cheibub, and Fernando Limongi,

> the expected life of democracy [in the developing world between 1950 and 1990] under presidentialism is approximately twenty-one years, whereas under parliamentarism it is seventy-three years.[16]

Presidential systems are more prone to coups than are parliamentary systems, and they also breed what Guillermo O'Donnell has called delegative democracy, in which

> whoever wins election to the presidency is thereby entitled to govern as he or she sees fit, constrained only by the hard facts of existing power relations and by a constitutionally limited term of office.[17]

Under Hugo Chavez in Venezuela, Robert Mugabe in Zimbabwe, or Vladimir Putin in Russia, delegative democracy devolved into autocratic rule. By contrast, Steven Fish has demonstrated that "the presence of a powerful legislature is an unmixed blessing for democratization" because it strengthens horizontal accountability and promotes the development of political parties.[18] In parliamentary systems, decision-making can be cumbersome, and direct accountability is far less than in presidential systems, where the people get to vote directly for the single most powerful person in the government. Yet, the advantages of parliamentary democracy and the disadvantages of presidential systems are numerous enough to undermine any claim of superiority by champions of the American model.

The American electoral system of voting for a single representative from an electoral district or state also has endured for two centuries, a real record of success.[19] Yet, other ways of electing officials to legislative and executive office are equally if not more democratic, and also foster stability. The electoral system of proportional representation in which voters select parties rather than individuals has produced stable and accountable government on the European continent for several decades. When minimum thresholds are not too high, proportional representation provides a tighter correlation between votes and seats. By contrast, first-past-the-post systems can generate a majority of seats in parliament for a party that won only a minority of the votes. A mixed electoral system that includes some direct elections of representatives and some party list voting is an alternative that blends the benefits of both.

Federalism is a third institutional feature of the U.S. system of government and was essential for launching American democracy in the first place. As the American political system evolved, federalism has provided a critical constraint on federal and executive power, a feature of the system that also has helped democracy endure in other larger, diverse countries.[20] However, federalism also helped sow the seeds of the American Civil War and then provided institutional protection for highly anti-democratic policies in the South for decades afterward. In other new democracies, such as Nigeria and Russia, federal structures have fueled secessionist movements and exacerbated ethnic conflicts. Corruption and federalism often go hand in hand. Democracy in unitary states, especially in smaller countries, has thrived and endured, leaving the jury out as to which design is best.

Many different democratic systems perform equally well. Although parliamentary systems with some degree of proportional representation tend to outperform other designs in stability and accountability, the exceptions are numerous enough to warrant caution about recommending one institutional blueprint for all countries. Different political challenges require different institutional solutions.

Democracy as the Best System of Government

From time to time, benevolent leaders have come to power in autocratic regimes and governed effectively and justly. European and Asian history is peppered with kings and queens who seemed to rule with an eye toward the common good. More recently, Lee Kuan Yew, Singapore's autocratic ruler for three decades, is credited by some with providing peace, stable government, and economic growth for his people without egregiously violating their human rights.[21] A few monarchs in the Middle East and Asia, as well as a couple of strongmen in Central Asia and Southeast Asia, also have provided public goods to those beyond their immediate families or entourages. At the same time, some democracies do not govern effectively, failing to protect human rights or represent the will of the people. Yet, on average, a democratic system of government benefits the populace more than any other system. Churchill was right.

First and foremost, democracy provides the best institutional arrangement for holding rulers accountable to the people. If leaders must compete for popular support to stay in power, they will respond to their citizens' preferences. Rulers who do not need popular support to gain or maintain power will likely be more responsive to whatever group—the family, the military, the mullahs, or the communist party—controls their fate. The larger the number of people needed to elect a leader, the more inclined that leader will be to pursue public policies that benefit the majority.[22] Not surprisingly, therefore, democracies "have consistently generated superior levels of social welfare" compared to autocracies at similar income levels.[23]

Second, the institutions of democracy prevent abusive rule, constrain bad government, and provide a mechanism for getting rid of corrupt or ineffective leaders.[24] Truly oppressive leaders cannot remain in power for long if they must seek the electoral mandate of those being oppressed. Autocrats face no such constraints. Mass terror and genocide occur in autocracies, not democracies.[25] Democracies do not prevent all abusive behavior, but over the centuries, democratic leaders have unquestionably inflicted less pain and suffering on their people than have autocratic leaders. Joseph Stalin and the Soviet regime sent 28.7 million to forced labor camps, 2.7 million of whom died while incarcerated.[26] Stalin consciously starved millions in Ukraine in the 1932-33 *holodomor*, and ordered the political execution of millions more during his bloody reign.[27] Adolf Hitler not only unleashed carnage through war, he murdered six million Jews and millions more Poles, gypsies, and others in his concentration camps. In China, Mao may have killed more than seventy million people during his reign, including the roughly thirty-eight million people who died during a horrific famine generated by government policies.[28] In only four years, Pol Pot exterminated roughly a quarter of Cambodia's population. Idi Amin in Uganda, Saddam Hussein in Iraq, and Slobodan Milošević in Yugoslavia also systematically slaughtered their own citizens.

The carnage within democracies during the same century is tragic, but its breadth is not on the same scale. In the twenty-first century, autocratic regimes in Sudan, Zimbabwe, North Korea, and Burma inflict pain on their citizens in a manner with no parallel in democratic countries.

Famine is also a phenomenon of dictatorships, not democracies. Amartya Sen notes in his work "the remarkable fact that, in the terrible history of modern famines in the world, no substantial famine has ever occurred in any independent and democratic country with a relatively free press."[29] Ironically, skeptics in the democracy promotion debate in the U.S., often argue that "bread and butter issues should come first," or "it is hard to care about your vote when you are starving."[30] What these critics fail to recognize is that people often starve because they do not have the power to vote.

More generally, democracies are better at guaranteeing human rights and individual freedoms than are autocracies, because they do not rely on the goodwill of leaders.[31] The correlation between Freedom House scores on political liberties and civil liberties is robust. For every liberal autocrat like Singapore's Lee Kuan Yew or the King of Jordan, there are several more Hitlers, Stalins, and Mugabes.

Finally, democracy stimulates political competition that helps to generate higher quality officials in government. Just as market competition leads to better products, political competition produces better leaders, ideas, and organizations. At a minimum, democracy provides a mechanism for getting rid of bad or incompetent rulers in a way that autocracy does not. The absence of political competition in autocracies produces complacency, corruption, and no mechanism for generating new talent.

The Decline of Ideological Challengers to Democracy

For most of history, non-democratic forms of government enjoyed normative legitimacy and were widely practiced. For thousands of years, monarchies (and the Supreme Leader in Iran still today) claimed that their authority to rule came from God, and their subjects often believed them. Earlier in history, monarchies also were considered to be effective regimes compared to other forms of government.[32] Colonial rulers claimed that spreading civilization to the savages was the normative justification for their non-democratic subjugation of others. Similarly, autocrats in ethnically divided countries have invoked ideas of ethnic superiority of one group over another as justification for dictatorship. In the twentieth century, fascist and communist regimes offered a new, modern alternative to both earlier forms of autocracy and democracy.

As serious ideological challengers to democracy, most of these earlier forms of government have lost their appeal. A handful of monarchies persists in the Middle East and Asia, but only just barely. Fascism thankfully disappeared after World War II, resurrecting its ugly head only intermittently since then.[33] The communist challenge lasted longer because the Soviet Union's command economy produced growth rates on par with or higher than those of capitalist economies for several decades, but eventually they faltered, and therefore so too that model of government.

Since 1991, new variants of autocracy have taken root in several states emerging from the USSR's dissolution, while autocrats who still call their regimes communist remain in power in China and Vietnam. Yet none of these dictators now champions an alternative form of government, claiming instead that their regimes are in fact democratic—just a particular kind of democracy such as the "sovereign" democracy in Russia.[34] Other rulers embrace an abstract idea of democracy, and contend they are moving their countries slowly and pragmatically towards developing this form of government.[35] In his speech to the 17th Congress of the Chinese Community Party on October 15, 2007, General Secretary Hu Jintao mentioned the word "democracy" sixty-one times.[36] In a similar spirit, Chinese Prime Minister Wen Jiabao argued in a September 2008 interview that China was progressing towards democracy:

> I believe that while moving ahead with economic reforms, we also need to advance political reforms. . . . When it comes to the development of democracy in China, we can talk about progress in three areas. No. 1: we need to gradually improve the democratic elections system so that state power will truly belong to

the people and state power will be used by the people. No. 2: we need to improve the legal system, run by the country according to law and [have] an independent and just judicial system. No 3: government should be subject to oversight by the people. . . . It's hard for me to predict what will happen in 25 years. That being said, I have this conviction: that China's democracy will continue to grow.[37]

In this interview, the Chinese premier was not challenging the desirability of a more democratic system of government in China and may even have hinted at the eventual necessity of pursuing one.

Illiberal creeds, racist norms, patrimonial rituals, and anti-democratic ideologies persist in pockets throughout the world, but only Osama bin Ladenism and its variants constitute a serious transnational alternative to liberal democracy today. Bin Laden is currently the world's most successful propagandist of a set of illiberal, anti-modern, anti-democratic, quasi-religious ideas.[38] Bin Laden and the more serious thinkers who preceded him, including the Egyptian Islamist Sayyid Qutb, reject democracy as the best system of government and recommend an alternative theocratic system. Bin Laden views democracy as a concept closely associated with the Judeo-American alliance, whose goal, he believes, is "to get rid of Islam itself."[39] In what he sees as a Manichean struggle to preserve his religion and way of life, bin Laden rejects all Western liberal concepts and instead promotes a form of governance that places religious laws he believes are dictated by God above man-made rules. Periodically, bin Laden also has called for the restoration of the Caliphate.[40] For radical Islamists, democracy is a foreign concept closely associated with non-Muslim cultures and religions, which makes its practice anti-Muslim. As Al Qaeda's second-in-command, Ayman Al Zawahari, put it, "Whoever labels himself as a Muslim democrat or a Muslim who calls for democracy is like saying he is a Jewish Muslim or a Christian Muslim."[41] More generally, adherents to this strain of Islamic fundamentalism "perceive democracy as the replacement of the will of Allah with the will of people; thus they deem it anti-Islamic."[42]

After decades of decline, Osama bin Ladenism gained new vibrancy after September 11, 2001 and the U.S.-led invasion of Iraq.[43] Yet the spike in Bin Laden's appeal did not last long, and this ideological alternative has been unable to challenge democracy's reputation as the world's most valued political system. Even as disdain for U.S. power in the Middle East skyrocketed, proponents of anti-democratic ideas and forms of government have not enjoyed a commensurate rise in support. In a survey conducted in six Arab countries in October 2005, Shibley Telhami found that 77 percent of respondents believed Iraqis were worse off since the American-led invasion, but only 6 percent of these respondents sympathized with Al Qaeda's goal of creating an Islamic state.[44]

Nor have political organizations sympathetic to Al Qaeda's anti-democratic theorems gained power. Terrorist organizations continue to attack citizens living in democracies, but they have yet to actually threaten any democratic regime's hold on power. In Iraq, Al Qaeda's presence rose in 2004-05 but declined precipitously in 2007-08. Hezbollah in Lebanon and Hamas in Palestine remain powerful actors, but their guns and social services—not their embrace of anti-democratic ideologies—are the determinants of their political success. In Afghanistan, the Taliban is gaining strength, but that is due in large measure to the ineffectiveness of the Karzai administration in Kabul, not to a renaissance in illiberal thinking among the Afghan people. In Iran, the actual institutions of dictatorship remain, but the ideological appeal of the Islamic Republic of Iran as an alternative regime has faded dramatically, and even Iranian government officials claim to be practicing a form of democracy.

Paradoxically, bin Laden's resurgence after September 11 has helped to provoke greater discussion about democracy in the wider Middle East. Arab intellectuals who contributed to the United Nations *Arab Human Development Report* propelled the issue of democracy to the forefront by stating boldly that the "freedom deficit [in the Arab region] undermines human development and is one of the most painful manifestations of lagging political development."[45] In recent years, Arab civil leaders and intellectuals have convened several international conferences to discuss and promote democracy's development. Even Islamist parties in the region, including the Muslim Brotherhood in Egypt, the Parti de la Justice et Developpement (PJD) in Morocco, and Islamist parties in Bahrain, Yemen, Kuwait, and Jordan have embraced a discourse about democracy as the best system of government.[46] Of course, Islamist leaders may interpret democracy very differently from those in the West, and may be using this tentative discussion of democracy as a tactical move to seize power.[47] But the fact that these Islamist groups propose no alternative to democracy represents a major and recent change in the ideological debate about democracy and its alternatives.

Democracy as a World Value

If clear-cut alternatives to democracy are not as prevalent or popular today as they were in previous eras, cultural arguments against the practice or promotion of democracy do continue from a peculiar alliance of American conservatives and liberal multiculturalists, as well as an array of ruling elites in autocracies and religious leaders around the world. Conservatives have argued

that Muslims do not want and are unfit for democracy.[48] Adam
Garfinkle has warned that Arab societies

> lack certain dispositional prerequisites for democracy;
> let us mention just three: the belief that the proximate
> source of political authority is intrinsic to the society;
> a concept of majority rule; and the acceptance of all
> citizens' essential equality before the law.[49]

Those on the left worry about shielding sovereign third world
states from American hegemony or preserving indigenous cultures from globalization. Thus they defend some anti-democratic
practices in the name of multiculturalism or anti-imperialism.
Autocratic leaders around the world also invoke culture—Asian
values, Islamic religion, or Slavic traditions—to explain why
their citizens do not want or are not ready for democracy.[50]
Some scholars also have tried to trace cultural sources of autocratic government.[51]

These cultural arguments were much more prevalent in
prior centuries. Hundreds of years ago, European thinkers developed sophisticated theories based on race and ethnicity to explain why populations in the colonized world (and slaves in the
first world) could not govern themselves. In retrospect, these
cultural arguments look archaic. Nonetheless, only half a century
ago, American politicians and analysts invoked ethnic arguments
to explain why Germans, Italians, and Japanese people embraced
autocratic rule. Only a few decades ago, scholars tried to develop theories to explain the autocratic tendencies of Catholics,
since there was a correlation in the 1960s and 1970s between
countries with a majority Catholic population and autocracy
(Spain, Portugal, and most of Latin America). More recently, analysts have advanced similar arguments to explain why Orthodox

Christian countries sustain autocratic governments. Today, immense popular and academic literature focuses on the autocratic elements of Islam.

That so many of these cultural arguments against democracy have not stood the test of time should give contemporary advocates pause. Proponents of the Asian values theory have a hard time explaining why Asian culture causes autocracy in China or Singapore, but not in Taiwan, Japan, or South Korea. Similar variations of regime type are present in the Christian Orthodox world. Autocratic rule is the norm in most Arab countries, but in the wider Islamic world, democracies and autocracies both exist, suggesting that religious values cannot be the sole cause of autocracy in the Middle East.[52]

Public opinion data also undermine these cultural arguments and instead suggest that democracy is becoming a universal value that cuts across all regions, religions, and cultures.[53] As Table One illustrates, majorities around the world agree with Churchill that democracy is the best system of government.

In some countries, respondents are ready to trade some democracy for more order, but in no country where survey work is conducted on this subject does support for dictatorship exceed support for democracy.

There are regional variations.[54] In the post-communist world, support for democratic values is less robust than the world average. The first democratic governments after the collapse of communism guided many of the countries through a painful, tumultuous, and uncertain period of economic transformation. Citizens in these countries equated the practice of democracy with economic decline, and not surprisingly expressed skepticism about the performance of democrats and democratic institutions. In Latin America, support for democracy has declined as new democracies have struggled to deliver economic development,

but democracy still remains the most popular system of government there. In the Arab world, the region with the fewest democratic regimes, surveys show solid majorities in support of
democracy, suggesting that commitment to Islamic ideas does not
hinder the embrace of democratic values.[55] The real values gap
between the Arab world and the West is not over the general idea
of democratic rule, but between men's attitudes about the rights
of women and liberal values more generally.[56] In Africa, support
for democracy varies among countries, but still remains robust.
In Asia, the once popular notion that Asian values were antithetical to democracy has not stood up to empirical tests. The wealthier an Asian country is, the more likely its population is to support
democratic values.[57] Democracy still faces ideological challengers, but these opponents are less popular today than at any
time in history.[58]

Percent Agree: "Democracy my have its problems, but it's better
than any other form of government."

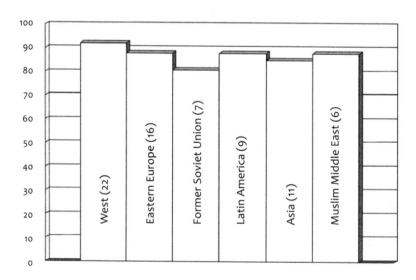

Percent endorse: "Strong leader who does not have to bother with parliament and elections."

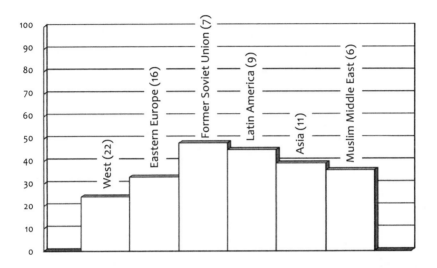

Although direct ideological rebuttals of democracy are rare, more subtle criticism remains prevalent both in the developing world and the developed world's policy debates about democracy promotion. Three charges are most common: (1) autocracies are better than democracies at producing economic growth, (2) democracies, especially new democracies, are unstable and war-prone, and (3) democracy is a worthy goal, but it only works after certain preconditions are met. Each of these arguments requires elaboration, engagement, and refutation.

Democracy and Economic Growth

The most powerful indictment of democracy today is that it fails to deliver what people most want: economic development. When given the choice between democracy and prosperity, so the argument goes, people prefer prosperity. In a similar vein, critics contend that people struggling to survive cannot afford the luxury of democracy.[59] Thus the most serious competitor to democracy in the past century and still today is the modernizing autocrat. In the 1930s, while the democratic West was languishing in a painful economic depression, the Soviet dictatorship was reorganizing national resources to sustain remarkable growth rates.[60] For several decades in the twentieth century, Moscow helped to inspire and export this model of state-led economic development under a communist party dictatorship. In the 1960s and 1970s, authoritarian regimes in Asia's tigers—Hong Kong, Taiwan, Singapore, and South Korea—provided a capitalist model for advocates of growth under autocracy.[61] Today, the Chinese economic miracle provides a serious alternative to the legitimacy and attractiveness of democracy.

The relationship between regime type and economic performance, however, is much more complicated than this select sample of cases suggests. Proponents of democracy overpromise and ignore empirical reality when they claim that democracies always and everywhere outperform autocracies in developing economies, but cheerleaders for the Chinese development model often overlook fundamental pitfalls in China's autocratic experience and overestimate the applicability of the model to other countries.

Just as democracy immunizes a society from the worst forms of governments, democracy also protects a society from the worst forms of economic disasters. Autocracies do not. No democracy has ever experienced the level of economic and social dislocation of Stalinism, Maoism, or Pol Potism. To be sure, democratic countries all suffered during the Great Depression, and economic downturns continue to occur in the democratic world. However, the frequency and the scale of these economic swings are much more moderate in the democratic world compared to the autocratic world. According to Bruce Bueno de Mesquita and Hilton Root, "[T]he variance in economic growth rates for autocracies is about twice what it is for democracies."[62] Or put another way, Mort Halperin, Joseph Siegle, and Michael Weinstein calculate that, "Over the past 40 years, autocracies have been twice as likely to experience economic collapse [that is, a shrinkage in annual GDP per capita of 10 percent or more] as democracies."[63] Really bad policies that can bring economic ruin occur less frequently in democracies.

In the long run, democratic regimes produce policies that favor sustained growth and prosperity just as well as authoritarian regimes do.[64] On average, democratic regimes also have higher levels of trade liberalization, which in turn generates higher growth rates. Democratic regimes also foster the accumulation of human capital, which has a positive effect on economic development.[65] Rulers in democracies also must be more responsive to the basic needs of their population, which does not always produce positive economic results in the short run, but does compel political leaders to pursue policies beneficial to majorities over the long run.[66] In contrast, authoritarian regimes are accountable to a powerful rich minority, and thus are more likely to prey on parts of society.[67] These regimes also have incentives to extract the maximum possible surplus to use for their own purposes, not for the welfare of the population as a whole.[68]

Contemporary comparisons of regime type and growth usually focus on the developing world, but leaving out the developed economies skews the sample. When all countries are included in the analysis, the oldest democracies in the world are also the richest countries in the world: only two of the twenty-five highest ranking countries on the Human Development Index—Hong Kong (if it is still counted as an independent political entity) and Singapore—are not democracies.

Among the poorest countries in the world, regime type varies considerably.

This correlation is not an accident of history. The rise of the Western world involved a complex interaction between institutional, cultural, and geographic factors, but a state constrained by democratic institutions and therefore capable of protecting property rights proved critical for market formation and expansion.[69] Countries such as Great Britain, the Netherlands, and the United States developed institutions that constrained the abusive power of the state and protected private property rights before they experienced rapid economic expansion. After 1688, England had in place a parliament capable of checking the Crown's power and compelling the state to consult its taxpayers before spending their money.[70] Of course, neither England in the seventeenth century nor the United States at its founding in the eighteenth century were full-blown democracies, since only a fraction of people in both countries at the time had the right to vote. Yet these regimes exhibited some degree of rule by the people (democracy) and some degree of checks and balances between different entities within the state (liberalism). This form of government provided the stable and predictable environment necessary for individual economic actors to make long-term investments.

The comparison between the United States and Canada on the one hand and the rest of the Americas on the other hand is also illustrative. Two hundred years ago, both of these regions enjoyed a similar set of rich endowments. Only 100 years ago, people living in Argentina enjoyed the same levels of prosperity as people living in the United States. Beginning in the nineteenth century, however, Latin American growth did not keep pace with North American growth. Many factors contributed to the increasing disparity, but political institutions, particularly the stability offered by democratic institutions in the North, played a major role.[71] As Douglass North, William Summerhill, and Barry Weingast have concluded,

> In the half-century following independence, the presence of widespread political instability and violence distinguished much of Latin America, especially Spanish America, from the United States. While the United States enjoyed an enduring set of political arrangements that both provided for stability and protected markets from predation, most of Spanish America erupted in internecine war. This instability imposed several types of costs. It diverted resources from economic activity and channeled them into caudillo ("strongman") armies and a variety of praetorian efforts. . . . Importantly, instability also made it impossible to establish institutions that could bring the expected private returns to investments close in line with social returns. The results were disastrous.[72]

This outcome was not anticipated. Back in the eighteenth and nineteenth centuries, many political theorists thought that democracy was incapable of securing private property to the extent necessary for investment and growth. Under majority rule, so the argument went, the average voter would have an incentive to ally with the poorer voters—the majority—in order to transfer income from the rich, the minority.[73] Universal suffrage was supposed to weaken property rights. These fears proved to be unfounded. By the twentieth century, the historical record demonstrated that democracies were capable of constraining populist appeals for redistribution and appropriation, and instead provided strong property rights essential for economic development.[74]

Richest Countries in the World

High Human Development	Country	Freedom Rating
1	Norway	Free
2	Iceland	Free
3	Australia	Free
4	Luxemburg	Free
5	Canada	Free
6	Sweden	Free
7	Switzerland	Free
8	Ireland	Free
9	Belgium	Free
10	United States	Free
11	Japan	Free
12	Netherlands	Free
13	Finland	Free
14	Denmark	Free
15	United Kingdom	Free
16	France	Free
17	Austria	Free
18	Italy	Free
19	New Zealand	Free
20	Germany	Free
21	Spain	Free
22	Hong Kong, China (SAR)	Not Free
23	Israel	Free
24	Greece	Free
25	Singapore	Partially Free

Least Developed Countries in the World

HDI Rank	Country	Freedom Ranking
177	Niger	Partly Free
176	Sierra Leone	Partly Free
175	Burkina Faso	Partly Free
174	Mali	Free
173	Chad	Not Free
172	Guinea Bissau	Partly Free
171	Central African Republic	Partly Free
170	Ethiopia	Partly Free
169	Burundi	Partly Free
168	Mozambique	Partly Free
167	Dem. Rep. of the Congo	Partly Free
166	Zambia	Partly Free
165	Malawi	Partly Free
164	U. Rep. of Tanzania	Partly Free
163	Cote D'Ivoire	Not Free
162	Benin	Free
161	Eritrea	Not Free
160	Angola	Not Free
159	Rwanda	Not Free
158	Nigeria	Partly Free
157	Senegal	Free
156	Guinea	Not Free
155	Gambia	Partly Free
154	Kenya	Partly Free
153	Haiti	Not Free

The positive influence of democratic institutions on economic growth in the developed world should not be overstated. After all, sustained growth in most of Europe started before full-fledged liberal democracy took root.[75] This sequence seems to support Lipset's famous thesis that "[t]he more well-to-do a nation, the greater the chances that it will sustain democracy."[76] The converse also is true. Democratic regimes in poorer countries are more likely to revert back to autocracies compared with democratic regimes in richer countries.[77] Furthermore, new democracies that produce economic growth are much more likely to consolidate than those that do not.

Some pivot from this relationship between wealth and democratic sustainability to suggest a sequencing of economic and political development: get richer first, worry about democracy later. For decades, this idea dominated thinking about development assistance in Western aid agencies and international financial institutions. The assumption behind this policy recommendation is that autocracies can sustain levels of economic growth similar to those witnessed in Europe before democracy and thereby prepare developing countries for democracy. In fact, some autocracies facilitate economic growth and development and some do not. On average, autocracies in the developing world have performed no better than democracies over the past four decades. Although some scholars have posited a positive relationship between democracy and growth,[78] others have found a negative relationship,[79] and a third school has found no relationship at all.[80] In the aggregate, this last finding seems most robust. In their study of the relationship between regimes and growth over four decades, Przeworski, Alvarez, Cheubub, and Limongi conclude that "there is no trade-off between democracy and development, not even in poor countries" and "[t]here is little difference in favor of dictatorships in the observed rates of growth."[81] Looking at all countries around the world over a similar period, Robert Barro comes to a similar conclusion: "[T]he net effect of more political freedom on growth is theoretically ambiguous."[82] John Helliwell also concludes that

> democracies are as capable as authoritarian regimes of combining redistribution and growth in such a way as to broaden markets and achieve economic expansion and economic growth.[83]

But what about China? Over the past three decades, autocratic China has maintained an average annual growth rate of 10 percent, making it the fastest expanding economy in the world.[84] That growth has occurred at a historically unprecedented rate, with the economy expanding eight-fold and per capita income increasing from $151 in 1978 to $1,740 in 2006 (measured by Purchasing Power Parity, the per capita figure is even more impressive: $7,600). No democracy has ever come close to matching this pace.

Growth under autocracy, however, is not the rule. For every China under Deng Xiaoping, there is a Zaire under Mobuto Sese Seko; for every Singapore, a Burma; for every South Korea, a North Korea; for every Uganda, a Zimbabwe. In the economic growth race in the developing world, autocracies are the hares and the snails, while democracies are the tortoises. On average, democracies have a slower rate of growth than the best autocratic performers but a much better rate of growth than most autocratic regimes. Democracies also grow at a steadier pace. In the past 10 years, Chinese growth accounts for the lion's share of growth generated under autocracy worldwide. Autocratic regimes in control of oil, gas, and mineral exports also have experienced growth rates in the past 10 years, but when raw material exporters are excluded from the equation, autocracies vastly underperform democracies.[85]

Even in China, the direct role of autocracy in steering economic growth is not so clear. Guided by progressive-sounding slogans like the Great Leap Forward and the Cultural Revolution, autocratic China in the 1950s and 1960s produced very different economic results, including famine, dislocation, and death for millions of innocent people. The 1961 famine may rank as the greatest man-made disaster in history. So even in China, autocracy was no guarantee of economic growth. In fact, the withdrawal of the state from the economy—not its guiding presence—helped to launch China's extraordinary run of sustained growth over the past 30 years.[86] Liberalizing political reforms—including greater rural self-government, a strengthened parliament, mandatory government retirements, and diminished controls on the media and civil society "either preceded or accompanied China's economic growth. It was not a result of economic success."[87] China's regime today is more constrained in its ability to influence Chinese society and Chinese citizens are freer today than at any time since the communist revolution.

The relationship between democracy and growth also varies over time after the introduction of democracy. In his seminal study, Barro found that when democracy is introduced in countries with harsh autocratic regimes, it tends to generate higher levels of growth than it does when introduced incrementally in middle-income countries that already have some degree of democracy in place. As he explains,

> One way to interpret the results is that in the worst dictatorships, an increase in political rights tends to increase growth and investment because the benefit from limitations on government power is the key mat-

ter. But in places that have already achieved a moderate amount of democracy, a further increase in political rights impairs growth and investment because the dominant effect comes from the intensified concern with income redistribution.[88]

A final economic attack against democracy pertains to transition. Some have posited that the transition to democracy makes people economically worse off.[89] They suggest that democratic leaders are bad at painful but necessary economic reforms because they fear electoral backlash.[90] Instead, leaders acquiesce to pressure for immediate consumption at the expense of investment and hence growth.[91] Authoritarian regimes, insulated from voter pressures, are purportedly more effective at mobilizing savings by reducing current consumption and implementing needed economic reforms, even if they hurt a majority of people in the short run.[92] In this model, political participation must be held down to promote economic development. Chile under Augusto Pinochet or China under the Communist Party today are often cited as the most efficient regimes at implementing painful economic reforms.[93]

The historical record, however, is much more complex. Again, in the aggregate over the past several decades, careful cross-national research does not support this popular assumption. Dani Rodrik and Roman Wacziarg's examination of the relationship between democratic transition and economic growth around the world shows that "major democratic transitions have, if anything, a positive effect on economic growth in the short run," and contrary to the pundits' claims, "this is especially true for the poorest countries in the world and those marked by sharp ethnic divisions."[94] Confirming Barro's earlier findings, Rodrik and Wacziarg also report that "democratic transitions are associated with a decline in growth volatility."[95]

It is difficult to see a clear pattern in which autocratic regimes decisively implement economic reforms more successfully than democratic regimes do. Instead, what we should admit is that we still have much to learn about the relationship between regime type and economic development. So many factors play a role in triggering economic growth in one country and stifling it in another that isolating the precise effects of democratic or autocratic institutions on economic development is complex and difficult. What we can say definitively is that the alleged benefits of autocracy for economic growth are not supported by empirical data. Denying people the right to select their government, therefore, cannot be justified in the name of growth or development.

Democracy and Security

A different set of democracy critics argues that dictatorships provide a more stable system of government. Amy Chua, for instance, has argued that in the multiethnic countries in which the minority holds a dominant position in the economy, "adding democracy to markets has been a recipe for instability, upheaval and conflagration."[96] In Africa, according to Fareed Zakaria, the introduction of democracy has produced "a degree of chaos and instability that has actually made corruption and lawlessness worse in many countries."[97] Democratization allegedly also weakens state capacity, which makes it difficult for these new democracies to provide basic public goods, or to fight terrorist organizations. In sounding caution about the deleterious consequences of democratic change, Jack Snyder and Edward Mansfield argue that "the beginning stages of transitions to democracy often give rise to war rather than peace. Since the end of the Cold War, this causal connection between democratization and war has been especially striking, but the fundamental pattern is as old as democracy itself, dating at least to the French Revolution."[98] In explaining why democratizing states are belligerent, Mansfield and Snyder focus on unleashed nationalism: "In democratizing states, nationalism is an ideology with tremendous appeal for elites whose privileges are threatened. It can be used to convince newly empowered constituencies that the cleavage between the privileged and the masses is unimportant compared to the cleavages that divide nations, ethnic groups, or races."[99] All these authors contend that while democracy may have many positive attributes in theory, its practice in the real world—and especially its introduction in countries formerly ruled by autocrats—is dangerous, destabilizing, and ultimately may cause war. They are wrong.

Democracy and Stability

Consolidated democracies have in place a predictable and peaceful mechanism for transferring power from one ruling group to the next: elections. Autocracies, especially in the contemporary era, do not.[100] Liberal democracies rarely unravel and wealthy liberal democracies almost never collapse. The longer a democratic regime survives, the less likely it will collapse. By contrast, autocracies that sustain economic growth continually face the challenge that an increasingly wealthy, educated, and urbanized society may eventually demand political change.[101] Conversely, autocracies that fail to generate economic growth can become unstable. The longer an autocracy survives, the more likely it will collapse.

Few argue that liberal democracies are unstable political systems. Rather, the critique is focused on democratization or new democracies, especially in the developing world. New democracies in poorer countries, are more likely to revert back to autocracy than are those in richer countries. Przeworski, Alvarez, Cheibub, and Limongi estimate that, in countries with per capita income below $1,000, the expected life of a democracy is eight years; in those with per capita income between $1,001 and $2,000, the expected duration of a democracy is eighteen years; and in countries with a per capita income above $4,000, the probability of democratic survival is nearly 100 percent.[102] Likewise, new democracies that fail to generate economic growth are much more likely to collapse than are new democracies that do generate economic growth.[103]

But these probabilities for new democracies' survival do not imply that autocracies are more stable. On the contrary, what is striking about the last three decades is autocratic instability. In 1973, forty of the 150 countries (26.7 percent) in the world were democracies. In 2007, 119 of 193 countries (61.7 percent) were democracies. This period represents the most radical decline in autocratic rule in world history. In addition, the survival rate for new democracies increased to roughly 75 percent in the 1980s and 1990s, a sharp increase over the rate in the previous two decades.[104] Moreover, the length of rule of new autocracies coming to power through military coups also has shortened dramatically in the past two decades as international norms about a return to civilian rule pressure these soldiers to get out of government and return to the barracks.[105]

Democracy and Peace

The second concern about democracies being more prone war is also exaggerated. Democracies do not go to war with each other. More precisely, Bruce Russett, one of the closest observers of this phenomenon, writes,

First, democratically organized political systems in general operate under restraints that make them more peaceful in their relations with other democracies. . . . Second, in the modern international system, democracies are less likely to use lethal violence toward other democracies than toward autocratically governed states or than autocratically governed states are toward each other. Furthermore, there are no clearcut cases of sovereign stable democracies waging war with each other in the modern international system.[106]

Reflecting on a vast academic literature on the causes of war, Jack Levy concluded that the democratic peace theory is "the closest thing we have to empirical law in the study of international relations."[107] Democracies are not pacifist regimes when dealing with autocracies. But democracies are peaceful when interacting with other democracies.

Why this pattern occurs remains the subject of heated academic debate. Some argue that democratic institutions compel leaders to pursue the natural, peaceful preferences of society at large.[108] Populations in democracies can hold their leaders more accountable than those in autocracies regarding the costs of war. If constitutional law governs relations between state leaders and societal groups, then rulers will be more cautious in engaging in costly military activity for which citizens must pay.[109] Others argue that democratic institutions create transparency regarding a state's international intentions, making them more predictable than those of an autocratic state whose leaders who do not reveal their preferences nor have to justify their preferences before publics. Like-minded democracies also encounter much less uncertainty when interacting with one another.[110] As a result, democracies neither fight each other nor tend to engage in arms races with one another.[111]

A related argument suggests this democratic peace results from norms in democracies against fighting other democracies.[112] These peaceful norms develop more slowly than democratic institutions, but once in place provide a more powerful constraint on belligerent behavior than the institutions themselves. Another line of argument posits that democratic states build up more linkages among one another, which raise the costs of conflict.[113] Over time, liberals argue, repeated, peaceful interactions between democracies produce self-enforcing habits and institutions, which every state has a stake in maintaining.[114] These democratic states form a Kantian "pacific union" or an international society in which interstate interaction is much more predictable and peaceful than interstate relations either between non-democratic states or between democratic states and non-democratic states. The international institutions that emerge from this peaceful interaction in turn help to keep the peace.[115] Other interactions that may serve to reduce uncertainty and thereby enhance peace include alliances, trade, and the presence of transnational actors. Among democracies, conquest does not pay.[116] In a related manner, peace among democracies in Europe may result from fifty years of a shared historical experience of containing communism, which nurtured a homogenization of interests and values, reinforced by robust international institutions.[117] In established democracies, those democratic norms that produce compromise within states also will spawn compromise between liberal democratic states.[118] Whatever the causal relationship between peace and democracies, the empirical correlation is robust.

Although few dispute the observation that liberal democracies enjoy peaceful relations with other democracies, some claim that the process of democratization instigates conflict and war. The evidence, however, does not support this sweeping generalization. Most importantly, countries making successful transitions to democracy rarely go to war. As Mansfield and Snyder themselves write, "[T]here is only scattered evidence that transitions culminating in a coherent democracy influence war."[119] In addition, democratizing states rarely initiate war. In the "third wave" of democratization, from 1973 to 2004, Freedom House catalogued 179 instances of democratization, defined as countries moving from either "Not Free" to "Free" (25 cases) or "Not Free" to "Partly Free" (154 cases).[120] In this same time period, only 30 of these democratizing states (16 percent) experienced political violence—civil war or interstate war—within five years after democratization, and the majority saw internal wars, not interstate wars.[121] Moreover, we do not know if these conflicts would have occurred anyway, irrespective of regime type or regime change.

But Mansfield and Snyder make the narrower argument that democratizing states are more likely to go to war than either stable democratic or authoritarian regimes. This narrower claim will seem counterintuitive to any student of twentieth-century history. In recalling the millions slaughtered in the twentieth century, we think of ruthless dictators like Stalin, Mao, Hitler, Pol Pot, Idi Amin, and Saddam Hussein, not leaders of democratizing states like Adolfo Suarez in Spain, Lech Walesa in Poland, or Nelson Mandela in South Africa. Mansfield and Snyder, however, are concerned not with democratizing countries in general but with a subset they call stalled transitions or incomplete democratizations.[122] They then make the universe of belligerent democratizers smaller by focusing only on those countries that have weak political institutions. Without the presence of this "weak institutions" variable, there is no statistical relationship between democratization and war. Once the importance of "stalled transitions" and "weak institutions" to the authors' causal argument becomes clear, one has to wonder why Mansfield and Snyder continue to name "democratization" as the causal force for war in these cases. In fact, what they are really explaining is why failed state-building and failed democratization lead to war. Most of the countries discussed in their analysis are not democratizing states, but ones with regime collapse or a return to autocracy, such as belligerent France in the nineteenth century, the Ottoman empire on the eve of World War I, war-prone Germany under the Nazis, the military junta in Argentina during the Falklands War, or Serbia under Milošević.[123] In these cases, democratization did not cause conflict. Rather, the failure of democracy allowed nationalist dictators to usurp power and then instigate conflict. The policy solution, therefore, is not to avoid democratization altogether, but to make sure it succeeds.

Sequencing and Preconditions

Another argument against democracy promotion is that some societies and countries are not ready for democracy. Proponents of this view invoke several preconditions.

Modernization is often cited as a prerequisite for democracy. Societies need to achieve a certain level of economic development, so the argument goes, before they can practice democracy. People can be too poor or too uneducated to participate effectively in democratic institutions.

A second school advocates the consolidation of liberal institutions as a precondition for the introduction of democracy. Liberal institutions are those laws, procedures, and norms that protect the individual against the indiscriminate power of the state or society (or in earlier times, from the church or society). Covenants and constitutions that establish liberalism have little to do with how to select a government and everything to do with how to define the relationship between government and the individual. As Fareed Zakaria, one of the most articulate proponents of this sequencing argument, rightly points out, "liberty came to the West centuries before democracy."[124] Institutions that checked the power of majorities such as the (unelected) Supreme Court in the United States or the House of Lords in Great Britain were part of the constitutional configuration before all adults were allowed to vote. By the time countries like Great Britain and the Nordics began to open the franchise to large numbers of voters, liberal practices had been in place for centuries.

Many suggest that a third precondition for democracy is the presence of a sovereign and functioning state. As Juan Linz and Alfred Stepan have argued categorically, "without a state, no modern democracy is possible."[125] Two dimensions of stateness must be present, or so the argument goes. First, there must be general agreement inside a country about who is in the state and who is not. "National unity," in Dankwart Rustow's formulation, "must precede all other phases of democratization" and works best as a precondition for democracy "when national unity is accepted unthinkingly."[126] Colonies of empires, therefore, cannot be democracies until they obtain independence. Ethnically divided societies cannot make the move to democracy until all sides agree who is a member of the polity. Second, the state must have some capacity to govern. Weak or collapsing states cannot sustain even minimalist forms of democratic governments.

In the extreme, all these arguments about preconditions are true. Societies in which the vast majority cannot read or eat will have difficulty practicing democracy effectively. As for liberty before democracy, elections in countries with no tradition of the rule of law, checks and balances within the state, or government constraint have little chance of making democracy work. Countries without states or well-defined nations are less likely to make successful democratic transitions. However, generalizing from these extremes is dangerous. Waiting for preconditions to appear under autocracy is neither practical nor necessary.

Regarding modernization, as discussed above, there is no reason to assume that autocracies are more likely than democracies to produce economic growth, development, or higher literacy rates. Przeworski, Alvarez, Cheibub, and Limongi found that

> . . . there is no trade-off between democracy and development, not even in poor countries. . . . [T]here was never solid evidence that democracies were somehow inferior in generating growth—certainly not enough to justify supporting or even condoning dictatorships . . . [T]here is little difference in favor of dictatorships in the observed rates of growth.[127]

Freedom is a luxury when you are starving, but you might very well be starving because you have no ability to control your government. To assume a sequence—first economic growth, then democracy—might very well relegate people to live in poverty forever.

In addition, levels of economic development or degrees of modernization are terrible predictors of when a country democratizes. The United States, after all, was a largely agrarian society with low literacy levels when it democratized. In the developing world over the past 50 years, there is no correlation between modernization and democratization.[128] Several successful democracies in the developing world, including Mali, India, and Botswana, made successful transitions to democracy at very low levels of development and have sustained democracy nonetheless. China, on the other hand, has experienced tremendous growth over the past two decades, yet democratization has not even begun. Over the past 10 years, economic modernization in Russia has undermined, not promoted, democratic development.[129]

As for the suggestion that liberalism must precede democracy, it is clear that elections alone neither make a democracy nor push a country along a path to liberal democracy.[130] Elections that occur in authoritarian regimes only sometimes have a liberalizing effect; they did in the Soviet Union in 1989, but did not in Egypt in 2005.[131] Especially in post-conflict settings, as the world learned tragically in Angola in 1992, Bosnia in 1996, Liberia in 1997, and Iraq in 2005, elections held prematurely can weaken liberal institutions.

But does the alternative—no elections—generate better or faster progress towards liberalism? There is no reason to assume today that autocracies are better than democracies at facilitating the emergence of constitutional liberalism. Leaders in Hong Kong and Singapore are the exception, not the rule. Many more dictatorships continue to impede the development of both liberal and democratic institutions.

And the introduction of elections can facilitate the emergence and consolidation of liberal democracy. As Barro observed in comparing 100 countries between 1960 and 1990,

> the civil-liberties variable is highly correlated with the democracy index: 0.8 in 1972, 0.93 in 1980, 0.94 in 1990 and 0.91 in 1994. . . . This result suggests that the economic and social forces that promote political rights are similar to those that stimulate civil liberties.[132]

In East Central Europe, liberalism did not develop under communism, but quickly took root after the first round of elections in 1989 and 1990. After the first wave of democratization, many other countries in the post-communist region did get stuck in the grey zone between democracy and autocracy. It was electoral breakthroughs—a mobilized opposition seeking to overturn falsified election results—not reforming autocrats, that jumpstarted the process of deepening liberal democracy in Serbia in 2000, Georgia in 2003, and Ukraine in 2004. In all three places, the quality of democracy improved after these so-called revolutions, which would not have occurred without elections.[133] In his analysis of nearly 200 elections in more than 30 African countries, Staffan Lindberg concluded that the introduction of elections did improve the quality of democracy, especially after the third round of elections.[134] Nikolay Marinov has demonstrated that elections even in semi-autocracies tend over time to have a democratizing influence on political systems.[135]

Very few autocratic regimes in the world today are building and strengthening liberal institutions. Hoping that eighteenth century England might be a model today is far more utopian than believing that these same countries might become democracies. Monarchies might be the only modern system of government that could sustain a liberalizing autocracy, since a benevolent king or queen might be able press for liberal changes before allowing democratic changes. Such regimes, however, are also rare, and include only a handful of the Gulf States, Morocco, and Jordan.

Those who pine for the European pathway to democracy via liberalism also forget just how bloody, volatile, and long the process of liberal state-building on the continent was. Liberalism in Great Britain did not evolve peacefully and gradually, but was forged over centuries of revolution, war, oppression, and rebellion.[136] The process in France was just as contentious, and more violent.[137] The emergence of a German liberal state occurred more rapidly, but also at a higher cost, both to the German people and to Europe as whole. More recently, South Africa's first democratically elected government did inherit much greater state capacity and constitutional liberalism when compared to many other states making the transition from colonial to black African leadership, but the human cost of building this capacious state under apartheid was enormous.

Finally, advocates of liberalism preceding democracy must acknowledge a practical political constraint: the people will not wait. As the Americans learned in both Afghanistan and Iraq, outsiders cannot ask or coerce people in another country to accept disenfranchisement until their elites build strong liberal institutions, especially when today's autocracies have such a poor record of actually building them. After the American-led invasion of their country, Afghan leaders demanded that elections occur sooner rather than later. In Iraq, the Grand Ayatollah Ali al-Sistani rejected the American-proposed procedure of indirect elections and insisted instead on direct elections. Once a process of political liberalization begins, denying citizens the right to vote is normatively indefensible and politically dangerous.

Stateness

Clearly, only people in a sovereign state with some minimal level of capacity can participate in democracy. This need for state sovereignty was exemplified in Africa and Asia in the twentieth century, where people first had to rid their lands of colonial rulers before they could begin to experiment with democracy.

Agreement about the borders of the state or nation most certainly facilitates democratic development.[138] When the national boundaries of the state are contested, democratization is less likely. But agreement is not a necessary precondition to democratic development. The Soviet Union, Czechoslovakia, Serbia, and Georgia are a few examples of countries that democratized before settling on new state borders. Ethnic conflicts over state borders made transitions in the Balkans and the Caucasus more difficult, but border disputes did not have to be resolved before democratization could occur. In Africa, local disputes about externally drawn borders have delayed and derailed democracy, but the introduction of regular, competitive elections has helped to reduce violent conflict within states and stimulate the development of "shared beliefs of citizenship and the rights, obligations, and benefits of collective action in both the political and societal spheres."[139] In countries where border disputes fester, there is little evidence and no guarantee that delaying democratization helps to resolve these boundary disputes.

Conclusion

If one were to argue that the United States is morally compelled to help make the world a better place, then it would follow that supporting democratic development in other countries should be a goal of American foreign policy. As a system of government, democracy has clear advantages over other kinds of regimes. Democracies represent the will of the people and constrain the power of the state. They avoid the worst kinds of economic disasters, such as famine, and the political horrors, such as genocide, that occur in autocracies. On average, democracies also produce economic development just as well as other forms of governments. Democracies also tend to provide for more stable government and more peaceful relations with other states compared to other regime types. Finally, most people in the world want democracy.

The central purpose of American power, however, is not to make the world a better place. Rather, American leaders must first ensure the security and prosperity of the American people. The next chapter explores how the promotion of democracy abroad serves these American national interests.

3
Democracy and American National Interests

The previous chapter outlined the benefits of democracy as an effective and just system of government, but also as a type of political regime that generates other valuable outcomes such as economic growth and security. We also saw that democracy and democratization are not as inimical to development and peace as is often claimed. In addition, public opinion polls demonstrate that most people in the world, regardless of income or culture, want democracy. The promotion of democracy, therefore, is morally justified. If American leaders want to practice an ethical foreign policy by supporting valuable and good causes, then democracy—like clean air, peace, and prosperity—is an international public good that the United States should promote.

Conversely, the normative defense for indifference to autocracy is weak. For several decades, American leaders and thinkers championed nonintervention in the internal affairs of other countries, and cited that norm to justify ignoring domestic abuses in autocratic regimes. In earlier eras of American history, doctrines against imperialism and in support of sovereignty carried moral weight, especially during the wave of decolonization that took place in Africa and Asia after World War II. Today, however, respecting the sovereignty of despotic regimes more often than not means doing nothing to stop human rights violations, be they the arrest of political dissidents in China, Iran, or Russia, or genocide in Rwanda in 1994 or in Sudan today. American foreign policy makers can invoke security or material interests to justify American inaction in such instances, but they are hard pressed to invoke ethical or normative arguments to justify their indifference to human rights abuses practiced by autocratic regimes.

The same is true regarding the active support of autocracies. When the United States provides billions of dollars in aid over several decades to prop up the Egyptian dictatorship, the sovereignty of the Egyptian people is being violated. Such a foreign policy may meet other American interests, but cannot be defended on normative grounds.[1] Likewise, when the United States provided military and financial support to Saddam Hussein so he could fight the Islamic Republic of Iran in the 1980s—a war that brought massive suffering to both the Iraqi and Iranian people— the policy had no moral defense, especially when Iraq used chemical weapons in the fight. American support for the apartheid regime in South Africa, Augusto Pinochet in Chile, and Mohammad Reza Shah Pahlavi in Iran are other examples in which norms were not the decisive factor shaping American foreign policy.[2]

In pursuing these policies, American leaders always have invoked the national interest. But what is the national interest, who defines it, and how is it best achieved? In digging down to the bare essentials, few would disagree that the central aim of American foreign policy must be to provide the greatest security possible to the American people. Division erupts over strategy.

Which foreign policies most effectively make Americans safer? For two centuries, American politicians, academics, and commentators have advanced very different answers guided by competing analytical assumptions.[3] The contours and cleavages of this contest over strategy are complex, but two fundamental issues have framed the debate: the degree of American involvement in the world and the nature of this involvement.

Isolation versus Engagement

The central cleavage in American foreign policy thinking for much of the country's first century was between advocates of isolation and proponents of international engagement. President George Washington's famous warning to avoid "entangling alliances" launched a longstanding and successful isolationist tradition of remaining detached from the unpredictable zigs and zags of international politics, especially in amoral, self-interested, and imperial Europe. The pursuit of this objective subsequently entailed repelling European advances into American affairs, defined at first narrowly to mean the territory of the United States and later, as codified in the Monroe Doctrine, to encompass the entire Western hemisphere. For more than a century, this isolationist and unilateralist doctrine dominated American strategic thinking. Geography and relative American weakness helped the isolationist cause. Back then, American leaders did not have the military or economic wherewithal to project power across the oceans and participate in global politics, even if they had aspired to do so. As late as 1885, President Grover Cleveland could declare in his first message to Congress:

> Maintaining, as I do, the tenets of a line of precedents
> from Washington's day, which proscribe entangling al-

liances with foreign states, I do not favor a policy of acquisition of new and distant territory or the incorporation of remote interests with our own.[4]

Just a decade after Cleveland's affirmation of Washingtonian isolationism, the imperial bug so widespread in Europe at the time finally infected American leaders. When the United States emerged as a genuine great power in the decades after the Civil War and reached the geographic limits of the continent, American strategic thinkers embraced a policy of "acquisition of new and distant territory," an impulse that eventually helped to produce the 1898 Spanish-American War and the creation of American colonies in the Philippines, Guam, Puerto Rico, and Hawaii. In deciding to enter World War I in 1917 and then subsequently participating in the post-war settlement in Versailles, President Woodrow Wilson broke firmly with Washington's warnings. Wilson joined with one set of European powers against another, and then helped create the archetypal entangling alliance: the League of Nations.[5]

Isolationism enjoyed one last surge of popularity in the inter-war period, especially in reaction to the Great Depression. During this period, Congress refused to ratify the Treaty of Versailles or join the League of Nations, and individuals such as Charles Lindbergh and groups such as the America First Committee forcefully articulated the American desire to stay out of World War II. However, the Japanese attack on Pearl Harbor on December 7, 1941, forever shattered the isolationist assumption that the United States could keep safe through disengagement. Since then, growing American power and emergent technologies that have made the world more connected (ballistic missiles, electronic trading in emerging markets, jet travel, the internet, etc.) have greatly diminished the analytic and prescriptive power of isolationist arguments. The isolationist impulse remains alive in both the Republican and Democratic parties, but only at the fringes of the debate, not the center.

Wilsonian Liberalism versus Realism

A second debate about strategies for making the American people safe and prosperous pits the so-called liberals and so-called realists—"so-called" because neither label actually captures the essence of either side's arguments.[6]

Wilsonian liberals—so dubbed in honor of Woodrow Wilson—contend that a country's internal political regime influences the way the country behaves externally.[7] Liberals have adopted a thesis first expounded more than 200 years ago by Immanuel Kant, arguing that democracies rarely go to war with each other, while autocracies are more likely to engage in conflict with both other autocracies and democracies.[8]

As discussed in the previous chapter, empirical research shows that democracies do not fight each other, even if the causes for this correlation are still poorly understood. As a result, the "democratic peace" thesis yields a clear prescriptive strategy: the United States (along with other democracies) has a national security interest in the expansion of democratic regimes throughout the world. In Wilson's famous formulation, the United States had to change the world to make Americans safe.[9] In Wilson's view, the best way to achieve American security was not to defend or isolate the United States from the outside world, but to change the political character of the outside world.

This approach to American foreign policy is not confined to the Democratic Party. During the Cold War, one of the staunchest Wilsonian liberals in foreign policy was Republican President Ronald Reagan, who also believed that the advance of democracy abroad enhanced American security at home.[10]

Realism is a second important tradition in American foreign policy and academia, one that has dominated American
thinking for most of the last century.[11] Realism as a theory of
international relations and ideological guide to foreign policymaking is based on three core assumptions.[12] First, states are the
central actors in an anarchic world. International institutions,
NGOs, multi-national corporations and other non-state actors
are either unimportant or a reflection of the interests of the
most powerful states. Second, domestic regime type does not
influence the external behavior of states. Third, rather than type
of government, the external behavior of states is determined
largely by their external environment, specifically, the balance
of power between the major states in the international system.
Realists believe that because power—not ideals or ethics—is so
central to a state's well being, states constantly compete to acquire more power relative to other states in the world. As John
Mearsheimer argues, "A zero-sum quality characterizes that
competition, sometimes making it intense and unforgiving.
States may cooperate with each other on occasion, but at root
they have conflicting interests."[13] American realists, therefore,
see any country with great or growing military and economic
power as a threat to the United States. Rising powers in particular such as Germany and the Soviet Union in the last century
and China today are especially frightening because they disrupt
the global balance of power and can trigger conflict between old
and new great powers.

This theory prescribes that the United States has a security
interest in increasing its military and economic power and fostering and maintaining alliances with powerful states to check
the influence of other great or rising powers. As President Nixon
once told Chinese leader Mao Zedong, "What is important is
not a nation's internal political philosophy. What is important is

its policy toward the rest of the world and toward us."[14] In Nixon's view, the balance of power was the crucial ingredient in international politics and therefore preserving America's power position, in this case by reaching out to China to balance against a rising Soviet power, was the best strategy to make Americans more secure.[15] To accumulate power to balance against potential challengers, realists argue that the United States needs access to oil, minerals, basing rights, and trade from all countries willing to cooperate, irrespective of whether they are autocratic or democratic.

This philosophy about world politics also prompts a policy prescription that it is best to refrain from democracy promotion. Realists argue that democracy promotion can undermine allies, empower anti-American forces, and generate both domestic and international instability. By pushing for democratization, so the argument goes, the United States "might help set forces in motion that it cannot control and that threaten its vital interests. . . . And even if it is accepted that stability has not brought [the US] security in all respects, it scarcely follows that instability will do so. That assumes that things cannot get worse than they are, a hazardous assumption for a statesman to make and one belied by much of human history."[16]

Like liberalism, realism as a guide for foreign policymaking is not confined to one political party in the United States.[17] The consummate realist of the twentieth century, Richard Nixon, was a Republican just like Ronald Reagan, the consummate Wilsonian liberal of the same century. Realism has a long tradition within the Democratic Party as well, recently energized in reaction to George W. Bush's alleged embrace of neoconservative or Wilsonian liberal policies.[18] In American academia, realism has dominated the study of international relations for decades.[19]

The Case for Wilsonian Liberalism
with a Realist Core

The realist premise that power matters is self-evident. The accumulation of military and economic power over the last two centuries has transformed the United States from a peripheral player in international politics to a world super-power. This accumulation of power has helped to deter and defeat foes. Conversely, countries with massive militaries and successful economies have impacted U.S. national security more directly over the past two centuries than weaker countries have, no matter what the internal composition of these great powers. Today, autocratic China and democratic India matter more to U.S. national security than autocratic Zimbabwe or democratic Honduras.

The stronger claim that only power matters is equally self-evidently wrong. Not all great powers have threatened American national security. Only great powers run by autocrats have posed real threats. At the other end of the power spectrum, very weak but highly motivated illiberal anti-democratic movements have threatened American national security. Neither America's armed forces nor its mighty nuclear arsenal—once thought to be the ultimate deterrent and preserver of peace in a rational world—prevented the Al Qaeda terrorist attacks on September 11.[20] As John Lewis Gaddis has observed,

> Neither [George W.] Bush nor his successors, whatever their party, can ignore what the events of September 11, 2001, made clear; that deterrence against states affords insufficient protection from attacks by gangs, which can now inflict the kind of damage only states fighting wars used to be able to achieve.[21]

Classic realist frameworks for assessing threats to U.S. national security fail to appreciate these kinds of very real threats.

To make Americans secure and prosperous, neither purely realist dogma nor purely liberal ideology provides good guidance. At times, the United States has needed to work with autocratic regimes to pursue vital national interests. Without French military intervention in the American Revolution (an instance of military intervention to promote democracy), the United States would not have become an independent country when it did. Without the Soviet Union as an ally, the United States would have suffered much higher casualties in World War II and could easily have failed to defeat the Nazi regime. Without the illiberal kingdom of Saudi Arabia as a trade partner today, the United States would not have enough affordable energy to support our current way of life. A foreign policy that refused French military assistance, an alliance with Stalin, or oil from Saudi Arabia would not have served American national interests.

At the same time, the claim that internal regime type of other countries has no impact on American national interests is ahistorical. The idea that promoting balance-of-power politics is a more prudent ideological guide for American foreign policy than promoting democracy is equally naïve. The history of the last 200 years, but especially the last 80 years, shows that American security, economic, and moral interests have been enhanced by the expansion of democracy abroad, while reliance on realpolitik frameworks as a guide for foreign policy has produced some short-term gains but many long-term setbacks for American national interests. The remainder of this chapter explains why, by looking at (1) the dangers of autocratic foes; (2) the tenuous benefits of autocratic allies; (3) the long-term security advantages from alliances with democracies; (4) the security benefits of democratization; (5) the security threats from democratic breakdown; (6) the economic dividends of democratic expansion; and (7) the positive reputational gains of supporting democracy abroad. These factors all point to America's security and economic interests being enhanced by the advance of democracy around the world.

Autocratic Enemies

Every foreign enemy of the United States has been a dictatorship. Autocracies, not democracies, have attacked and threatened the United States. The consolidation of democratic regimes in states ruled by formerly anti-American, autocratic regimes has transformed such countries from enemies into allies of the United States. Over the last two centuries, the advance of democracy abroad has made Americans safer at home.

The first war fought by Americans as independent citizens (or, more precisely, people striving to become independent citizens) was sparked in part by a disagreement between autocrats and democrats. The American Revolution is often portrayed as an anti-colonial war of independence, compared with later struggles for sovereignty in Africa and Asia in the twentieth century. However, the "Americans" who fought the British were in large measure colonialists on the North American continent. (Thus the appropriate analogy is not Indians fighting to regain their independence, but white Rhodesians breaking with their native country in an attempt to establish a new country). As Robert Kagan has written, "Mid-eighteenth-century Anglo-Americans thus became the most enthusiastic of British imperialists . . . . [C]olonial elites, far from seeking separation from the Old World, aspired to be more British in their habits, their manners, and their dress."[22] The manner of rule—not ethnic conflict or anti-imperialism—precipitated conflict. A British autocracy sought to sustain and expand antidemocratic practices in the American terri-tories. The American colonialists who eventually led the struggle for independence mobilized initially to resist King George III's attempts to abrogate their rights as Englishmen. Under the battle cry, "no taxation without representation," Americans rebelled as a means of ending perceived antidemocratic practices in the American colonies.

Victory in the War of Independence did not eliminate the British threat to American national security; British troops burned the White House to the ground in 1814. But regime change in the United States did help to make Americans more se-cure, first and foremost by limiting radically the scope of British interference in the lives of American citizens. The initial institu-tional design for American democracy—the 1781 Articles of Confederation—failed to create an effective state capable of sus-taining economic growth or defending American citizens, but the subsequent 1787 democratic Constitution provided the institu-tional structure for sustaining one of the most successful economies in the modern era.[23] In addition, the type of govern-ment established by this constitution eventually (though not im-mediately) provided the framework for accumulating military power capable of deterring most American foes. Other kinds of regimes, including most prominently the Soviet dictatorship in the twentieth century, have replicated this concentration of co-ercive power, but in trying to sustain superpower capacities by means of a command economy and a totalitarian political system, the Soviet state eventually collapsed.[24]

In the 100 years following the War of 1812, the American republic faced minor threats and encroachments from European autocracies. Of these European threats, the one that diminished most dramatically over time and then disappeared altogether was Great Britain. Despite a tumultuous beginning, bilateral ties be-

tween Great Britain and the United States evolved into a cooperative relationship capable of settling international disputes
through negotiation rather than military conflict. England was always more liberal than the rest of Europe. The Magna Carta of
1215, Henry VIII's break with Rome, and the Glorious Revolution in 1688 were historic milestones on the path to creating a
liberal state, from which both British and American political institutions evolved in the eighteenth and nineteenth centuries. This
common liberal heritage provided the glue for a deep and lasting
relationship. By the end of the nineteenth century, Arthur Balfour,
the leader of the British Tory Party, rightly predicted that "the day
would come" when "statesman of authority" would "lay down the
doctrine that between English speaking peoples" war was "impossible."[25] In the twentieth century, British-American ties developed
into a "special relationship" that anchored a strategic alliance in
World War I, World War II, and the Cold War. As powerful ideological challengers to democracy emerged in the twentieth century, the United States and Great Britain worked closely to defend
and later expand liberal democracy.

America's relations with France were more volatile, not because of France's fluctuating power capabilities, but rather because of internal dynamics in the French Republic. American
revolutionaries had no qualms about accepting military assistance
from a French monarch, but the French Revolution presented a
dilemma for American statesmen. Thomas Jefferson and his Republican allies applauded the revolutionaries and wanted to provide assistance to "the freedom struggle," while John Adams,
Alexander Hamilton, and their Federalist friends lamented the
loss of an ally in the *ancien régime* and worried about antagonizing
Great Britain. The debate resulted in American neutrality, driven
mostly by American weakness, but also by American ideological
division. However, the restoration of absolutism that followed the

Napoleonic wars appeared threatening to the new American republic. At the time, the United States lacked the military capacity or inclination to become involved in Europe's wars, but American elite sentiment clearly turned against France as the regime governing this former U.S. ally became increasingly autocratic.

In the early 1820s, the great powers in Europe colluded to squash rebellions in Italy, Portugal, and Greece. Contemporary and subsequent champions of realist philosophy applauded these military interventions on the grounds that they preserved the balance of power on the continent.[26] More generally, the Concert of Europe, which maintained the balance of power in Europe for most of the nineteenth century, is often celebrated as a brilliant application of realist ideology in the name of world peace.[27] The relative peace on the continent kept Americans out of war with rising European powers for several decades.[28] Europe's imperial impulses during the nineteenth century, which fundamentally reshaped borders and governance in most of Africa and parts of Asia, did not threaten American security or sovereignty directly. American leaders, however, viewed the Concert's autocratic actions as potential threats to the American experiment with democracy. As John Quincy Adams warned in 1816, "All the restored governments of Europe are deeply hostile to us."[29]

During this period, American presidents applauded and sometimes aided the movements of independence in South America, thereby indirectly pitting the United States against absolutist regimes in Europe. As eventually codified in 1823 in the Monroe Doctrine, American leaders sought to push all European actors—irrespective of regime type—out of the American hemisphere. Rhetorically, U.S. officials framed this policy in moral terms: fledgling American republics battling against absolutist monarchs.

In the nineteenth century, the real autocratic threat to American security, prosperity, and territorial integrity came from within the U.S., not from Europe.[30] The political regimes in place in the American South before the Civil War can only be understood as an autocratic, just as South Africa under apartheid was a dictatorship, even though white elites in both places enjoyed some liberal and democratic rights. When drafting the 1787 Constitution, northern leaders compromised with their southern counterparts, believing that northern acquiescence to slavery was the only way to preserve the Union. They did so, however, knowing full well that this "grand compromise" threatened the long-term future of American democracy. As Washington warned, "nothing but the rooting out of slavery can perpetuate the existence of our union, by consolidating it in a bond of principle."[31] Over time, the northern and southern systems of government grew further apart, and so too did their conceptions of American foreign policy. For instance, in a debate about democratization and stability with echoes today, northern antislavery politicians applauded Haiti's successful struggle for independence in 1804, while southern leaders denounced the slave rebellion as destabilizing and threatening to American national interests. Later, northern leaders applauded the Monroe Doctrine as an assertion of American power in the name of republicanism, while southern leaders saw the doctrine and efforts to expand it as dangerous examples of the federal government wielding its power to influence the internal politics of foreign governments. Eventually, some northerners aspired to use American power to promote "regime change" in the South. "Realist" southerners, in contrast, wanted to preserve the balance of power within the republic and avoid using federal power to meddle in the internal affairs of states. It was only with the elimination of this regime type in the South, after a long and tragic civil war, that the illiberal threat to

American democracy from within disappeared. Over time, the advance of democracy in the South made the United States a more secure and wealthier country.

The North's occupation of the South after the Civil War might be considered the first instance of the United States using military force to pursue democratic regime change and nation building. Before the war, southern states enjoyed tremendous autonomy from the federal government, and during the Civil War itself, of course, these states declared their independence from the United States. The North's post-war occupation aimed not only to reincorporate these states into the Union, but also to establish more democratic practices in the occupied territories, including first and foremost the extension of the franchise to former slaves. Like future attempts to use military force for democracy promotion, the results were limited; early gains were eventually undermined by more enduring anti-democratic social and political institutions in the South, which circumscribed the human and democratic rights of African-Americans for decades after the Civil War. Only a major grassroots social movement launched nearly a century later completed the South's transformation from autocracy to democracy.

The Civil War aside, other American military conflicts in the nineteenth century can hardly be blamed on a supposed threat emanating from autocracies. Presidents did concoct arguments about the spread of civilization as an excuse for seizing the land of indigenous nations in North America and Hawaii. Even before independence, American settlers championed the virtues of empire and the legitimacy of expanding Western civilization through conquest. After the creation of the United States, American leaders saw little contradiction between their democratic values and the expansion of their country across the continent, even when this expansion meant the destruction or relocation of indigenous nations or going to war with Mexico. Not all American leaders agreed with these tactics or the arguments that justified them, but those in favor of using force to enlarge the country prevailed.[32] These conflicts had little to do with the internal organization of the Mexican or Native American governments and everything to do with the American desire for more territory.

Beyond North America, American leaders did perceive new threats emanating from the expansionist impulses of European and Asian empires in the nineteenth century. This new global competition for colonies and resources compelled American leaders to reexamine the relationship between American power and principles. By the end of the nineteenth century, the United States was no longer a fragile new state, but a major industrial power. Given this new level of power and the growing international interests of Americans producers that accompanied it, some American leaders wanted to join the international scramble for new territory, believing that colonies would make the United States stronger and richer. Others supported imperialism because they believed in a special missionary role for the United States as a promoter of civilization in lands occupied by barbarians.

As a result of this new American flirtation with imperialism, conflict eventually erupted in 1898. American leaders framed the Spanish-American War in moral terms—Spanish tyranny versus American liberty. Similar brushes with conflict with the more liberal British Empire, for instance in the border dispute between Venezuela and Guyana at the end of the nineteenth century, did not lead to war. On the contrary, the peaceful resolution of this crisis proved to some that the prospect of war between Great Britain and the United States would be similar to the "unnatural horror of civil war."[33] Nonetheless, it would be a stretch to argue that Spanish autocracy precipitated the Spanish-American War, or even that autocratic Spain threatened the democratic United States in Cuba. American leaders wanted this war as a way to get into the colonial game.

After a quick victory, the United States acquired Puerto Rico, established a protectorate in Cuba, and occupied the former Spanish colonies of Guam and the Philippine islands. As with North American territories annexed earlier and the occupation of the South after the Civil War, American leaders proclaimed the promotion of freedom a core objective of the American presence in the Philippines.[34] The mission did not go well. In the Philippines, American forces fought a prolonged war against insurgents, resulting in the deaths of 220,000 Filipino soldiers and civilians and 4,000 American soldiers over 14 years.[35] Such bitter experiences with colonization and state-building tempered further American imperial aspirations. President Woodrow Wilson in particular rejected the imperial ambitions and "gunboat diplomacy" of Theodore Roosevelt, promising instead to restore American traditions of anti-colonialism.[36] Never again did the United States seek to obtain colonies, and once this anti-colonial norm in American foreign policy was reaffirmed, the United States clashed increasingly with those non-democratic regimes that continued to seek territorial gain through military conquest.[37]

World Wars Against Dictatorships

For most world leaders and political analysts, World War I represented the breakdown of the brilliantly orchestrated *realpolitik* as practiced on the European continent for a good part of the nineteenth century. In President Wilson's view, however, the war erupted not only because of changes in the balance of power in Europe, but also because of the distribution of ideas and political systems on the continent. The United States, according to Wilson, was threatened not simply by German military power, but by German autocratic power. After seeking in vain to preserve American neutrality and to negotiate a "peace without victors," Wilson eventually responded to German submarine attacks on American ships by joining the war on the side of Great Britain, France, and Russia. In explaining American motivations for joining the war, Wilson emphasized that the U.S.

> seeks no material profit or aggrandizement of any kind. She is fighting for no advantage or selfish object of her own but for the liberation of peoples everywhere from the aggressions of *autocratic* force.[38]

Wilson argued for American involvement in World War I as a defensive move, a way to protect America's freedoms and republican system of government from the autocratic, illiberal ways of Germany and its allies. Of course, World War I was not solely a conflict between democracies and autocracies. Great Britain and France allied with tsarist Russia, one of the most rigid autocracies in Europe at the time, to fight Germany and the Austrian-Hungarian Empire.[39] Nonetheless, in making the case for joining this foreign war, Wilson explicitly framed American interests in normative terms, emphasizing that the United States "had no quarrel with the German people" but instead aimed to repel the belligerent behavior of Germany's autocratic regime.[40] Wilson saw American involvement in the war as a means to expand freedom for all mankind:

> The tragic events of the three months of vital turmoil through which we have just passed have made us citizens of the world. There can be no turning back. Our fortunes as a nation are involved, whether we like it

or not. . . . And yet we are not the less American on
that account. We shall be the more American if we
but remain true to the principles in which we have
been bred. They are not principles of a province or
of a single continent. We have known and boasted all
along that they were the principles of a liberated
mankind.[41]

It is difficult to imagine that the United States would have
fought in World War I if Germany had been a liberal democracy.
Even more virulent forms of autocracy defined the nature
of the threat to the United States in World War II. All American
foes in this war were autocracies. The conflict was not simply a
struggle between the world's great military powers, but a war
that pitted Western democracies against German and Italian fascism as well as Japanese imperialism.[42] The nature of the settlement that ended World War I helped to fuel German nationalism
well before Hitler derailed the Weimar Republic and seized power
in January 1933.[43] Hitler took advantage of elections and a relatively pluralist political system to build his Nazi party. Yet, Hitler
invaded Poland six years after Germany had become a full-blown
dictatorship. Moreover, his blitzkrieg on Poland's western border
was so effective in part because he had an autocratic ally, the Soviet Union, invading Poland from the east. The secret Molotov-
Ribbentrop pact would not have been concluded between a
democratic and fascist regime.

Nonetheless, the same totalitarian regime that colluded with
Hitler in 1939 to start World War II eventually played a decisive
role in defeating the Nazi regime. Without question, the United
States, Great Britain, and the rest of the free world needed the
highly undemocratic Soviet regime to save the democratic world.
For Roosevelt, cooperating with Stalin was part of a strategy for

minimizing American casualties.[44] More than 27 million Soviets died during World War II, most of them civilians felled by disease, deportation, or conflict; Red Army deaths exceeded 8 million.[45] According to John Lewis Gaddis, "for every American who died in the war . . . fifty-three Russians died."[46] Had Roosevelt refused to cooperate with the Soviet Union at the time because of Stalin's inhumane methods of governing at home, American national security interests would have suffered.

The Cold War

The anti-democratic nature of Stalin's regime, however, doomed Roosevelt's desire for long-term cooperation with the Soviet Union after World War II. Roosevelt hoped for collective security, embodied first in his concept of the "Four Policemen" and later in the creation of the United Nations Security Council. But it did not work in large part because of the ideological conflict between American democracy and capitalism on the one hand and Soviet communism on the other.[47] To be sure, the notion of collective security was also derailed by mutual distrust over the massive military power amassed by the United States and the Soviet Union—which eventually spawned the Cold War. But the key obstacle was the fact that these Soviet military resources lay in the hands of a competing political and economic system that presented a tremendous threat to American national security for several decades after World War II.[48] Because both countries believed their respective systems were superior, they actively promoted the replication of these political and socio-economic systems in other countries and resisted expansion of the other's system elsewhere in the world.[49] The Soviet Union and the United States were rivals not only because they were the two greatest military and political powers in the international system, but because they were two powers with antithetical visions about how domestic polities and economies should be organized.

Realists sometimes reflect fondly on the stability of the Cold War era, and the supposedly more manageable threats facing the U.S. compared to our current era.[50] In fact, the Cold War was anything but stable and peaceful for the United States or the rest of the world. By one estimate, 120 wars killed roughly 20 million people during this period of bipolar "stability."[51] The nuclear stalemate did keep the Soviet-American rivalry from becoming a full scale third world war, yet millions of people in the developing world, as well as American and Soviet soldiers fighting in these wars, died during this so-called Cold War to preserve this so-called stability. To contain communism, American soldiers fought directly in wars in Korea and Vietnam and the U.S. provided military advisors and assistance to dozens of proxy armed forces fighting against Soviet-sponsored proxies (sometimes real, sometimes imaginary) in all corners of the world, from Greece to Turkey, from Iran to Guatemala, from Cuba to Laos, from Angola to El Salvador, from the Dominican Republic to Zaire.[52] For the people of these countries, as well as those living in Korea, Hungary, Congo, Vietnam, Czechoslovakia, Cambodia, Chile, El Salvador, Angola, Afghanistan (all non-democracies at the time of these conflicts) or for the American and Soviet soldiers who died fighting in many of them, the post-war international system did not provide stability or peace.

Miscalculations about the nature of the communist threat also undermined American national security interests. American presidents initially treated the entire communist world as monolithic, a mistake with disastrous consequences for American strategic interests, especially in Asia. Oftentimes U.S. leaders confused means and ends, so that all users of violence against non-communist states were considered part of the world communist movement. Nelson Mandela, for instance, was considered for decades to be a "communist terrorist." The American inability to distinguish between anti-colonial movements struggling for independence and Soviet proxies struggling for world communist revolution also led to many strategic errors in fighting the Cold War, including most tragically in Vietnam. The overzealous search for communist enemies from within in the 1950s also weakened the American model of democracy, a valuable tool in fighting against real ideological enemies. These challenges to American security all emanated from a perception of ideological threats that would not have existed in a world governed only by democratic regimes.

Viewing communism as a global threat also prompted most American presidents to court anti-communist regimes around the world, including many unstable and unpredictable dictatorships. During this period, the Shah in Iran was a great ally of the U.S. for 37 years, but a terrible ally that 38th year, when the radical mullahs removed him from power and transformed the Islamic Republic of Iran into a serious enemy of the United States and its allies. In trying to recover from the loss of the Shah as an ally, the United States subsequently embraced Saddam Hussein in Iraq as he waged an inhumane war against Iran in the 1980s. Soon after the conclusion of the Iran-Iraq war, Saddam Hussein turned against the United States, invaded Kuwait, and thereby triggered the largest deployment of American military power since World War II. The American embrace of both of these autocratic rulers produced some ephemeral benefits for U.S. security, but the short-term gains were outweighed by the long-term negative consequences. Had both Iran and Iraq been ruled by democratic regimes at the time, they would have posed no great challenge to American national security interests.

As part of a strategy to roll back communism at its weakest links, President Reagan agreed to provide military assistance to national liberation fighters with dubious democratic credentials fighting against communist regimes in Angola, Afghanistan, Cambodia, and Nicaragua.[53] The strategy had some success in weakening Soviet imperialism, but little success in nurturing new American allies, in large measure because of inattention to the internal governing structures in these countries and indifference to the norms that anti-communist movements embraced. By 2008, democracy had taken root only partially in just one of these four countries, Nicaragua, and ironically, Daniel Ortega, the Sandinista leader the American-backed *contras* sought to depose, was the democratically elected president.[54] Cambodia in the twenty-first century does not pose a threat to American national security, but the regime in place there is not democratic and remains one of the most corrupt in the world. In Angola, the Reagan administration made a tragic error in backing the undemocratic Jonas Savimbi, who succeeded in prolonging a civil war for decades, which enabled him to stay in power in the territory he controlled until his death.[55] The most detrimental error for American security, however, was Operation Cyclone, the program of covert U.S. support for the *mujahadeen* during the Soviet war in Afghanistan. These so-called freedom fighters were useful U.S. allies in driving the Soviets out of Afghanistan, but they were hardly Jeffersonian believers, as the world learned when they tried to govern Afghanistan in the early 1990s. On the contrary, their failure to build stable, accountable government helped to bring to power the Taliban, which in turn invited Al Qaeda to set up shop in Afghanistan. That alliance eventually yielded devastating consequences for American national security on September 11, 2001.[56]

In the name of containing communism at various times during the twentieth century, American foreign policymakers also helped to empower and sustain dictatorships in Argentina, Brazil, Chile, Egypt, El Salvador, Indonesia, the Philippines, Portugal, Saudi Arabia, South Africa, South Korea, Taiwan, and Zaire, to name just a few of the most notorious regimes. None of these alliances posed direct or indirect threats to short-term national security interests, but they did undermine American moral standing in the international community, which subsequently constrained American efforts to promote democracy in other countries during the Cold War era.

After the Cold War

Since the end of the Cold War, America's enemies have continued to be drawn from the ranks of autocratic regimes and antidemocratic movements. In the 1990s, no state directly threatened the United States, but American security interests in peace and stability in Europe were threatened by Serbia's autocratic ruler, Slobodan Milošević, who wreaked havoc in the Balkans through war with his neighbors and ethnic cleansing in Kosovo.[57] Milošević never threatened American security directly, but his wars did undermine security in the backyard of America's closest European allies. Consequently, American armed forces eventually became involved in the Balkan wars, including a major peacekeeping operation in Bosnia-Herzegovina and a NATO bombing campaign against Serbia in the spring of 1999 to stop Milošević's forced expulsion of ethnic Albanians from Kosovo. Today, American troops remain in Bosnia-Herzegovina and Kosovo.

In September 1994, the United States led a U.N.-sanctioned military intervention called Operation Uphold Democracy to overthrow a dictatorship in Haiti. Again, the Haitian military junta did not represent a direct threat to American national security, but the regime's policies did constitute an assault on American values and a possible economic burden from tens of thousands of Haitians seeking refuge in the United States. American military interventions in Panama and Somalia were likewise not in response to direct threats to the United States, but both regimes were non-democracies.

In the 1990s, Iran, North Korea, Afghanistan, Iraq, Cuba, and Libya did not have the military capacity to threaten the United States directly. Nonetheless, relations that had been tense and confrontational with these countries during the Cold War remained so in the decade that followed. The only common feature among all these countries is autocracy. Certainly it is not the power capabilities of these countries that led American leaders—Democratic and Republican alike—to consider them threats to the United States. Even before September 11, 2001, U.S. military budgets were many times greater than the combined military spending in these countries.[58]

Military Budgets (in billions)

U.S. ████████████████████	281.0
Iran ▌ 6.9 (R)	
Syria ▌ 4.5 (e)	
North Korea ▌ 4.3 (P, R)	
Iraq ▎ 1.3 (R)	
Cuba ▎ 0.6 (E, e)	
Sudan ▎ 0.4 (E)	
Libya (NA)	

(e): Major share of total mil expenditures believed omitted, probably including most expenditures on arms procurement
(E): Estimate based on partial or uncertain data
(NA): Data not available
(P): Value data converted from national currency at estimated PPP
(R): Rough estimate

To deter impoverished North Korea, the United States has maintained more than 35 thousand troops in South Korea for over half a century, while also supplying South Korea with billions of dollars in military and economic assistance.[59] To contain Iran, the U.S. has supplied billions of dollars in military equipment and deployed the U.S. Navy in the Persian Gulf. Iran's annual military budget is less than one-eightieth that of the United States.[60] To counter future ballistic missile threats from North Korea and Iran, American military planners have spent billions of dollars to develop national and theater ballistic missile defense systems. These asymmetric responses by American foreign policymakers to relatively minor military powers can only be explained if regime type in Iran and North Korea is part of the threat analysis.

After September 11, the Bush administration calculated wrongly that the future military threat from autocratic Iraq was so great that the United States had to intervene preemptively to overthrow Saddam Hussein's dictatorship. An assessment of threats based only on the balance of military power between Iraq and the United States would have produced a different conclusion.[61] Think, however, of the other counterfactual: Had Iraq been ruled by a democratic regime, no amount of intelligence about Iraq's secret nuclear weapons program would have convinced the American people to support a preemptive war.

U.S. policy toward Cuba can likewise be explained only with reference to Fidel Castro's dictatorship.[62] Cuba has virtually no military capacity to threaten the United States, and yet, for more than four decades, president after president—Democrats and Republicans alike—have maintained a sanctions regime against this island country, to the detriment of American economic interests.

The People's Republic of China has lingered somewhere between friend and foe of the United States since the end of the Cold War. China's current military capacity and potential for even greater military might create the possibility of serious confrontation with the United States, yet China's regime type also plays a direct role in exacerbating Sino-American tensions.[63] Despite the enormous amount of trade and investment traffic between China and the United States, American leaders continue to support Taiwan's security, both by selling military hardware and by maintaining a deliberately vague commitment to defending the island against attack from the mainland. This American support began when an autocratic regime ruled Taiwan, but has continued in part because Taiwan made the transition to democracy in 2000. Taiwanese leaders and diplomats constantly stress the democratic values they share with the United States as a central reason for close military cooperation. If mainland China were to become a democracy, then the case for defending Taiwanese sovereignty would be weakened.

The current successful management of American-Chinese relations underscores the important observation that conflicts between democracies and autocracies are not inevitable.[64] The Bush administration's casting of China as a "stakeholder" in the international system—that is, a force for the status quo rather than a revisionist power—produced stabilizing results. Nonetheless, there is no question that managing China's rise will remain a central concern of American presidents for the next century. For the past 15 years, China has increased military spending steadily and gradually, a pattern that suggests China is seeking to counter if not challenge American military might.[65] American concern about this military buildup is driven in large measure by the nature of the Chinese regime. A rising democratic China would be less threatening.

In the 1990s, non-governmental movements dedicated to nondemocratic ideologies also posed threats to the United States and its allies. As discussed in chapter 2, Al Qaeda espouses a set of beliefs antithetical to democracy, which Osama bin Laden and his followers associate with the evil West.[66] In their quest to push the

United States out of the Middle East, bin Laden and his followers attacked the United States numerous times in the 1990s, culminating in the horrendous terrorist attacks on American soil on September 11, 2001.[67] Once again, the United States is at war with a transnational, ideologically motivated enemy, whose core beliefs are anti-democratic, anti-liberal, and therefore anti-American.

Political organizations that use terrorism as a weapon do not all embrace the same antidemocratic political objectives as Al Qaeda. Hezbollah in Lebanon has participated in elections and followed the rule of law at times, while also pursuing a parallel terrorist campaign against Israel and justifying extra-constitutional acts within Lebanon when convenient. Hamas has followed a similar dual track strategy in the Palestinian Authority. Most absurdly, Hamas participated in and won the January 2006 parliamentary elections, then executed a coup d'etat to seize power in Gaza the following year. Neither Hamas nor Hezbollah can be considered democratic organizations or part of democratic governments. Both are adversaries of the United States and its democratic allies in the Middle East.[68]

Autocratic Allies: Short-Term Necessities and Long-Term Liabilities

All enemies of the United States have been and are autocracies, but not all autocracies have been or are enemies of the United States. As just discussed, the United States has benefitted from a variety of alliances through the years with monarchists (in France during the American Revolution), and autocrats (in Russia during World War I and the Soviet Union during World War II). Autocratic allies, however, have posed three major national security problems for American leaders: sustainability, consistency, and cost.

Regarding sustainability, most autocratic regimes have no predictable or legitimate way to hand over power, meaning that transitions from one leader to the next can be precarious. Generally, though not always, democracies make leadership transitions more predictable. Even more problematic, autocrats often struggle to stay in power. In the face of societal unrest, autocrats typically resort to additional repression to hold onto power, a response that sidelines moderates and strengthens extremists, be they communists, fascists, or Islamic fundamentalists. These explosive situations often end in revolution, civil war, or state collapse, outcomes that almost never serve American interests. The fall of several autocratic allies, including Chiang Kai-shek in China, Fulgencio Batista in Cuba, the Shah in Iran, and Anastasio Somoza in Nicaragua all produced new autocratic regimes hostile to American interests. In these cases, new extremists came to power and blamed the United States for propping up the *ancien régime* they had just toppled.

Second, autocratic leaders can change their allegiances quickly. Because they do not answer to parliaments or voters, they can move much faster and in much more unpredictable ways to reverse their international orientation.[69] Stalin terminated cooperation with the western allies quickly after the end of the World War II, rejecting U.S. economic assistance offered through the Marshall Plan even though the Soviet economy at the time was in desperate need of such aid. Egyptian leader Gamal Adbul Nasser flip-flopped repeatedly in his relations with the United States before finally deciding to cast his lot with the Soviet Union.[70] Saddam Hussein was eager to cooperate with the United States during his war with Iran from 1980 to 1988, but quickly and easily abandoned his American allies when he decided to invade Kuwait in 1990. Uzbekistan's strong man, Islom Karimov, is a more recent flip-flopper: both Presidents Clinton and George

W. Bush courted him for years, but he dumped the U.S. abruptly in 2005 after ordering his troops to fire on protesters and blaming the United States for fomenting a supposed "insurrection."[71] Even strains in U.S.-Saudi relations underscore the difficulties of relying on autocrats as enduring and reliable allies. American and Saudi leaders share interests in trading energy resources and containing Iranian influence, but also struggle to manage major disagreements over the Israeli-Palestinian conflict, non-governmental Saudi assistance for fundamentalist religious movements, or more recently the lack of Saudi support for the Shia-dominated government in Iraq.[72] And Saudi Arabia has remained a major supplier of anti-American terrorists not only for the September 11 attacks, but in Iraq as well.[73] American relations with Pakistan have followed a similar topsy-turvy course of cordial relations followed by tenser phases, though it could not be argued that relations are better when democratic governments are in power in Pakistan and worse during periods of autocratic government. It goes without saying, however, that Pakistan has not always acted as a reliable ally of the United States. Support for the Taliban from Pakistan's Inter-Services Intelligence or ISI (their equivalent of the CIA) and the country's continued reluctance to move aggressively against Al Qaeda camps inside Pakistan underscore just how problematic such alliances can be.[74]

A third problem in working closely with autocratic allies is the cost Americans have to incur. Realist thinkers often argue that balancing against threats and supporting other countries to balance against American enemies (called by scholars "offshore balancing") amount to a less costly strategy for pursuing American national security interests compared to promotion of democratic change. Yet maintaining balances of power favorable to the U.S. through the engagement of autocratic allies is an extremely expensive and inexact policy. During the Cold War, in addition to

American spending on its own military forces, autocratic allies extracted tremendous military and economic subsidies from the United States as a price for maintaining their allegiance to the international anti-communist coalition. Maintaining regional balances of power between autocratic regimes or between autocratic and democratic regimes also proved costly in both financial and human terms. To maintain a balance of power in the Middle East, the United States has supplied billions of dollars in military and economic aid to both Israel and Egypt. American efforts at tweaking the balance of power between Iraq and Iran not only resulted in the death of more than one million Iraqi and Iranian soldiers in the Iran-Iraq war, but ultimately resulted in regimes hostile to the United States in both countries.[75] In Asia, the U.S. strategy of balancing Soviet and Chinese power by supporting autocratic allies in Vietnam and Korea proved very costly in American lives and resources. There may have been no other options; for example, had the United States not defended autocratic South Korea against North Korean aggression, a democratic South Korea may never have emerged. But to assume that the embrace of autocratic allies to balance against autocratic enemies is always a more efficient means for pursuing U.S. security interests is also wrong. The short-term benefits of embracing autocratic allies are almost always overshadowed by the long-term costs.

Finally, when the United States embraces autocratic allies, its reputation as a country committed to democratic values suffers greatly. The people of Iran still remember bitterly Operation Ajax and the overthrow of Prime Minister Mohammed Mossadeq in 1953 as well as American support for Saddam Hussein during the Iran-Iraq war. Citizens throughout Latin America still associate the United States with embracing military dictators. Close American associations with Mobutu in Zaire or the apartheid regime in South Africa have made Africans suspicious of American inten-

tions and skeptical of American pronouncements on democracy
and human rights. The Bush administration's embrace of dictators
in Egypt, Pakistan, Saudi Arabia, and Kazakhstan undermined its
calls for greater freedoms in Iran, Burma, and Russia.

Enduring Democratic Allies

Not every democracy in the world was or is a close ally of
the United States, but no democracy in the world has been or is
an American enemy. And all of America's most enduring allies
have been and remain democracies.

As mentioned above, Great Britain lingered as the most serious threat to the American republican experiment for decades
after the revolution. Over time, however, the common liberal
values that united Great Britain and the United States eventually
eclipsed the differences and paved the way for a peaceful transition from British to American hegemony, a very rare occurrence
in world history. The Anglo-American alliance gradually consolidated to anchor the free world, while the United States has benefited enormously from its military, economic, and cultural ties
to Great Britain. The two countries have not sided together on
every major foreign policy issue. In 1861, they inched close to
conflict during the so-called Trent affair involving the North's
blockade of Confederate ports into which British ships sailed, and
again in 1895–1896 over a border dispute between Great Britain
and Venezuela.[76] After World War II, the United States and Great
Britain clashed intermittently over various decolonization issues;
perhaps most amazingly, the United States sided with the autocratic Soviet Union in supporting Egyptian dictator Nasser against
democratic Britain and France during the Suez canal crisis in the
fall of 1956. The Suez crisis, however, stands out as a rare exception in Anglo-American relations over the past century. Despite

possessing roughly 200 nuclear warheads in its stockpile, Great Britain has posed no military threat whatsoever to the United States, and on most issues of war and peace, the United States and Great Britain have stood closely together.

The convergence of British and American foreign policy interests took place as both countries were deepening their democratic practices. Of course, they also share a common culture and history, which further contributed to the development of close relations. However, as relations today between Ukraine and Russia, for example, or North Korea and South Korea demonstrate, cultural and historical connections are not sufficient conditions for forging an alliance. Democratic consolidation in both the United States and Great Britain contributed significantly to the deepening of their "special relationship."

The United States also has enjoyed enduring alliances with other European and Asian democracies. In both world wars, it was not mere coincidence that the United States sided with the most liberal regimes. During the Cold War, American presidents developed ties with anti-communist autocrats as part of an international strategy of Soviet and communist containment, but the bedrock American allies during this decades-long struggle were European democracies, Canada, Australia, New Zealand, and Japan.

In the aftermath of the Soviet collapse and the disappearance of a common enemy, some predicted that ties developed among Western (and Asian) democracies during the Cold War would weaken and would be replaced by multi-polar competition among these former allies.[77] According to this realist analysis, the new multiple powers in Europe and the international system would be compelled to balance against each other by forming shifting alliances akin to the Concert of Europe in the nineteenth century.[78] To date, however, none of this predicted behavior among the great powers in Europe or among the democracies in the world has occurred: no arms races, spiraling threats, or even trade wars. Nor has balancing occurred between the United States and Europe. The democratic countries that composed the core of the alliance to contain communism have continued to co-operate to address common security threats, while democracies outside this Cold War alliance system—most notably India— have moved closer to the United States. Relations between states in this democratic core have been driven by a different dynamic than balance-of-power politics.[79] Despite realist predictions of its demise, the NATO military alliance has persevered and ex-panded, enlarging and protecting the democratic community of states in Europe.[80]

The American decision to invade Iraq placed a serious strain on the democratic community of states, since several important democracies, including France and Germany, vehemently ob-jected to the war. When these divisions crystallized in the spring of 2003, some predicted a return to balance of power politics in Europe, with France and Germany siding with Russia as one new constellation, and the United States, Great Britain, and Poland providing the backbone of an opposing axis.[81] This new power configuration never coalesced. Instead, relations between the democracies started to improve well before the war was over and even while President Bush was still in office. As newly elected French president Nikolas Sarkozy perceptively stated upon his arrival in the U.S. for a meeting with Bush in August 2007, "Do we agree on everything? No. . . . Even within families there are disagreements, but we are still the same family."[82]

The United States has also maintained close military and economic ties with the one democracy in the Middle East, Israel. Common Judeo-Christian values, American sympathy for the plight of the Jews during World War II, and a large Jewish population in the United States have helped to fortify this special American relationship with Israel, a bond that would probably persist even if Israel were a dictatorship. Nonetheless, Israel's unique status as the only liberal democracy in the region provides an added reason for close ties, and one that U.S. leaders frequently invoke as a justification for the deep American commitment to Israeli security. That traditional realist thinkers have questioned the utility of this alliance and cannot explain this close bilateral relationship using traditional metrics of state power suggests that the regime type in both the United States and Israel is critical in explaining this unique alliance.[83]

The United State never developed an alliance with democratic India during the Cold War. The world's most populous democracy instead maintained formal neutrality between East and West. This anomaly resulted primarily from the American decision to embrace Pakistan as a Cold War ally. However, the end of the Cold War opened the possibility of developing deeper ties with democratic India.[84] In the new context of their "global war on terror," Bush administration officials perceived India as an important ally both in combating Muslim terrorists and as a model regime in which 100 million Muslims participated relatively peacefully in a democratic system of government. This rapprochement became so extensive that American and Indian diplomats negotiated a deal in July 2007 that will provide India with U.S. nuclear technology for civilian purposes, even though India has refused to the sign the Non-Proliferation Treaty (NPT) and has successfully developed and tested nuclear weapons. American critics of the deal rightly claimed that the Bush administration's decision weakened the nonproliferation regime.[85] Given this rancor, the deal could only have been negotiated with a democratic regime—one seen as posing no current or future threat to the United States or its democratic allies.

Security Benefits from Democratic Change

Perhaps the most compelling evidence that democracy's advance serves American national interests comes from those countries that have changed from autocratic to democratic regimes. In every case, the country in transition has developed better relations with the United States after consolidating democracy.

World War II Enemies to Allies

As autocracies, Germany, Japan, and Italy were enemies of the United States. As democracies, all three have developed into important American allies.[86] Immediately after World War II, these three countries were occupied; their governments did not choose to ally with the United States. With time, all three countries put in place democratic institutions and in parallel gained greater sovereignty. As sovereign, democratic countries, Germany, Japan, and Italy all sought to maintain deep military ties with the United States. To be sure, these three countries sided with the United States in part as a response to the communist threat, compelling some to argue that the driving force behind these alliances was a common enemy.[87] But why were they all threatened by communism in the first place? It is because they were democracies. Moreover, these alliance relationships persisted well after the collapse of communism and the disintegration of the Soviet Union.

After communism's demise in Europe, transitions to democracy in East Central Europe, southern Europe, and the Baltic states also produced security benefits for the United States. Poland, the Czech Republic, and Hungary all joined NATO at the first opportunity in 1999, and seven more countries in the region joined in the second wave of enlargement in 2004. Every new liberal democracy in the region has decided to seek NATO membership. Initially, the benefits of NATO expansion seemed to accrue only to the new members, which were eager to counter a perceived Russian threat. NATO also provided a multilateral bridge for these new members as they pursued European Union membership. With time, however, the security benefits to the United States have grown. East European members of NATO were most vocal in supporting the American-led war in Iraq, including a famous "letter of eight" signed by three East Central European leaders in support of Bush and in opposition to "Western" or "old" European resistance to the military intervention.[88] At varying levels and for different periods of time, several new American allies in Europe, including Albania, Bulgaria, Croatia, the Czech Republic, Estonia, Hungary, Latvia, Lithuania, Poland, Romania, Slovakia, and Slovenia, provided troops in Afghanistan and Iraq. In 2006, Poland agreed to expand its forces fighting under NATO command in Afghanistan to one thousand, making Poland one of the largest contributors to the mission.[89] Some of these new allies, including Slovenia and Hungary, also have supplied troops to the peacekeeping mission in Kosovo. The Czech Republic and Poland agreed to participate in a ballistic missile defense system aimed at thwarting a future threat from Iran.[90] Romania and Bulgaria have agreed to provide territory for new NATO bases.

Soviet Transformation

American national security benefited from democratic transformation in East Central and Southern Europe only because of regime change inside the Soviet Union started by Mikhail Gorbachev. Conventional American accounts explain the end of the Cold War as a victory of American economic and military prowess.[91] Ronald Reagan's military spending increases, including his plans to build a space-based missile shield, bankrupted the Soviet system and forced its collapse, or so the narrative goes.[92] Like all tall tales, this triumphal explanation of the Cold War's end has elements of truth embedded in it. Most certainly, the Soviet economy was not in good health by the 1980s and American increases in military spending did produce demands from the Red Army to increase its arsenal at the expense of civilian sectors of the economy.[93] But Gorbachev was not forced to make the decisions he did in reaction to American power. After all, many dictatorships endure for decades with low economic growth and high levels of poverty. The Soviets could have done the same. The Soviet military also had several options to easily counter Reagan's Strategic Defense Initiative.[94] In other words, the Soviet Union's collapse in 1991 was not inevitable, but occurred because Gorbachev initiated a process of political change, which then spun out of his control.[95]

This political change within the Soviet Union ended the Cold War, which in turn had a profoundly positive impact on U.S. national security.[96] Speaking to the British parliament in 1982, President Reagan argued that

> there are new threats now to our freedom, indeed to our very existence, that other generations could never have even imagined. There is first the threat of global war. No president, no congress, no prime minister, no parliament can spend a day entirely free of this threat.[97]

Reagan was referring to the threat of war between the West and the Soviet Union. By the summer of 1991, President Bush was not spending much time worrying about world war with the Soviets. The specter of a nuclear holocaust faded, even if Russia maintained the ability to obliterate the United States overnight. The international contest to contain communism in far away places such as Angola or Nicaragua ended. Threats to American allies in Europe subsided.

In the wake of Soviet dissolution, some worried about war and instability resulting from democratization in the post-Soviet region.[98] At the time, the collapse of the Federal Republic of Yugoslavia underscored the potential for war in the wake of state collapse. And in the early 1990s, especially after the stunning electoral victory of nationalist Vladimir Zhirinovsky in Russia's 1993 parliamentary elections, fascist forces within Russia were visible enough to evoke comparisons to the Weimar Republic.[99] These nightmare scenarios did not unfold, however, because the nature of the political system that emerged in Russia in the 1990s was a weak form of democracy.[100] In the 1990s, radical political and economic change in Russia produced leaders, political forces, and economic interest groups that identified with and benefited from liberal ideas, specifically democratic and market practices at home and integration into Western institutions abroad. Russia's new leaders also rejected communist and fascist ideologies, building instead economic institutions (including first and foremost, private property rights) and to a lesser extent political institutions designed to constrain illiberal, anti-democratic forces. This new regime dramatically diluted the threat from Russia to the United States, to the point that leaders in Washington and Moscow began to refer to each other as strategic partners and friends.[101] It was not Russia's military decline that lessened the threat to the United States, but rather internal democratic change.

Because of their Western orientation, Russia's leaders in the 1990s also cooperated with the United States in weakening other potential threats to the United States and its allies in the re-

gion.[102] Most importantly, President Yeltsin cooperated closely
with President Clinton to negotiate the transfer of nuclear
weapons from Ukraine, Belarus, and Kazakhstan to Russia. Yeltsin
opposed NATO expansion—his foreign minister, Yevgeny Pri-
makov, called the decision to enlarge NATO "probably the worst
since the end of the Cold War."[103] Negative Russian responses to
NATO's war in Kosovo also threw a considerable chill over U.S.-
Russian relations.[104] Yet Yeltsin eventually played a critical role in
pressuring Milošević to capitulate in Kosovo.[105] Despite the perceived threats to Russian security and the up-and-down quality
of the U.S.-Russian relationship, the general thrust of Russian
foreign policy in the 1990s was integration into rather than balancing against the international community of democratic
states.[106] Had Russia been ruled by a communist or fascist leader
during the 1990s, the United States would have been less likely
to pursue NATO enlargement or the bombing of Yugoslavia because of concerns about the potential for armed conflict with
Russia. Had a radical nationalist been in the Kremlin during the
NATO war against Serbia in 1999 or the American-led war in
Iraq in 2003, Slobodan Milošević and Saddam Hussein might have
received Russian military assistance.[107] In fact, under a communist or fascist dictatorship, Russian troops might still be stationed
in Poland or the Baltic states.

The Bulldozer Revolution in Serbia

State collapse in Yugoslavia helped to produce one of the
worst military conflicts in Europe since World War II.[108] The
federal dissolution coincided with greater political liberalization
in the region, prompting some analysts to blame democratization for the Balkan wars in the 1990s.[109] Yet, by the time Milošević launched his project of ethnic cleansing in Kosovo in 1999,

the Serbian regime was neither democratic nor democratizing. Milošević was a dictator, albeit a weak one, who threatened the security interests of American allies and innocent civilians in the region. Milošević eventually lost power in a dramatic democratic moment. After he tried to falsify the outcome of a presidential election in October 2000, his own people mobilized against him to protect the actual voting results and eventually organized a massive demonstration that toppled his dictatorship.[110] This breakthrough made the regime more democratic, though still not a consolidated democracy. Nonetheless, since October 2000, Serbia has not initiated any wars. Democratization has made Serbia more peaceful and American allies in the region more secure, and it has facilitated a rapprochement between Serbia and the United States, an improving relationship that even survived American recognition of Kosovo's independence in 2007.

Toppling the Taliban Regime in Afghanistan

In the 1990s, an autocratic regime in Afghanistan emerged as an unlikely threat to American national security. Using traditional military and economic measures, Afghanistan did not rank as a major power in the international system. Instead, the threat to the United States came from the nature of the Taliban regime, which wholeheartedly embraced illiberal, totalitarian ideas and established an ideological alliance with another anti-democratic force, Al Qaeda. The Taliban regime offered Al Qaeda logistical support and a territorial base, which in turn aided Al Qaeda's terrorist activities abroad, including the attacks on the United States on September 11, 2001.

By eliminating a base of operations for a major American enemy, the American-led military effort to destroy the Taliban regime in Afghanistan following the September 11 attacks produced immediate security benefits for the United States and its allies. Both the Taliban and Al Qaeda remain threats to American national security, but they are lesser threats because they no longer control a nation-state—a valuable asset for plotting, preparing, and launching terrorist attacks. Even in this weak, peripheral country, the nature of the regime governing Afghanistan produced a profound and direct effect on American national security interests. Whether Afghanistan emerges once again as a threat to American national security will depend heavily on what kind of regime eventually takes hold there.

Deepening Alliances after Democratization

During the Cold War, some American strategists argued that the United States had to defend autocratic allies who helped the United States pursue vital national interests, including containing communism, providing energy resources, protecting trade routes, or securing American investments.[111] In the case of the Philippines, for instance, senior officials in the Reagan administration, including the president himself, worried that democratization would bring anti-American forces to power. A similar argument was advanced about the negative consequences of democratic change in Chile, Portugal, South Africa, and South Korea.[112] In these countries, so the argument went, the process of democratization would bring to power communist forces, which would turn against the United States and undermine democracy. A very similar argument is made about the threat of anti-American, anti-democratic Islamists coming to power through elections in the Middle East.

However, transitions from autocracy to democracy in Chile, Portugal, South Africa, and South Korea, as well as Argentina,

Brazil, Indonesia, Spain, and Taiwan, did not damage American strategic interests as predicted. Instead the transitions served to consolidate deeper, more lasting relationships with the new democratic regimes in these countries.[113] New democracies often face threats from autocratic regimes in their neighborhoods, making them more likely to become allies of the United States.[114] Fears of pro-American autocrats giving way to anti-American democrats have been largely unfounded.

Threats from the Failure to Consolidate Democracy

The collapse of autocracy does not always lead to democracy. The end of tsarism in Russia in February 1917 created permissive conditions for the Bolsheviks to seize power in October of the same year. The dissolution of the Qing dynasty in China in 1911 resulted in an era of chaos, invasion, and civil war, which culminated in 1949 in the emergence of a more robust form of autocracy in the People's Republic of China. The non-democratic outcomes of both the Russian and Chinese revolutions produced very real and serious threats to American national security.[115] Similarly, the breakdowns of democratic regimes in Spain and Germany in the interwar years precipitated internationalized wars.[116] In the past 50 years, the failure of democracy to replace fallen autocracies in Iraq, Cuba, Vietnam, Nicaragua, Iran, Afghanistan, and Uzbekistan has created threats to American national security. Three of America's most recent and serious security threats—from Iraq, Iran, and Afghanistan—are byproducts of Cold War decisions to befriend and support autocrats in the struggle against communist enemies (perceived or otherwise) which were then replaced by autocracies even more hostile to American national interests.

During the Cold War, American covert and overt interventions also interrupted transitions from authoritarian rule in Latin
America, Africa, and the Middle East. Although few of these interventions produced threats to American national security,
nearly all of them damaged America's image abroad as a defender
of democracy. American support for the coup against Salvador
Allende in Chile in 1973 is the most glaring example. The United
States never faced a real military threat from Chile either during
or after Augusto Pinochet's rule, but supporting the coup exacted
enormous costs to America's reputation.

In the case of Iran, however, America's involvement in dis-
rupting democratic change generated more direct threats to its
national security, albeit delayed. In August 1953, a CIA covert
operation codenamed Ajax helped to topple Prime Minister
Mossadeq from power and replaced him with the Shah. Not all
of Mossadeq's methods of wielding power were democratic, but
his ouster in a coup orchestrated by the United States and Great
Britain sealed his legacy as a democrat and nationalist toppled by
"anti-democratic" imperial powers.[117] After the removal of
Mossadeq, the Shah of Iran remained a reliable U.S. ally for nearly
four decades. But his eventual fall from power ushered in one of
the most anti-American regimes in the world. During the Iranian
revolution in 1979, U.S. support for the 1953 coup against
Mossadeq served as a rallying cry for anti-American forces in Iran
among both leftist leaders and the clergy.

In Afghanistan, as already discussed, the collapse of communist dictatorship from 1989 to 1992 did not lead to a democratic
or stable form of government, which eventually allowed the Taliban to seize power by 1996. Whether or not democracy had any
chance of taking hold in Afghanistan after the fall of communism
is difficult to know. What is clear is that the United States dramatically reduced support to and engagement with the new

Afghan government once it came to power in 1992. Before the war against the Soviet occupation in the 1980s, according to Ahmed Rashid, "Islamists barely had a base in Afghan society."[118] They gained a foothold only because Pakistan channeled American funds to the most extremist parties in the anti-Soviet coalition. The Pashtun-based Taliban came to power not because all of Afghanistan embraced their totalitarian interpretation of Islam, but because they offered a Pashtun alternative both to the Tajik-Uzbek dominated government that controlled Kabul after the fall of the communist regime in 1992, and the anarchic warlords who prevailed under the Rabbanni government between 1992 and 1996.[119] The negative consequences for U.S. national security of this failed democratic transition were profound.

Democracy's failure to take hold in Iraq also resulted in direct threats to American security interests. Again, as in Afghanistan, it is not clear that democracy ever had a chance in the wake of the American-led military invasion that toppled Saddam Hussein's regime.[120] Democracy's failure in Iraq stimulated civil war between Sunni and Shia groups, which in turn pulled American forces back into combat within the country. The absence of a legitimate democratic regime also helped to compel disaffected Iraqi Sunnis to ally with Al Qaeda and other anti-American, anti-democratic transnational movements. Beginning in 2005, new participation in a political process—the so-called Sunni Awakening—helped to quell violence in the Sunni regions of Iraq. In combination with an American spike in military forces in 2007, the Awakening helped to reduce threats to Americans based in Iraq and to weaken transnational movements like Al Qaeda that also threatened Americans in Iraq and around the world.

In the post-Cold War era, the negative security implications of failed democratic transitions in Afghanistan and Iraq dwarf all other threats to the U.S. caused by democratic breakdown.

However, a few other prominent democratic erosions have produced lesser, but direct and negative consequences for U.S. national security.

In Russia, democracy emerged but never consolidated in the
1990s.[121] When Vladimir Putin became president in 2000, Russia's democratic institutions were still weak and vulnerable. Putin
weakened them further by undermining the power of Russia's regional leaders, the independent media, both houses of parliament, independent political parties, and genuine civil society.
According to Freedom House, the Russian regime slipped from
"partially free" in 2000 to "not free" in 2005. In parallel and not
coincidentally, Russia's relations with the West and the United
States in particular have become increasingly belligerent, culminating in Russia's invasion and subsequent dismemberment of
Georgia in August 2008. Along the way, Putin has blamed the
United States for terrorist attacks inside Russia and accused the
U.S. of fomenting "color" revolutions in Georgia and Ukraine and
of crafting a similar plan for Russia. He even compared the
United States to Nazi Germany. In a speech on the 62nd anniver-
sary of the end of World War II, Putin said,

> In our days, these threats [to Russain security] are not
> diminished. They are only transformed. And in these
> new threats, like in the time of the 'Third Reich' there
> is the same disdain to human life, the same claim for
> the world supremacy.[122]

Putin has not championed an alternative economic model
to capitalism or even an alternative political model to democracy,
but he does see great power competition in international affairs
in zero-sum terms. What is good for the U.S. is bad for Russia,
and vice versa.

In Venezuela, the correlation between democratic erosion under President Hugo Chavez and greater tensions with the United States is also more than a coincidence. American covert efforts to overthrow Chavez in 2002 not only exacerbated bilateral tensions but also provided an excuse for Chavez to implement even deeper autocratic changes. As Chavez has consolidated his autocratic grip on the country, Venezuela has become a more active participant in many anti-American causes, including increases in aid for autocratic Cuba, economic support in the form of contracts for the purchase of military equipment from Belarus, and greater economic, military, and political ties with Iran. Chavez even has threatened to disrupt oil exports to the United States.

In all of these cases, the erosion of democracy inside the country eventually has produced greater hostility toward the United States. The correlation is more than coincidence.

Economic Benefits of Democratic Expansion

In addition to making Americans more secure, the expansion of democracy abroad also has made Americans richer. Most obviously, the transformation of autocratic foes into democratic allies has reduced the need for military spending—the famous "guns and butter" trade-off. As John Owen IV has observed, "The near absence of wars among mature liberal democracies . . . means that democratic states need not prepare for war against one another. This allows them to invest in resources elsewhere that might have been used on such preparations."[123] Although some economists argue that defense expenditures stimulate growth, most conclude that the levels of taxation required to maintain large military budgets impede investment in more productive sectors of the economy.[124] For instance, the spike in military spending at the beginning of World War II helped to pull the United States out of the Great Depression. By the end of the war, economists estimate that roughly 40 percent of America's GDP was tied to the war effort.[125] Maintaining such a ratio for decades, however, would have retarded growth in civilian sectors of the economy. The end of World War II and subsequent decreases in government spending on the military freed up resources that sustained an amazing growth period in the United States in the post-war era.[126] By one account, the post World War II demobilization infused $68 billion into the post-war economy.[127] Military spending reductions after the Cold War's end had a similar positive impact on the U.S. economy in the 1990s. By some estimates, the "peace dividend" from the end of the Cold War resulted in more than a 20 percent decrease in military spending between 1986 and 2004.[128] Companies dependent on Pentagon contracts suffered as they tried to navigate the difficult and usually unsuccessful path of defense conversion, while many communities also suffered as military bases important to the local economy closed.[129] However, the overall economic benefits of defense expenditure reductions were enormous. They helped to produce balanced budgets and sound fiscal policy and fueled one of the greatest periods of economic growth in American history. Economist Anders Åslund has calculated the American peace dividend resulting from the Cold War's end to be more than $1.3 trillion.[130] A study conducted for the International Monetary Fund found more broadly that a sizable "peace dividend" resulted for all countries that cut military spending since 1985.[131] Conversely, increased military expenditures to finance American wars in Afghanistan and Iraq contributed to major budget deficits and financial imprudence during the Bush administration. Joseph Stiglitz and Linda Bilmes have calculated that the range of the total cost of the Iraq war will be anywhere from $3 trillion to $5 trillion.[132] Yet as Stiglitz explains, the negative impact of this war does not end with the direct costs:

> To the extent that the war caused the price of oil to go up, and the fact that the war expenditures don't stimulate the economy as much as domestic expenditures would have, the economy is weaker. . . . So, we have more of a mountain of debt in order to offset the negative effects of war spending, and that mountain of debt is now the problem we're dealing with. There is a clear connection between the two. We're spending money abroad that we could have spent at home.[133]

In addition to reducing the pressure on government spending for defense purposes, the transformation of former foes into new allies opens new markets for trade and investment for American firms. Democratic states trade more openly and to a greater extent than non-democracies.[134] New democracies tend to reduce trade barriers, especially in developing countries endowed with cheap labor, as the majorities in these countries seek the benefits of trade with the developed world. As Helen Milner and Keiko Kubota concluded in explaining the correlation between democratic regime change and reduced trade barriers in the developing world since 1990,

> Democratization opened up new avenues of support for freer trade. Leaders recognized that previously disenfranchised groups had become part of the voting public; . . . these groups benefited more from trade liberalization than continued protectionism. . . . Democratic leaders in a number of developing countries chose trade liberalization a means for gaining broader political support.[135]

American trade with and investment in Germany, Japan, and Italy expanded exponentially after World War II. When democratic regimes first replaced communism in Eastern Europe and the former Soviet Union, analysts predicted that the masses now in control over the government would resist liberalizing economic reforms.[136] Yet the exact opposite happened: the fastest democratizers were also the most aggressive economic reformers, whose actions in turn created tremendous trade and investment opportunities for the United States and other European democracies.[137] And even with the more closed and less developed economies of the former Soviet Union, U.S. exports to these states increased 18-fold from 1989 to 2007.[138] Democratization in the developing world contributed directly to the spike in international trade flows in the developing world since 1990.[139]

Democracy in Germany, Italy, or Japan was not a necessary condition for this expansion of economic activity. In South Korea, U.S. trade and investment skyrocketed well before democratization, which did not occur until 1987. A similar sequence occurred with the Philippines and Indonesia. However, the data demonstrate that democratization, when it did occur in these countries, did not hinder U.S. trade and investment, and in fact in some instances increased it. In the former communist world, American firms are just as involved in new autocracies such as Kazakhstan, Azerbaijan, and Russia as they are in democratic Poland, Estonia, or Ukraine. Most obviously, American companies trade and invest heavily in autocracies around the world, including most importantly, China. Nonetheless, in all of these countries, including those still considered autocratic, a more open political system started economic liberalization. Azerbaijan's political regime today is much more open than it was 30 years ago. The same is true in China.

Finally, as discussed before, democratization often facilitates the strengthening of checks on executive power, more transparent government, and in the long run, stronger legal institutions. All of these components of a liberal democracy in turn create positive conditions for foreign investment and trade, including American trade and investment in new democracies. Autocrats can nationalize foreign companies, demand bribes from foreign investors, and treat domestic economic actors more favorably than foreign entities to a much greater extent than can democratic leaders.

The Benefits of a Moral Foreign Policy

American support for democratic change abroad aligns the United States with the preferences of the vast majority of people around the world. As discussed in the previous chapter, public opinion surveys of people throughout the world show that solid majorities in every country support democracy. When Americans argue instead that the U.S. should support autocrats in the name of "stability," whose preferences does that serve? Whose stability? It is obviously not the preferences or stability of a majority of people living under these autocracies. And that raises the question of which policy is more imperial: one that supports the aspirations of a people, or one that shores up the power of a dictator who is willing to serve the interests of the global hegemon in return for the survival of his autocracy? As we have seen, democracies do not commit genocide, do not generate refugees, and do not permit wide-scale famines, so by supporting democratic change abroad, the United States also will be supporting a more ethical and just foreign policy.

The direct security and economic benefits of such a moral foreign policy are hard to measure. Famines, genocide, and state collapse often end up costing the United States financially, and have even pulled the U.S. into conflict, as in Somalia and Haiti in the 1990s. Investing in democratic government in other countries today can be thought of as helping to prevent more costly interventions in the future.

Less directly but more importantly over the long haul, a more moral U.S. foreign policy increases America's standing in the world, which in turn increases American leverage on all issues of international politics, including those with more direct consequences for U.S. national security and prosperity. Especially after the United States emerged as a world power, other countries were willing to accept American leadership because of a genuine belief in the American commitment to "doing good" in the world. American leaders were allowed to take the lead in building international institutions that benefited American security and prosperity in part because the United States was the most powerful country in the free world, but also because other leaders trusted the United States as a moral force for good. Conversely, U.S. foreign policies that have undermined American commitment to democracy—by supporting autocrats, undermining democratically-elected leaders, or ignoring international human rights norms—have weakened American influence and standing more generally regarding international affairs.[140]

Finally, Americans—foreign policymakers and citizens alike—may gain some sense of satisfaction by seeing their country do the right thing, or stand on the right side of history. Although impossible to measure, the feeling of pride or contentment with one's country's international standing must register as a benefit to the American people.

4
Is More Democratization Good for the U.S.?

The historical relationship between the expansion of democracy and the enhancement of American security should encourage cautious optimism about the future benefits for the United States of democracy's advance worldwide. But that optimism is based on an analogy drawn mostly from the European experience, and analogies do not always travel well between different regions or historical eras. At the same time, to state with certainty that future democratization is impossible and will not bring security and economic benefits to the United States is to be unduly pessimistic about the current state of affairs in the world and unduly romantic about the European experience. The process of making Europe free and whole took centuries, involved dreadful wars, and required overcoming deep ethnic and religious divides. The same may be true in the Middle East and Asia. Yet, just as Europe eventually succeeded, so too can these more autocratic and more unstable regions change, and in turn enhance U.S. security.

A Democratic Middle East?

In the long run, the consolidation of democratic regimes in the greater Middle East will likely make the American people more secure. In the early twenty-first century, autocratic powers in the Middle East pose threats to each other—as did autocratic rulers in Europe in the past century. Some of them and their proxies also threaten the one democracy in the region, Israel. Also like Europe in the past century, some of these autocratic powers have global ambitions motivated by ideological doctrines. Because of allies and economic interests in the region, the United States has been pulled into these conflicts intermittently since the beginning of the Cold War.[1] Occasionally, American forces have engaged in direct combat, as they did in the Gulf War in 1991 or the post-September 11 wars in Afghanistan and Iraq. More often, the United States has supplied military and economic aid to various countries to counter threats from other states in the region. The United States aids Israel to help protect this democracy from threats presented by various autocracies in the region, while at the same time providing military assistance to regimes in Saudi Arabia, Pakistan, and Egypt, in part to counter threats from another dictatorship in the region: Iran.[2] American forces also have been stationed in the region to help defend American allies from threats from other autocracies. These missions of peacekeeping and deterrence have stimulated a sequence of violent responses, from the attack on the U.S. Marine barracks in Beirut, Lebanon, on October 23, 1983, to the Khobar Tower bombings in Dhahran, Saudi Arabia, on June 25, 1996, the suicide attack on the USS Cole in the Yemeni port of Aden on October 12, 2000, and the terrorist assaults on New York and Washington on September 11, 2001.

Imagine for a moment if democratic regimes governed the major countries in the Middle East. The first important change would be that interstate war would be less likely. A democratic Middle East would present a hard test for the democratic peace thesis. Some frame the conflict between Israel and Palestine or Israel and the rest of the Arab world as a contest about borders and cultures that can never be resolved. Others speculate that the divide between Sunni and Shia is so fundamental that no degree of democracy in either Iran or the rest of Sunni world in the Middle East would defuse this conflict. By the logic of these arguments, the U.S. would be engaged forever in the struggle to defend Israel and maintain the balance of power between Sunni and Shia both within and between states in the Middle East.

This might be the future for the region. But it is important to remember that similar fatalistic predictions were made about irreconcilable disputes in Europe between Catholics and Protestants, French and Germans, or fascists and communists. European conflicts over territory, religion, and ideology flamed and ebbed for centuries, only ending after the deadliest war ever. And for nearly half a century after World War II, the continent remained poised to fight yet another world war, this time with the possible use of nuclear weapons on a massive scale. Yet remarkably, democracies now rule almost of all of Europe (except in Belarus and Russia), and as a result, the probability of interstate war on this bloodiest of continents has declined dramatically. The "perpetual peace" that seems to have taken root in Europe resulted in large measure from the expansion of democracy on the continent. The idea, therefore, that countries in the Middle East are trapped permanently in conflict is short-sighted. Should democracy take hold in the region, there is no reason to believe that Middle Eastern democracies would not enjoy the same benefits of cooperation and face the same domestic constraints on engaging in wars that European democracies do today.

Certain benefits for U.S. security resulting from democratic development in the region are easier to imagine than others. Iran, for instance, exhibits many structural characteristics that make it conducive to, if not ripe for, democratization.[3] In a comparative context, the state and nation of Iran are well defined in terms of territory, culture, and history.[4] Unlike neighboring Iraq, imperial powers did not create the country from scratch a century ago. Iran is also a middle-income country, with levels of wealth, education, information, and independent social organizations sufficient to sustain a democracy.[5] The illegitimacy of the current theocracy in the eyes of most Iranians offers another positive factor for democratization. The Iranian opposition today embraces democracy, the West, and the United States. If it came to power as a result of a democratic transition, it would quickly seek closer ties to the United States, just as Poland and other parts of Eastern Europe vigorously pursued closer relations with the West after communism fell. As a regional hegemon, autocratic Iran currently provides military assistance to Shia militias fighting American troops in Iraq, gives military and economic support to Hezbollah in Lebanon and Hamas in Palestine, and may even be preparing to threaten the United States directly someday through the acquisition of nuclear weapons technology and the development of long-range ballistic missiles. As a regional hegemon, a democratic Iran could help to stabilize Iraq and Afghanistan, weaken Hezbollah and Hamas (recall how Soviet support for communist proxies in the developing world quickly evaporated after Gorbachev's reforms), and reduce dramatically the probability of an Iranian nuclear threat to the United States or its allies in the region. Moreover, it is unclear that a democratic Iran would continue to pursue a nuclear weapons program, since a central strategic motivation for obtaining a nuclear weapon is to deter American military intervention.[6] A democratic Iran would no longer fear an American attack.

More generally, a more democratic Middle East might reduce the demand for nuclear weapons among all countries in the region. Egypt and Saudi Arabia have hinted that they will join the nuclear arms race if Iran goes nuclear.[7] If all these countries eventually developed democratic institutions, then the threats they currently generate with respect to each other would decline.

A more peaceful region in turn would reduce the demand for American troops in the Middle East just as the end of the Cold War dramatically reduced the need for American troops in Europe. A smaller U.S. presence in the region would eliminate one of the central justifications for jihad against the United States that Al Qaeda and other terrorist organizations have advanced.[8]

Sound fanciful? No crazier than dreaming the same for Europe in 1948. It is easy to forget that Europe was the most war-torn continent in the world for hundreds of years, especially in the twentieth century. Only after the spread of democratic government throughout Europe—a process that unfolded slowly and is still not complete—did the region became more stable and the need for American military involvement there decrease.

Democratization and Terrorism

In the long run, the advance of democracy around the world and especially in the Middle East also would reduce the appeal and capacity of extremist Islamic organizations that practice terrorism. Obviously, not all political movements practicing terrorist tactics come from the Middle East or live under dictatorships. But terrorists are more likely to come from autocracies, or more precisely, according to Alan Kruger and David Latin, from countries with limited civil liberties.

A country's GDP per capita is unrelated to the number of terrorists originating from the country. A country's degree of civil liberties, by contrast, is associated
with participation in terrorism: countries with a lower
level of civil liberties have a higher participation rate
in terrorism, on average. Thus, low civil liberties are
associated with greater participation in terrorism
while economic factors are unrelated.[9]

Most anti-American terrorists—including those who executed the September 11 massacres—have come from dictatorships.[10] Not all terrorists are themselves poor, oppressed, or
living in autocratic countries with Muslim majorities, and the
problem of radical Islamic alienation in Europe is increasingly evident and troubling.[11] But ideologically and symbolically, violent
Islamists gain support from the perception that regimes in the
Middle East are illegitimate because they are corrupt, abusive,
and unaccountable to the people or to any higher law or code.
Criticizing autocratic regimes in the Middle East is a central focus
of extremist propaganda, while overthrowing these dictatorships
is trumpeted as a key objective of these terrorist groups. A Middle
East governed by more legitimate, democratic regimes would rob
these fanatical groups of a key enemy.

Democratic development also would provide an outlet for
political expression for those currently disenchanted with the existing order. These disillusioned and alienated citizens of Middle
East autocracies constitute the backbone of support for terrorist
organizations. Democracy is the only reliable constraint on abusive state power, the only tonic for illegitimacy, and the only political system that offers the disenfranchised a way to participate
nonviolently in the political process. With more avenues open for
peaceful political participation, organizations that practice ter-

rorism would be forced to make strategic decisions about whether or not to pursue their political objectives in accordance with the democratic rules of the game or to remain extra-constitutional, anti-systemic movements. Because democracies reward centrists and political leaders who appeal to the majority of citizens, extremists groups also might be compelled to moderate their political views.[12] Some groups might decide to continue to pursue extra-constitutional strategies for achieving their ends, but they would risk marginalization in a democracy.[13] Over time, those organizations that continue to challenge the political system will find it more difficult to maintain societal support in the face of elected rulers with legitimacy acquired through the democratic process. Thus far, the incremental steps towards political liberalization in the Arab world have produced mixed results in reducing terrorist acts, but nowhere yet in the region have serious democratic reforms been attempted, leaving us to guess what the long-term implications for security might be.[14]

Democratic breakthroughs in highly repressive regimes also have triggered substantial economic growth in other regions of the world.[15] There is no reason to predict that the Middle East would not follow a similar trajectory. Recent economic surveys of the Middle East, including the seminal United Nations Development Program report in 2005, have underscored the close connection between bad government and stagnant economies, declaring boldly that "freedom is pivotal to human development."[16] Development economists Paul Collier has gone so far as to label "bad governance" a "poverty trap."[17] Economic growth in turn would provide greater economic opportunity to those now disillusioned and likely to support extremist organizations as an expression of their frustration.

Finally, democracies are more transparent societies, making it harder (though certainly not impossible) for terrorists to operate in them. At a minimum, the expansion of democracy means the elimination of autocratic regimes that support terrorist activities, like the Taliban in Afghanistan before 2001 or the Islamic Republic of Iran. No democratic government in the world supports non-state terrorist organizations.[18]

In the short run, however, democratization has not reduced terrorist attacks either in the Middle East or against Western democracies.[19] Given the limited progress toward democratization in the Middle East, we simply cannot predict with any certainty that more democracy in the region would produce less terrorism in the short run. The bold claim made frequently by President George W. Bush and his administration, that democracy is the "long-term antidote to the ideology of terrorism today,"[20] is a hypothesis about the future, not an observable pattern.

Although the expansion of democracy throughout the world would clearly have long-term benefits for U.S. security, it would not eliminate all terrorist threats. Consolidated democracies, after all, have been the birthplace and residence of extremists who resort to terrorism as a political tool or an expression of rage. Just as democratic institutions did not stop the Ku Klux Klan, the Unabomber, or Timothy McVeigh, or prevent the terrorist attacks in Madrid in March 2004, London in July 2005, or Mumbai in November 2008, the emergence of democratic regimes throughout the wider Middle East—a development that is still decades away—will not eliminate all security threats to the United States from the region.[21]

But we also must be careful not to blame democratization for terrorist threats to the United States: to restate the obvious, terrorist organizations attacked the United States well before any process of political liberalization in the Middle East began. Democratization in Saudi Arabia or Afghanistan did not trigger the emergence and development of Al Qaeda. On the contrary, the monarchy in Saudi Arabia has chosen not to seek legitimacy through the ballot box, opting for other means that include indirect financial and political support for fundamentalist religious organizations at home and abroad. The Saudi government never directly financed Al Qaeda, but Saudi charity organizations with close ties to the government, including charities headed by government officials, did provide direct and indirect support for Al Qaeda and like-minded political groups.[22] A U.S. government official described Saudi Arabia as "the 'epicenter' of financing for Al Qaeda and other terrorist organizations."[23] In Afghanistan, autocratic consolidation under the Taliban—not democratization—created a sympathetic environment for Al Qaeda's activities. The collapse of the Taliban dictatorship and subsequent political liberalization in Afghanistan have made it more difficult, not easier, for Al Qaeda to operate in the country.

We do not know how democratization in the Middle East will influence the rise or fall of terrorist activity because political liberalization in the region has been so minimal. To date, however, incremental steps towards democratization in Egypt, Bahrain, Kuwait, Yemen, and Morocco have not produced any traceable increase in terrorist activities from groups or citizens from these countries. Terrorist attacks skyrocketed in Iraq in the first years after the American-led invasion; the driver of these activities was not democratization, however, but state breakdown, foreign occupation, and political and ethnic rivalries. All these factors would still be present after the American-led invasion in 2003, with or without the implementation of democratic reforms. Afghanistan is a similar story.

The real puzzle about the relationship between democracy and terrorism is in Europe, not the Middle East. The majority of terrorists who have attacked the United States have been citizens of autocracies, but a number of these attackers, as well as terrorists who have attacked European targets, have lived for a considerable time in European democracies. Addressing the problem of alienated Muslims living in Europe requires policy responses well beyond deepening democratic development.

Democratization as a Generator of Threats to U.S. Interests

In the short run, democratization has not produced more stable U.S. allies in the Middle East. As of 2007, the Iraqi regime was not classified as a democracy.[24] However, Iraq by 2007 did have a more democratic government than it did under Saddam Hussein, and the new regime was friendlier toward the United States than was the previous one. The Iraqi government's limited ability to govern its own territory effectively still generates threats to Americans, primarily towards those Americans stationed and working in Iraq. The current Iraqi government, however, does not threaten the United States as a country or American citizens around the world.

The same is true in Afghanistan. The current Afghan regime is more democratic than the Taliban dictatorship, and President Hamid Karzai and his government are obviously closer partners with the United States than was the previous regime.[25] Yet the Afghan government's inability to defeat the Taliban and its reliance on United States and NATO forces to do most of the fighting on the ground creates a lingering threat to American security. That the Taliban and Al Qaeda must operate from the mountains of Pakistan rather than from downtown Kabul benefits American national security. At the same time, these anti-American groups continue to gain strength as the Karzai regime continues to struggle to build an effective state or a democratic regime.

Speculations about future threats to U.S. national security stemming from democratization rest on questionable logic and a miscoding of current cases. The general claim that democratization leads to increased conflict was discussed and refuted in the previous chapter. However, the more specific claim that democratization in the Middle East has produced threats to the United States profoundly shapes the contemporary U.S. debate about democracy promotion and therefore deserves special attention here.

Autocratic allies in the region make a very simple argument: real democracy in the Middle East and South Asia will bring to power radical Islamists, who will threaten U.S. security interests. In Egypt, supporters of President Hosni Mubarak claim that the Muslim Brotherhood would win a free and fair election and use its political power to threaten Israel and the U.S. In Morocco, King Mohammed VI has argued that his regime is the stalwart defender of American interests in the region, just as his grandfather's was when it defended Morocco against the communists during the Cold War. In Saudi Arabia and other Gulf states, those in power warn that free and fair elections would legitimize Al Qaeda sympathizers, who would cut off oil to the United States and offer increased funding to anti-American terrorist organizations. Even in Pakistan, whose political system is more developed than that of most Arab states, General Musharraf used to warn before his downfall that he was the only bulwark against anti-American extremists in his country.

Oftentimes, American government officials have followed the logic of these dictators. When pressed to choose between the democratic forces or autocratic incumbents in Egypt, Saudi Arabia, and Pakistan, the Bush administration stood with the autocrats. Middle East analysts provide an intellectual rational for such a policy. Martin Kremer contends that the "the chief beneficiaries of every political opening [in the Middle East] have been Islamist zealots with fascist tendencies who detest America.[26] In their call for a "return to realism," Steve Simon and Ray Takeyh argue that

> "the U.S. defeat in Iraq should finally squelch the appealing but naïve belief that promoting democracy is a panacea for the Middle East's ills. Washington faces a bleak choice: It can push its values or realize its interests. It cannot do both. The problem in trying to build democracy in the Arab world is not solely that Islamic radical groups such as Hamas tend to win the elections; it's also the absence of secular liberal parties who support U.S. policies."[27]

Using a similar line of reasoning, Gregory Gause speculates that

> the advent of democracy there [the Middle East] seems likely to produce new Islamist governments that would be much less willing to cooperate with the United States than are the current authoritarian rulers. . . . The emphasis on electoral democracy will not, however, serve immediate U.S. interests either in the war on terrorism or in other important Middle East polices.[28]

A handful of historical analogies undergird these predictions about threats from democratization: Germany under Hitler, the Algerian elections in 1992, and the Hamas electoral victory in Palestine in 2006, and perhaps Hezbollah's electoral successes in Lebanon. We can learn important lessons from all these cases, but we must not conclude that democratization produces threats to American national security.

The first lesson to remember about Nazi Germany, Algeria in the early 1990s, or Hamas's electoral victory in 2006 is that these three tragic chapters are not instances of democratization. They are the opposite: cases of democratic breakdown. Hitler did compete successfully in electoral politics in Weimar Germany, and his Nazi party's success did help him to become chancellor of Germany in 1933.[29] One can speculate as to whether his Nazi movement could have come to power in a full-blown autocracy or if the Nazis could have maintained their popular support if compelled to compete at the ballot box over a longer period of time.[30] But even if democratic institutions contributed to Hitler's rise, he did not attack his neighbors as the leader of a liberal democracy or even an electoral democracy. Rather, Hitler destroyed democracy in January 1933 and eventually consolidated a repressive dictatorship. Only after six years of Nazi dictatorship did Hitler invade Poland. After the war, it was successful democratization in West Germany that made this country a more peaceful neighbor (American military occupation helped, but as we know from contemporary Iraq, occupation does not ensure peace).

Algeria is an even stranger analogy. To be sure, a political movement with dubious democratic credentials—the Islamic Salvation Front or FIS (the acronym in French)—threatened to come to power through democratic elections in 1991. In the first free and fair elections in Algeria at the local and municipal level in June 1990, FIS scored remarkable victories against the ruling National Liberation Front or FLN. After a volatile year of strikes, rallies, martial law, and government reshuffles, the ruling FLN eventually decided to go forward with parliamentary elections in December 1991. When FIS won the first round of this parliamentary vote, the military intervened, removed the incumbent government, and declared another state of emergency. In response, FIS and other Islamist parties took up arms, a move that thrust

Algeria into a brutal, decade-long civil war.[31] This conflict did not start because democratization began, but because democratization was interrupted. No one knows how brutal life in Algeria might have become had FIS come to power in 1992, but it is hard to imagine that the outcome could have been worse than the civil war that destroyed the country in the 1990s.

In the Palestinian territories, parliamentary elections in January 2006 gave the Palestinian organization Hamas a majority of the seats, which exceeded expectations and eventually led to formation of the first Palestinian government headed by a Hamas leader. The postponement of democracy, not a rush to democratic government, nurtured fertile ground for Hamas' popularity. Had elections occurred as scheduled throughout this period, Fatah, the governing party at the time of the 2006 vote, might have ruled in a less corrupt manner while other more liberal challengers might have been able to take advantage of the election process to emerge and grow.[32] Moreover, whether Hamas' participation in this election could be considered democratic is debatable. Ideally, parties are only allowed to participate in elections after they pledge allegiance to the democratic rules of the game and also recognize the state's monopoly on the legitimate use of force.[33] Hamas did neither. As their subsequent actions revealed, Hamas had no intention of either disarming or acquiescing to democratic rules, but instead took advantage of the election to obtain assets from the Palestinian state to use against its "partners" in the government, Fatah. Eventually, in June 2007, Hamas staged a coup in Gaza, with aspirations of also seizing power in the West Bank. These moves cannot be characterized as democratization.

A particularly worrying case is Hezbollah's continued electoral strength in Lebanon, a country with stronger democratic institutions than those in Germany in 1939, Algeria in 1991, or Palestine in 2006. Elections in Lebanon have not forced radicals to the sidelines, but through a very particular electoral system, have instead entrenched a deliberate balance of power among Shia, Sunni, and Christian forces.[34] Hezbollah has taken advantage of this electoral system to keep one foot in the electoral process and another foot in the so-called "armed struggle" against Israel. Democratization has not helped to reduce the Hezbollah threat to an American ally, Israel. Because Lebanon's electoral system does not require or even allow any single group to seek a majority, democracy has not induced Hezbollah leaders to moderate their views to obtain more votes.

Islamist parties, including those tied to militias, also won the first set of elections in Iraq. Yet, it remains too early to know if either of these parties will moderate over time or lose power or both.

A second lesson from these cases is that only one—Hitler's rise to power in Germany—directly threatened the United States. Algeria's civil war was an epic tragedy, but not a threat to the U.S. or its allies. Hamas' electoral victory in 2006 helped Hamas to seize power in Gaza in 2007, an act that triggered conflict between Israel and Hamas at the end of 2008. But it is too soon to tell whether Hamas's election victory in 2006 will increase security threats to Israel. Military battles between Hamas and Fatah intensified after the election, becoming by some definitions a civil war. The presence of a terrorist organization in control of territory on Israel's borders certainly threatens America's democratic ally. Hamas has continued to launch sporadic missile attacks from Gaza against Israel, and Israel responded militarily at the end of 2008 in a tragic escalation that did not serve the interests of the United States and its allies. At the same time, it must be remembered that these kinds of attacks by Hamas occurred before the January 2006 vote and before Hamas seized control of Gaza. Although Hamas has gained a temporary military advantage by controlling Gaza, the terrorist organization also has suffered a setback to its reputation among Palestinians and the Western world for its antidemocratic behavior. In the long run, the January 2006 election might be seen as a critical boost in empowering Hamas in the Palestinian territories, but the election and Hamas' subsequent participation in government may also have revealed the true anti-democratic and destabilizing intentions of the organization, which in turn could help to marginalize Hamas as a political organization and weaken it as a terrorist group.

The third and most important lesson is to underscore how rare are the instances in which democratization is claimed to have threatened American national security. Throughout the Cold War, dictators in Chile, El Salvador, Greece, Guatemala, Indonesia, Portugal, the Philippines, South Africa, South Korea, and Taiwan all made the claim that elections would bring to power anti-American forces. After the Cold War, military leaders in Turkey, supporters of the monarchies in Saudi Arabia, Morocco, and Jordan, and defenders of autocracy in Egypt made the same claim, this time threatening that anti-American Islamists posed the danger. However, in countries where some political liberalization has occurred, it has not undermined democracy, weakened the state, or abrogated a security relationship with the United States.

The successful integration of the Justice and Development Party, or AKP party, into Turkey's democracy offers a counter narrative to the Hamas experience. For years, Turkish military leaders and their Western supporters treated AKP as a radical Islamist party with anti-democratic proclivities. AKP eventually was allowed to participate in local elections, and in 2002 won a shocking electoral victory in national parliamentary elections, after which AKP party leader Recep Tayyip Erdogan became Turkey's first "Islamist" prime minister. Erdogan did not close down secular courts, institute *Shariah* law, or suspend democratic institutions. Instead, he and his party strengthened the idea of rule of law for all, including the military, and promoted the separation of church and state. They pushed aggressively for Turkey's membership in the European Union through implementation of several human rights reforms, including greater protection for minorities and women and the elimination of the death penalty. And they affirmed AKP's electoral mandate by capturing 47 percent of the vote in parliamentary election in 2007, 13 percentage points more than in 2002.[35]

In Morocco, the story is more similar to that of Turkey than that of Palestine (or Algeria in the 1990s or Nazi Germany). When given the chance to vote in free and fair elections in September 2007, Moroccans did not sweep Islamists into power. The Islamist Party of Justice and Development (PJD) won only 14 percent of the seats in parliament, coming in second behind a secular party. Even if the PJD had won a majority, the result would not have been an end to democracy. The PJD's participation in elections and in parliament has moderated the party's orientation and spurred important intraparty debates on the relationship between Islamist political principles, opposition tactics, and democratic values.[36] The Moroccan case of Islamist political participation suggests no evident conflict, and perhaps some congruence, between democracy and stability—an outcome amenable to American security interests.

Election results in Jordan in December 2007 showed a decline for the major Islamist party, the Islamic Action Front (AIF), which won only six of 110 parliamentary seats, down from 17 in the previous election. The electoral context was highly constrained, and considered to be the "least free and fair elections" since Jordan's "democratic opening" in 1989.[37] Knowing that it would not be allowed to win a majority, the AIF contested only 22 seats, but still managed to lose most of these, due not only to internal squabbles between "hawks" and "doves," but also to its limited appeal.[38] No one knows for sure how the IAF would perform in a genuinely free and fair election, but an Islamist landslide seems highly unlikely.

Even the 2005 parliamentary elections in Egypt did not sweep anti-democratic, anti-American Islamists into power. Candidates affiliated with the Muslim Brotherhood won 88 seats—substantially more than in the previous election—but this number still constituted only 20 percent of all parliamentary seats. The 2005 election was not free and fair and Brotherhood affiliates deliberately decided to contest only 150 seats. Nonetheless, the Brotherhood's modest gains suggest that a more democratic regime in Egypt would not automatically bring radicals to power. Moreover, the assumption that a Muslim Brotherhood government would be anti-democratic and antagonistic to American interests is plausible, but not certain. Since the 1990s, Brotherhood politicians have abided by the political rules of the game in Egypt, and have not pursued extra-constitutional strategies to change the regime. Politicians affiliated with the Muslim Brotherhood in Egypt have abandoned (at least rhetorically) their commitment to creating an Islamic state and implementing *Shariah* law. Brotherhood leaders no longer identify their organization as an Islamist party but instead as "a civil movement with an Islamic reference," a change in emphasis that Amr Hamzawy, Marina Ottaway, and Nathan Brown interpret to suggest that the Brotherhood

> accepts the civil nature of the political system and that it will draw on Islamic teachings for its positions . . . . It will pursue its goals by working through rather than around constitutional and democratic procedures.[39]

Brotherhood leaders still claim the right to "resistance" in defending their friends in Palestine, but also contend that they respect Egypt's international legal commitments, which include recognition of Israel.

The Justice and Development Party in Morocco, the Muslim Brotherhood and the Al-Wasat (Center) Party in Egypt, the Islamic Action Front in Jordan, the Islamic Constitutional Movement in Kuwait, and the al-Wefaq Society in Bahrain are all distinguished from Hamas and Hezbollah in another critical respect: these Islamist parties are not waging a struggle for statehood or a war against a neighbor, but instead have agreed to participate in electoral processes to shape domestic political decisions. These parties have calculated that their political agendas are better served by participating in electoral politics than by using violence.[40] For some, such as the Muslim Brotherhood, this embrace of democracy over terrorism represents a change in tactics, compelling some to warn that the change is temporary. But who knows for sure? We will never know what the Egyptian Muslim Brotherhood, the PJD in Morocco, or the Islamic Action Front in Jordan will do in power until they actually come to power or share power through a democratic process. Holding these parties to a higher standard than the dictators ruling their countries, however, is problematic. As Nathan Brown has written,

> Islamists in the Arab world are asked to demonstrate their fealty to a set of democratic rules that simply do not exist and to embrace democratic ideals that others in their society (most of all rulers) fail to practice. How can they prove their democratic credentials if there is precious little democracy to uphold?[41]

The only way out of this paradox is to start the democratization process, preferably in an evolutionary manner, with real checks on the power of those first elected (even anti-democratic checks, such as a monarchy in charge of the armed forces). The anti-democratic status quo, after all, gives the Islamists an advantage over liberal groups in these countries, since the Islamists can use the mosques to propagate their ideas and recruit supporters, whereas the public space for liberal politicians is much more constrained under autocracy. To assume that the likely outcome of democratization will be democratic destruction is to draw worst-case analogies from a very small set of cases. Even in the Arab world, the Hamas scenario is the exception, not the rule.

Another potential outcome could be the weakening of the radicals' appeal as the political space for other kinds of ideas opens up. In many dictatorships in the Arab world, politics are polarized between those who control the state and those who control the mosque. The political space and information platforms needed to nurture moderate and liberal ideas are highly constrained. As Tamara Wittes explains,

> . . . Islamists' privileged position in the opposition is a result of an artificially constrained political marketplace, a duopoly of regimes and undifferentiated Islamists. Freedom of press, speech, and association will not only allow non-Islamist political movements to emerge, advertise, and build support but also encourage diversification within the broad stream of political Islam, creating greater clarity and competition between Islamist groups and reducing the salience of Islamism as a catchall category for political dissent. Public support for Islamists will become more differ-

entiated and will likely shrink overall, and the Algeria scenario will become increasingly unlikely.[42]

Of course, Wittes' analysis presents a hypothesis about the future, not a certainty, but so too does the assertion that democratization will empower anti-democratic jihadists.

Finally, critics of democratization assume that the status quo can be preserved: that the monarchy in Morocco can rule forever, that Mubarak's son can maintain power for another 50 years, that the Saudi family can rule for another 100 years. In fact, societies in all the countries in the greater Middle East are changing rapidly, presenting a dynamic challenge to all regimes in the region. Demographic pressures coupled with modernization pressures from globalization already threaten the stability of existing political institutions.[43] To pretend that the status quo can be maintained indefinitely is wishful thinking. The real question is not whether existing political institutions will change, but how they will change. Will the process of political change be evolutionary, as were the transitions from authoritarian rule to democracy in southern Europe in the 1970s, or revolutionary, as in the case of the transition from monarchy to theocracy in Iran after 1979? Assuming that the current configuration of autocratic regimes in place today will persist 50 years from now is much more naïve than believing that some of these regimes might succeed in making the transition to democracy.

Possible Positive Effects of More Democracy in Asia and Eurasia

Beyond the Arab world, the specter of radical Islamists seizing power through the ballot box seems even less likely. In Bangladesh in 2001, the Bangladesh Nationalist Party defeated its Islamist rival, *Jamaat-e-Islami*, by a wide margin. In 2004 in Indonesia, the right of center parties won a majority, while the Islamist party, the Islamist Prosperous Justice Party (PKS), captured only 8 percent of the vote. In Malaysia in 2004, the ruling party the United Malays National Organization (UMNO) and its coalition partners won nearly two-thirds of the vote, whereas the Islamic Party (PAS) captured a dismal 3 percent. In 2008, the ruling coalition popularity declined dramatically but Islamists did not surge in parallel. Instead, PAS shared electoral gains with the secular Democratic Action Party (DAP) and the People's Justice Party, whose leader Anwar Ibrahim—a secular democrat—was poised to become Malaysia's next leader. In 1997, in the last parliamentary election before Musharraf's coup, the Pakistan Muslim League crushed its Islamist opponent, winning two-thirds of the vote. Despite a decade of military rule, Pakistan's secular parties captured an overwhelming majority in the February 2008 parliamentary elections, while the militant Islamist party, Muttahida Mjles-e-Amil or MMA, won only three seats. Islamists are not surging to power in democracies in Asia, but rather, participating in the electoral process as one of several political powers.

In the long run, democratic development in Asia also would enhance American security. Like democratization in East Germany, genuine democratic change in North Korea eventually would lead to unification and eliminate the regime altogether as a threat to the United States and its allies. In the long run, relations between a democratic Taiwan and a democratic China would defuse tensions, and might even create permissive conditions for unification. A democratic China also would undermine support for some of the most ruthless dictators in Asia, including those in North Korea and Burma, and in such places as Sudan and Zimbabwe in Africa.

In Eurasia, a democratic Russia could become a force for regional stability and even an inspiration for democratic activists in the region, not unlike the role that Russia played in the beginning of the 1990s. A democratic Russia seeking once again to integrate into Western institutions also would cooperate more closely with the United States and Europe on international security issues, from securing "loose nukes" and stopping the proliferation of nuclear technologies—thereby slowing Iran's nuclear ambitions—to fighting terrorist groups in Afghanistan.

All of these changes obviously would produce positive effects for American national security. The disappearance of the North Korean regime would eliminate the specter of either a nuclear threat or nuclear blackmail from this state. The diffusion of tension between Taiwan and China would remove from the U.S. strategic map a potential tripwire for conflict with the fastest growing military power in the world. Democratic development in Russia and China also would reduce the likelihood that these two powers would pursue balancing policies against the United States.

Of course, these are all speculations about the future based on analogies from the past. But assumptions of stability in all of these regions are also forecasts about the future based on historical metaphors. Given that democracy's advance over the last 200 years has delivered payoffs for American interests, the burden of proof should remain with those who believe or predict that the positive trajectory will not continue.

5
We Can Do Better: Supporting Democratic Development More Effectively

This book has offered a set of arguments for why the United States should promote democracy around the world. The next step is for President Barack Obama and his administration to recognize the limits of American instruments for fostering democracy abroad, learn from past successes and mistakes in efforts to promote democracy, and then develop a sophisticated, comprehensive strategy to effectively facilitate democratic development abroad. This chapter offers a set of recommendations for achieving these objectives.

Restoring the American Example

From the beginning of the American republic, American leaders have believed that their experiment in democracy could inspire others. As Benjamin Franklin predicted in 1782, "Establishing the liberties of America will not only make that people happy, but will have some effect in diminishing the misery of those, who in other parts of the world groan under despotism."[1]

During the nineteenth century, American subjugation of indigenous peoples, wars for territorial expansion, and the Civil War did not illustrate the best virtues of democracy. Yet the United States still entered the twentieth century as a democratic model revered by those seeking better government, from liberals in Czechoslovakia, Germany, and Russia, to those leading the struggles for independence in India, China, and throughout the African continent.

During the Cold War, the communist model of government, as practiced first in the Soviet Union and later in China, Cuba, and other parts of the developing world, presented an alternative to the American example, especially because Soviet leaders devoted tremendous propaganda resources and economic incentives to help promote their model abroad.[2] As American leaders began to understand the scope of the Soviet ideological challenge, they began to dedicate government funds to promote the virtues of American democracy abroad, using new tools such as Radio Free Europe, Voice of America (radio and television), Radio Marti, and Radio Liberty (similar to Radio Free Europe but aimed at the Soviet Union), and Radio Free Asia (started in 1950 and aimed at communist countries in Asia). They also employed the U.S. Information Agency and its network of offices overseas, which provided free access to American publications and daily viewings of American news broadcasts before the dawn of satellite television; an array of publications such as *Problems with Communism, Encounter, Partisan Review*, and *The New Leader*, which sold the American example and undermined the Soviet competition with varying degrees of bluntness.[3] During the Cold War, programs that stimulated American travel abroad

(Peace Corps, student fellowships) or foreign travel to study or work in the United States (Rotary scholarships, student exchanges, business internships through the Marshall Plan) also indirectly stimulated interest in the American democratic model. In parallel to these government-sponsored activities, an army of American private institutions such as universities, civic organizations with international chapters, the private advertising and movie industry, and some private corporations also indirectly helped to champion the American political system during the twentieth century.[4]

Yet to contain communism, American leaders compromised their commitment to democratic practices by supporting anticommunist dictators and political movements abroad.[5] In Africa, for instance, American presidents celebrated struggles for independence as echoes of the American Revolution and at the same time supported Portuguese colonial rule and grotesquely antidemocratic regimes in Rhodesia and South Africa—purportedly to fight communism.[6] During the Cold War era, McCarthyism's assault on individual liberties and the tumultuous struggle for civil rights in the American South also tarnished America's democratic image.[7]

Some American leaders recognized how illiberal practices at home weakened the appeal of the American model abroad and tried to address the hypocrisy. For instance, in 1948, President Harry Truman stressed his dedication to a new civil rights agenda in part for national security reasons. "We know that our democracy is not perfect," Truman admitted, but "if we wish to inspire the people of the world whose freedom is in jeopardy, if we wish to restore hope to those who have already lost their civil liberties, if we wish to fulfill the promise that is ours, we must correct the remaining imperfections in our democracy."[8] After the dark days of Watergate, President Ronald Reagan sought to rescue the

American model by devoting considerable rhetorical attention to the virtues of U.S. democracy, arguing how the advantages of democracy in the West might inspire the emergence of democracy in the East.

The American model outlasted the communist alternative and served again as a main source of emulation for post-communist leaders throughout Eastern Europe and the Soviet Union. In the late 1980s, constitutional drafters from South Africa to Poland carefully studied the U.S. Constitution. However, American hegemony after the Cold War also produced resentment. Instead of simply inspiring others by the power of example, critics charged that the United States deliberately and sometimes coercively exported its model of government in the post-Cold War era with no other great power around to resist American imperialist impulses.

The demonstration effects of the American model diminished even further as a consequence of anti-democratic policies adopted by President George W. Bush and his administration to fight what they labeled the "global war on terror." Critics charged that Bush not only practiced an extreme version of unilateral foreign policy, including most dramatically an American-led, preemptive war against Iraq that was not sanctioned by the United Nations Security Council, but also ignored many international norms and rules in the execution of his global war on terror.[9] Most controversially, President Bush issued a military order two months after September 11 allowing for the indefinite detention of noncitizens, including not only Al Qaeda members but anyone who "has engaged in, aided or abetted, or conspired to commit, acts of international terrorism, or acts in preparation therefore."[10] Many of these detainees eventually ended up in a prison at Guantanamo Bay, Cuba, where they were denied any right to a speedy trial in either a civilian court or a military tribunal.[11]

Some American soldiers, supported by their civilian leaders, interpreted the global war on terror as a license to torture and humiliate detainees, as the world learned when photos of prisoners at Abu Ghraib prison in Iraq, were released in 2004. These graphic depictions of American abuses delivered an enormous blow to America's image around the world. Equally damaging to America's reputation were Bush administration orders to torture detainees.[12] The Bush administration also shipped secretly detainees to other countries whose police, military, and intelligence forces then used torture techniques to try to obtain information about terrorists and their activities.[13] Once these practices became public, America's international standing in the world declined precipitously.

The imperfect practice of American democracy at home over the last decade added further damage to the U.S. as a model for democracy. The 2000 presidential election, in which the candidate with the largest number of votes did not win, underscored the arcane qualities of the Electoral College, while the numerous counting mistakes in Florida called into question the American commitment to free and fair elections.[14] The Bush administration's decision to listen in on calls made by American citizens for national security reasons dealt a further blow to America's image as a protector of civil liberties.

Taken together, all of these actions tarnished the American image as a model democracy, weakened America's standing in the world, and made it much harder for American leaders to call for more democratic practices in other countries. By the end of the Bush administration, public opinion polls around the world captured a real decline in the appeal of the United States and the American form of democracy. The change of administration in Washington in 2009 offers the United States an opportunity to renew the American system of government as a model for democracy by reversing course in the problematic areas, from closing the Guantanamo Bay prison to reaffirming U.S. commitment to its treaty obligations to addressing voting rights issues at home.

Better Reconciling Our Rhetoric and Actions

Over the course of American history, presidents, diplomats, and non-governmental leaders have delivered speeches that frightened autocrats and emboldened democrats through the world. Thomas Paine's writings and activities to promote liberty might constitute the first one-man American NGO dedicated to democracy promotion. Presidents Abraham Lincoln, Woodrow Wilson, Franklin Roosevelt, John F. Kennedy, Ronald Reagan, and Bill Clinton all delivered speeches about the virtues and benefits of freedom that resonated well beyond America's borders.[15]

After September 11, President George W. Bush delivered some very ambitious, breathtaking speeches about the importance of defending and promoting freedom around the world. As texts, they cannot be criticized. Yet, however well-intended, Bush's sweeping speeches often did more harm than good, raising expectations well beyond what he and his administration were prepared to pursue or capable of doing.[16] Inspired by Bush's rhetoric, democratic activists in Egypt, Iran, Belarus, Syria, Russia, and Azerbaijan took chances and challenged their regimes, believing that Washington would come to their defense. They were let down. Nowhere is this tragedy more apparent than in Egypt, where Ayman Nour had the opportunity to become a presidential candidate in part because of American pressure for democratic change, but now is imprisoned for the crime of standing as a presidential candidate. President Bush and his administration not only failed to bring democracy to Egypt, they did not even succeed in getting Nour out of jail.

The American president must continue to speak out in support of democracy and human rights. Shying away from the "d" word in favor of more euphemistic phrases like "good governance" or "human dignity" would send a terrible signal to the activists around the world fighting for human rights and democratic change. Certainly, the United States has to cooperate with illiberal and authoritarian regimes on a wide range of economic, security, and political issues. Americans need Saudi oil, Russian cooperation on reducing the world's nuclear arsenals, and Chinese computer chips and textiles. In pursuing these transactions, however, American diplomats must not check their values at the door. Consistency also matters. The worst of all worlds is when one cabinet official gives a speech about democracy promotion as a U.S. priority and another senior official downplays its significance.[17]

Too much talk without commensurate action hurts the democratic cause. Likewise, expectations about the speed and magnitude of democratic change have to be managed. Most importantly, the U.S. government must focus on promoting concrete steps towards political liberalization or democratic consolidation and move away from grandiose pledges of fostering full-scale regime change in autocracies or creating overnight liberal institutions in new democracies. As former National Security Advisor Anthony Lake wrote more than 20 years ago, "By promising less, Washington can accomplish more. U.S. influence is diminished only when results fall short of rhetoric."[18]

American officials also must adopt a broader definition of democracy and use a wider vocabulary of related concepts to promulgate democratic ideas more effectively. Senior foreign policy officials in the Bush administration rarely mentioned ideas such as equality or justice, values that past American leaders considered fundamental to our system of government.[19]

Fostering accountability and transparent government also must assume greater priority. Western definitions of liberalism must be stretched to allow for more universal notions of human rights as well as more specific regional and cultural conceptions. In particular, the reverential focus on the individual prevalent in Anglo-American thinking cannot be exported blindly to cultures that place greater value on collective and communal practices.

The promotion of economic development also must accompany efforts to advance democracy, since simultaneous progress on both fronts can create a virtuous circle of sustainability. In the developing world, new democracies without economic growth are much more likely to fail than are democracies that produce economic growth.[20] Likewise, as Carles Boix suggests,

> Democratization and, particularly, democratic consolidation have been systematically bolstered by high levels of income equality and a fair distribution of property in the countryside across the world in the last two centuries.[21]

In other words, the reduction of poverty and even the promotion of economic equality are policy goals that also can foster democratic development. The same intertwined relationship holds true for the rule of law and democracy.

As discussed earlier, the desire to sequence a reform process—such as state building first, economic development second, and democracy third—is often misplaced both because our own theories about what should come first are contradictory but also because the United States rarely has the power or influence to dictate to another country a particular sequence of change. At the same time, rhetorical recognition of the interre-

lationship among these various goals could help to make democratization sound more like a development goal and less like an
imperial mission.

Renouncing Military Intervention as a Tool of Democracy Promotion

Most of the world, as well as a good many Americans, equate
the American-led invasions of Afghanistan and Iraq with democracy promotion. During the Bush administration, the American
armed forces assumed a leading role in fostering democratic
regime change. This close association between war and democracy promotion is unfortunate, not only because these American-
led wars are unpopular and therefore undermine support for
democracy promotion among the American people, but also because they overshadow the more traditional means for supporting
democratic development in other countries.

Only in rare circumstances have American presidents ordered American soldiers into battle for the purpose of promoting
democracy.[22] The few exceptions, such as Panama in 1989 or
Haiti in 1994, were hardly real military conflicts. All other military interventions in American history, including the American-
led military interventions in Afghanistan and Iraq, aimed to
achieve some more immediate security objective, not democracy
promotion. The reason for this is clear: the American people have
not and will not support the invasion of another country for the
cause of democracy promotion.

If American presidents almost never initiate military conflict
to promote democracy, they also rarely withdraw American
troops before first seeking to alter the political institutions in the
occupied country in a more democratic direction. After American
soldiers have lost their lives in war, replacing one dictator with

another is not a politically attractive outcome, especially after a long war. Rarely can American presidents justify the sustained occupation of another country in the name of preserving the balance of power or advancing narrow American geo-strategic interests such as access to oil or other strategic resources. Instead, the post-war objective must be a moral one, which usually involves the creation or restoration of democratic institutions. Bush's use of preemptive military force to eliminate Saddam Hussein's regime in Iraq may have been a strategic innovation.[23] His quest to promote democracy inside Iraq after American forces occupied the country is an old American tradition.

Analysts count the number of American military interventions in different ways, but most studies, no matter how the dataset is constructed, have concluded that the American use of military power has rarely succeeded in installing democracy in the aftermath of conflict.[24] A 2003 RAND study of seven nation-building cases praised two as successes: Germany and Japan; deemed two more to be partial successes: Bosnia and Kosovo; and labeled three as failures: Somalia, Haiti, and Afghanistan. Written the same year the U.S. invaded Iraq, the study hinted that that case would be a failure. In a more expansive study of seventeen U.S. nation-building missions after military occupation going back to 1898, Minxin Pei, Samia Amin, and Seth Garz identify only four countries that sustained democracy 10 years after the departure of American forces: Germany, Japan, Panama, and Grenada.[25] Jeffrey Pickering and Mark Peceny review all cases of U.S. military interventions from 1946 to 1996, dividing these campaigns between those in support of the target government and those hostile to the target government. Regarding the first category of cases, they find that "not a single country that experiences a supportive U.S. military intervention became a democracy within 5 years of intervention."[26] Pickering and Peceny find that a hostile U.S. intervention increases the probability of democratization by 18 percent five years after the military action. Yet, they also note that these results are driven by only three successful cases: the Dominican Republic in 1961, Panama in 1989, and Haiti in 1994.[27] And of these, only Panama can be considered a clear case of democratic success.[28]

The system of government that emerged in Afghanistan after the American-led invasion in the fall of 2001 is mostly certainly more democratic and more liberal than the Taliban dictatorship it replaced. Elections have played a role in determining who governs, independent media and civic organizations have sprouted, and modest progress towards establishing the rule of law has been made. At the same time, the ethnically based networks of patronage that have dominated Afghan politics for centuries still remain the dominant political institutions in the country—a condition that was strengthened by American reliance on warlords to govern and assist in fighting Al Qaeda.

In early 2009, Iraq was a similar story. The American-led occupation in Iraq demonstrated the extreme limits of American strategic thinking about building democratic regimes in the wake of fallen autocratic regimes.[29] Once the political decision was made to invade Iraq, Pentagon planners drafted a comprehensive plan for destroying Saddam Hussein's autocratic regime. The Department of Defense then had the resources to execute this plan with great success. Nowhere in the United States government, however, did a parallel organization draft an integrated, comprehensive plan for constructing a post-war democratic regime. Although many agencies drafted proposals, the Department of Defense eventually drove post-war stabilization efforts.[30] The resources for post-war regime construction were poorly organized, too few, and improperly deployed. Even the official history of post-war reconstruction has described a futile effort.[31] Regarding the narrower task of building democratic institutions, planning and execution was ad hoc and constantly changing.[32] Someday Iraq may become a democracy and the three-week, American-led war to topple Saddam Hussein's dictatorship may be seen as a necessary beginning of this democratization process. But the subsequent years of American occupation and then the counterinsurgency war—fueled in large measure by poor post-war stabilization and reconstruction planning—will also be seen as having impeded rather than consolidated democracy's eventual success.

After the invasion of Iraq, the Bush administration realized the limits of the U.S. government's ability to plan ahead and organize for post-war reconstruction and responded by creating the new Office of the Coordinator for Reconstruction and Stabilization (S/CRS). This new bureau borrowed professionals from the State Department, USAID—especially its Office of Transition Initiatives (OTI), the Defense Department, and other parts of the government to "lead and coordinate U.S. Government planning, and institutionalize U.S. capacity, to help stabilize and reconstruct societies in transition from conflict or civil strife so they can reach a sustainable path toward peace, democracy and a market economy." This office did not get involved in either Afghanistan or Iraq, but instead aimed to prepare for future situations. Several years later, however, the new office remained woefully underfunded and the head of the office did not hold the rank equivalent to an assistant secretary of state. Whether this office should be located within the State Department was also hotly debated.

More generally, it is difficult for traditional democracy promotion programs to work in dangerous war zones. American NGOs involved in political party training, NGO development, and assistance to independent media have worked in conflict zones from Liberia to Bosnia to Afghanistan to Iraq. The obstacles to effective work are enormous. In Iraq, many American democracy promotion organizations have refused to work in country, and those that do spend up to 40 percent of their budgets on security. U.S. military intervention usually has not facilitated democratic development, but it is untrue that military intervention has never has aided democratic change. A few famous occupations—Germany, Japan, and one might add Italy and Austria as well—have produced positive democratic results. Some conditions are more likely to produce democracy after interventions than others. As with all instances of democratization, the new democratic regime is more likely to endure in rich, urban, developed countries and less likely to take hold in poor, underdeveloped countries.[33] The probability of democratic consolidation in rich Germany, Austria, Italy, and Japan was much higher than in poor Philippines, Vietnam, Somalia, Haiti, or, more recently, Afghanistan and Iraq. Second, countries with some prior experience with democracy have an easier time restoring democratic institutions after intervention than countries with no history of democratic governance. Restoring democracy to Panama was easier than trying to build democratic institutions from scratch in Bosnia and Herzegovina. Third, U.S. intentions matter. In Germany and Japan (as well as in Italy and Austria), American leaders defined democratic governance in these occupied countries as a strategic objective—part of the fight against communism. In Vietnam and Somalia, democracy promotion was never considered a high priority. Finally, in cases where both the regime and state collapsed after intervention, American occupying forces have to pursue both state-building and democracy promotion, but with a premium placed on state-building and security in particular. In countries where civil wars are ongoing, elections can exacerbate tensions and fuel polarization. In other words, when a strong state already exists and when the targeted country is small, rich, and experienced in democracy, military intervention can successfully promote democracy. It is in the more difficult cases—poor states with weak infrastructure and a totalitarian history—in which American military intervention has failed to facilitate democratic change.

The lesson for the future is simple: never invade a country to promote democracy. In surveying the list of contemporary autocracies with strained relations with the United States—North Korea, Iran, Syria, Cuba, Venezuela, Zimbabwe, Burma, and possibly Russia and China—the use of military force or even covert aid to surrogate forces would have disastrous consequences for democratization.[34] Especially in the wake of Iraq and Afghanistan, the deployment of American military power to foster regime change is so unimaginable that President Obama should codify a new U.S. foreign policy doctrine: the United States does not use military force to promote democracy, period. He could quote Ronald Reagan's famous speech before the British parliament on June 8, 1982, in which Reagan rightly observed that "regimes planted by bayonets do not take root." Humanitarian interventions to interrupt genocide or famine must remain an option, but only when the military action can stop human suffering.

Covert and overt military assistance to "freedom fighters" also has a poor record in fostering democratic change.[35] Democracy rarely follows from these kinds of interventions. Discontinuing them except in the rarest of special circumstances, therefore, should become U.S. policy.

The Limits of Sanctions for Aiding Democracy

When governments violate human rights or deny democratic practices to their citizens, the United States and other democracies increasingly respond by imposing economic sanctions.[36] The theory is that economic sanctions enforced by the world's largest economy will restrict those resources controlled by the autocratic regime, thereby undermining the popularity and legitimacy of the targeted dictator, especially if sanctions can spark an economic crisis. The use of sanctions to punish autocratic behavior is growing. While only 3 percent of illiberal regimes endured sanctions for anti-democratic behavior in 1983, 21 percent of those regimes were targeted in 2000.[37] In the last decade, economic sanctions were applied virtually every time democratic rights and freedoms were suspended, human rights were grossly abused, or a civil war broke out.[38] A country in Latin America that experienced a lapse in democracy in 2000 had a greater than 80 percent risk of being punished by economic sanctions.[39]

Even if one goal of sanctions is democratic change, others goals often coexist. For instance, American sanctions against the Soviet Union also aimed to weaken Soviet military capacity and increase Jewish emigration. International sanctions against South Africa focused first on ending apartheid, but also aimed to end South African military aggression in the region.[40] American sanctions have purportedly aimed to undermine the Cuban and Iranian regimes, but also to punish the way autocrats in these two countries seized power. Presidents also have applied sanctions frequently to alter the behavior of states without seeking regime change. For instance, sanctions against Iraq in the 1990s aimed to punish Saddam Hussein for invading Kuwait, impede his regime from acquiring weapons of mass destruction, and weaken Iraq's capacity to threaten other countries in the region.[41] More recently, many who advocate sanctions against Iran explicitly argue that regime change has to be taken off the table if sanctions are to work in curtailing Iran's nuclear weapons programs. In general, the United States often applies economic sanctions as a

way to do something rather than nothing or to appease a particular domestic constituency, sometimes without tying sanctions
to a desired policy outcome.

These multiple objectives make it hard to evaluate the role
of sanctions on fostering democratization. The very premise that
sanctions weaken autocrats must be questioned. Some sanctions
may weaken the democratic opposition more than the regime.
Other sanctions might serve to rally society behind the ruling autocrats. Not surprisingly, therefore, the literature on the efficacy
of sanctions shows rather limited results. In one survey, Clifton
Morgan and Valerie Schwebach report that "most studies in political science have concluded that sanctions do not 'work' at least
not in the sense of bringing about a desired change in the policy
of the target country. . . ."[42] In summarizing the academic literature on whether sanctions are effective, Nikolai Marinov says,
"The consensus view seems to be somewhere between 'no' and
'rarely.'"[43] Their effectiveness has been limited especially when
in place over long periods of time. They work most effectively
when deployed against a country to restore democracy after a
coup. They also work best against countries with deep economic
connections to the United States and the West. Sanctions played
a positive role against South Africa only after decades of uninter-
rupted trade and investment with the West—that is, because
South African companies had much to lose from their application.
In countries like Burma, Cuba, and Iran, where the United States
interrupted trade and investment decades ago, the United States
has weak levers of economic coercion. Sanctions also only work
when pursued multilaterally. High energy prices immunize oil
and gas exporters like Iran, Venezuela, and Russia from economic
sanctions, while America's high levels of trade, investment, and
debt with China also undermine the credibility of threatening
sanctions there.

Symbolically, sanctions must be applied from time to time to demonstrate American moral outrage when human rights and democratic activists in the targeted country demand them.[44] Economic sanctions, however, should never be enforced alone as a policy for supporting democratic development.

Engaging Autocratic Friends for Change

Close American relationships with authoritarian regimes in Saudi Arabia, Egypt, and Jordan, and cordial relationships with autocratic rulers in Kazakhstan, Azerbaijan, and Equatorial Guinea, undermine U.S. credibility when criticizing similar types of autocratic regimes with less friendly ties to Washington.[45] Only the truly naïve, however, would advocate a termination of diplomatic relations with these countries in the name of a more ethical foreign policy. Nonetheless, American leaders can do more to distinguish between material and strategic interests in the short term and our deeper values over the long run, while simultaneously doing more to encourage evolutionary change in these kinds of regimes.

To demarcate more clearly our interests from our values, American diplomats have to maintain more vigilance in curtailing flowery, friendly language to describe the leaders and governments of these authoritarian regimes. American foreign policy officials also must reject the false linkage between cooperation and silence on human rights abuses that autocrats try to make a condition of engagement, and instead U.S. leaders must go out of their way to engage democratic activists in these same places. Our autocratic friends in power must understand that we respect their democratic challengers. Historical experience has confirmed that U.S. engagement with opposition leaders can help protect them from harassment and imprisonment. And only in rare cases has a friendly autocratic regime stopped working with the United States on a strategic issue of mutual benefit because an American official criticized this same regime for antidemocratic practices. Arrests or crackdowns on democratic forces in these countries demand commensurate responses from American officials.

In addition, American aid to these regimes should be disaggregated into one channel of support for geostrategic cooperation and another channel for democracy and development assistance. Bribes paid in the pursuit of geostrategic ends should not be dressed up as "democracy assistance."[46] To the extent possible, these kinds of transfers also must be reduced as they amount in essence to the American promotion of autocracy. For instance, American aid to Egypt jumped to roughly $2 billion a year after 1979 as a payment for Egyptian recognition of Israel. Thirty years later, does the U.S. really need to pay Egypt not to harm to Israel? Such transfers with no strings attached also produce little economic development or political liberalization—the very kinds of changes that could save regimes in Egypt and Pakistan from revolutionary challengers.

Over the long term, the United States must engage more actively in pressing our autocratic friends to initiate political liberalization, however incremental, and eventually to pursue pacts, negotiations, and roundtable discussions with democratic forces in their societies.[47] In many successful transitions from authoritarian rule to democracy, interim settlements between the incumbent autocrats and challenging democrats have helped to smooth political change and then consolidate stable democratic institutions afterwards.[48] In particular, pacts often have been crafted to limit the agenda of change to political institutions only and not infringe on the property rights of existing economic actors tied to the ancien regime. Successful pacts often include highly undemocratic features, which serve to bridge the gap from one regime type to the next. For instance, as a condition for democratic transition in Chile, General Pinochet was allowed to stay on as the commander of the military. Pacts also can be used to insure the safety of leaders from the exiting autocratic regime. In crafting these delicate and unjust pacts, external actors such as the United States can play pivotal roles as mediators and as guarantors of the terms of the pacts. In the 1980s, for instance, President Reagan and his administration leveraged their close relations with autocrats in the Philippines, South Korea, Chile, and South Africa to help foster evolutionary democratic change. In the margins, these American efforts helped to nudge these dictators to relinquish power.

In the Philippines in 1986, Reagan reluctantly signaled to his good friend, Ferdinand Marcos, that the United States would no longer support any further attempts to crush the "People Power" movement, which had filled the streets of Manila with hundreds of thousands and then millions of protesters demanding that Marcos step down after he stole an election.

When visiting South Korea in 1984, Reagan made clear his idea that "the development of democratic political institutions is the surest means to build the national consensus that is the foundation for true security. . . ."[49] When protests teetered towards mass violence, Reagan signaled that he would not support repression and at the same time encouraged his diplomats to meet directly with the opposition.[50]

In Chile, Reagan and his Secretary of State George Shultz eventually pressured Pinochet to take some measures to legitimate his regime. As Shultz recalls,

> By the start of the second Reagan term, however, I was convinced that the U.S. approach [supporting

Pinochet without qualification] was not working. We
understood Pinochet; he was not changing. But he did
not understand us; we wanted a more open government, rule of law, and a government headed by elected
officials.[51]

In reaction to this pressure, Pinochet called for a plebiscite on
his rule in 1988, a vote that he was convinced he would win.
When he lost, the process of democratic restoration began.

Reagan proved more reluctant to push the apartheid leadership in South Africa to change. Still worried about the communist threat emanating from Angola and Mozambique, Reagan
vetoed the Comprehensive Anti-Apartheid Act (CAAA), which
became law in October 1986 after a congressional override.[52]
Nonetheless, in parallel to this support for the South African
regime, Shultz became the first American Secretary of State to
meet with an African National Congress (ANC) leader, Oliver
Tambo, on January 28, 1987—a gesture that started a process of
removing the ANC from the State Department's terrorist list.[53]
The following year, Chester Crocker brokered a peace settlement
in Namibia that included the South West Africa People's Organization (SWAPO)—a one-time communist and terrorist organization—as a key interlocutor. His successful negotiations for
Namibian independence in 1988 underscored how cooperative
diplomacy, not coercive sanctions, could produce democratic
outcomes.[54] Incrementally, American leaders encouraged their
South African counterparts to do the same: abandon their "war
on terror" against the ANC and its allies inside South Africa and
begin negotiations with the more moderate elements of the democratic opposition before the radicals seized power.

In all these cases, many specific conditions were necessary
for this strategy to succeed. First, the American president and

top diplomatic officials consciously defined democratization as a goal of engagement. Otherwise, the targeted regime and the American diplomats executing an engagement policy can interpret the goal as "stable" relations and nothing more. Second, senior officials in the American government were involved in these efforts. This kind of strategy for democracy promotion cannot succeed if assigned to lower-level diplomats. Third, this strategy has worked best when the other regime was friendly to the United States, and it was especially potent when targeted at autocracies that relied on the United States for legitimacy, arms transfers, economic assistance, and security guarantees. Fourth, this strategy succeeded when the United States government and American NGOs sought to engage and at times support in parallel the democratic forces inside the targeted autocratic regime. In the Philippines and Chile, aid and technical assistance from the National Endowment for Democracy (NED) and the National Democratic Institute (NDI) helped to expose electoral fraud, and in Chile, to assist the opposition in running a successful "NO" campaign during the referendum.[55] In South Africa, AID as well as NED, NDI, and other American NGOs provided support and solidarity to the opposition forces.[56] This second track was needed not only to keep the pressure on the autocrats but also to make sure that the democratic opposition understood and supported the American strategy.

Today in the Middle East, Central Asia, and South Asia, the challenge is not only to nudge friendly autocrats towards democratic change, but also to engage unfriendly social movements— Islamists in particular—by seeking their participation in negotiations about democratic change. Some lessons from successful democratic transitions are clear; others are not. Most importantly, all Islamists—just like all leftists during the Cold War—are not alike.[57] Al Qaeda seeks the re-creation of the caliphate and uses terror as a means to achieve its political objectives. Other groups, including Hamas and Hezbollah, focus on specific local political grievances while embracing both Islamist tropes and violent means. It makes little sense to negotiate with organizations that do not seek democracy as a final objective or that use violence as an instrument for achieving political goals. But many Islamist parties have embraced democracy (even when their governments do not) and denounce violence as a strategy for achieving their ends (even if some in this category still condone violence carried out by others against American or Israeli targets). As Amr Hamzawy has explained,

> It is both desirable and feasible for the West to reach out to Islamist movements in the Arab world now that there are signs that some of these groups embrace nonviolence, pragmatism, and democratic procedures. Those who still insist that there is no such thing as a "moderate Islamist" miss the reality that activist organizations in Morocco, Algeria, Egypt, Jordan, Kuwait, and Yemen have evolved after decades of failed opposition to repressive regimes. Instead of clinging to fantasies of theocratic states, Islamist movements in these countries now see the wisdom of competing peacefully for shares of political power and working within existing institutions to promote gradual democratic openings.[58]

These parties compare themselves to Turkey's AKP and Europe's Christian Democrats. They must be part of any negotiated transition from authoritarian rule.

Doctrinal statements and analogies do not signal clearly what these parties would do should they come to power. Commitments to nonviolence and procedural democracy are not enough. Assessing an Islamist movement's compatibility with democratic politics also requires determining that movement's attitudes toward pluralism, alternation of power, individual rights, and the equality before the law of women and religious minorities. Although internal democracy and transparency can help others make these judgments, ultimately only participation in the democratic practice will provide a true test. A group's commitment to democracy cannot really be known without a political process open enough to put them into positions of authority and responsibility.

The genius of negotiated or "pacted" transitions is that incumbents can dictate the pace of change and insulate certain state institutions such as the army or the monarchy from immediate exposure to democratic control. The democratic credentials of new participants in the political process can be tested in the parliament, for instance, before handing over control of all executive institutions to the democratic process.

Consequently, U.S. officials should encourage leaders of friendly autocratic regimes to start the process of pacted transition now, while they still can help to manage the process of change, rather than waiting so long that revolutionary actors in society gain strength. U.S. leaders should encourage their counterparts in the Middle East to emulate the evolutionary transition from autocracy to democracy that occurred in Spain and avoid copying the revolutionary transition from autocracy to a new form of dictatorship that transpired in Iran.

In the past, autocratic friends of the U.S. consistently exaggerated threats to American security interests from democratization. In transitions from authoritarian rule in Portugal, Spain, the Philippines, South Korea, Chile, and South Africa, the threat turned out to be much less radical than originally imagined, and as democracy took root, the threat faded still further. In none of these cases did democratization produce anti-American governments or fundamentally undermine American national security interests. Of course, we cannot know with certainty if a similar process would unfold after political liberalization in the Middle East or South Asia, but processes of evolutionary change already launched in Turkey, Indonesia, Morocco, Jordan, and Kuwait suggest that a similar result could be achieved.

Successful democratizers must be rewarded generously with economic assistance and security guarantees. In 2007, Senators Joseph Biden and Richard Lugar proposed a "democracy dividend" of $1.5 billion annually for Pakistan as a reward for restoring democracy.[59] This is a mechanism that should be established to respond quickly to other countries undergoing democratic breakthroughs.

In special circumstances, U.S. officials must be prepared to offer falling autocrats exit out of the country and safe haven to enjoy their retirement from politics. However unjust, safe passage out of the country for an autocratic ruler sometimes can be a necessary condition for peaceful democratic change.

Trying to avoid change forever in these friendly autocracies is simply not an option. Throughout the latter half of the twentieth century, American leaders tried to pursue American interests in the Middle East by aligning with authoritarian regimes as a strategy to maintain the existing balance of power in the region. Results of this approach included the taking of hostages in Tehran, a protracted war between Iraq and Iran, the slaughter of French and American soldiers in Beirut, the invasion of Kuwait by our former ally Saddam Hussein (an ally who ruthlessly slaughtered tens of thousands of his citizens to maintain the "status quo"), the rise of the Taliban in Afghanistan, and the gradual, almost imperceptible growth of one of the most ruthless and violent terrorist organizations ever known, Al Qaeda. Now, before incumbent dictatorships face serious challengers, U.S. officials must deploy the tools of diplomacy to nudge democratization forward. By doing so, American leaders will enhance the probability of evolutionary change and lessen the likelihood of revolutionary change.

Engaging (and Sometimes Coercing) Autocratic Foes to Advance Democracy

It is not coincidence that American leaders have pursued more confrontational strategies for promoting democratic change against those countries with strained relations with the United States, while adopting policies of engagement to induce democratic change with American friends and allies. This hypocrisy in American foreign policy is accentuated when American presidents actively use coercive tools to promote regime change in the first category of countries, but not the other. President Reagan provided financial and military assistance to "freedom fighters" seeking to undermine communist regimes in Angola, Afghanistan, Nicaragua, and Cambodia, but did not extend such support to freedom fighters in Indonesia, Mexico, Taiwan, or South Africa. President George W. Bush's axis of evil speech threatened autocratic regimes in Iraq, Iran, and North Korea, while conspicuously leaving Pakistan, Egypt, and Saudi Arabia off this list.

This bifurcated strategy has produced uneven results. Although useful perhaps for achieving other American policy objectives, coercive strategies such as military force or sanctions have not worked very often as instruments for promoting democracy in autocracies that have antagonistic relations with the United States. More generally, periods of high tension or disengagement between the United States and authoritarian foes rarely have facilitated internal democratic change in these countries and more often have created a pretense for greater levels of political repression. Conversely, policies of engagement with autocratic foes have sometimes created the permissive conditions for democratization.

U.S.-Soviet relations are illustrative.[60] The conventional story on the collapse of the Soviet Union celebrates President Reagan for using a military buildup and the threat of "Star Wars" to pressure Moscow to change. In fact, it was Reagan's own Secretary of State, George Shultz, who recognized the folly of isolation and the necessity to engage both the Soviet leaders and Soviet society. As Schultz wrote in his memoirs about the start of 1983, "I wanted to develop a strategy for a new start with the Soviet Union. I felt we had to try to turn the relationship around: away from confrontation and towards real problem solving."[61] Shultz's new strategy met resistance but he was "determined not to hang back from engaging the Soviets because of fears that the 'Soviets win negotiations.'"[62] In reengaging Moscow,

> We were determined not to allow the Soviets to focus
> our negotiations simply on matters of arms control.
> So we continuously adhered to a broad agenda: human
> rights, regional issues, arms control, and bilateral is-
> sues.[63]

Once Gorbachev came to power, Shultz's strategy reaped benefits. As relations between the United States and the Soviet Union became less confrontational and more cooperative during the Gorbachev era, Gorbachev felt more emboldened to pursue radical political and economic reform at home. Gorbachev announced his most revolutionary democratic reforms at the nineteenth conference of the Communist Party of the Soviet Union, in June 1988—years after the thaw in U.S.-Soviet relations had begun, and a month after Reagan's historic trip to Moscow. By that time, Reagan was not seeking to confront the "evil empire," but was instead developing a friendly, personal relationship with Gorbachev. Shultz and Soviet Foreign Minister Eduard Shevardnadze established a similar bond. To be sure, the United States continued to supply Stinger missiles to insurgents in Afghanistan, and Reagan went out of his way to demonstrate solidarity with those inside the Soviet Union persecuted for their religious and political beliefs. But compared to the hostile and tense atmosphere surrounding American-Iranian relations today, U.S.-Soviet relations at the dawn of political liberalization inside the USSR were downright friendly. President George H.W. Bush continued to support Gorbachev, not wanting to do anything that might weaken or undermine America's trusted friend in the Kremlin.[64] Even after the August 1991 coup had failed and the collapse of the Soviet Union was obvious to everyone, Bush still tried to persuade other European leaders to support Gorbachev and his quest to preserve the USSR.[65]

This relatively benign international context made it easier for Gorbachev to pursue his radical domestic agenda of change.[66] During this period of warm relations with the United States, Gorbachev did not worry that his "enemy" would try to take advantage of his country's weakness as the USSR underwent the chaotic transformation from communism to something else. A more hostile international environment might have made Gorbachev more cautious. The West's embrace of Gorbachev in turn made Gorbachev more powerful inside the Soviet Union, at least for a time, in his struggles with both the left and the right.

In parallel to greater engagement with the Soviet regime was greater engagement of the democratic opposition inside Russia and the other republics. The former was a precondition for the latter. During more tense eras in U.S.-Soviet relations, groups such as NED had a difficult time operating inside the USSR. As diplomatic relations thawed, however, non-governmental activity to promote democracy became possible. During this period of detente, NED, NDI, the International Republican Institute (IRI), and the AFL-CIO established working relationships with and provided limited financial assistance to leaders and organizations of Russia's opposition. The AFL-CIO gave assistance to striking coal miners in 1989 and again in 1991 and later helped to establish the Independent Miners Union in Russia.[67] During the same period, NED grants provided fax machines, computers, and advisers to the Russian Constitutional Commission, support for human rights organizations, and a printing press for Democratic Russia, the coalition of opposition parties and organizations spearheading the grassroots movement for democratic change in Russia. And while President Bush issued warnings about the dangers of nationalism, NED was offering assistance to national democratic movements in the Baltics, Ukraine, Azerbaijan, Armenia, Georgia, and Russia.[68] Similarly, NDI initially directed "its efforts towards the institutions which are spearheading democratic reform—the city soviets and the republics of Russia and Ukraine."[69] The NDI avoided direct financial transfers to Russian organizations at the time but did provide technical assistance, training, and limited equipment to Democratic Russia during this period. The IRI (called the National Republican Institute at the time) engaged in party-building programs with Russian counterparts well before the Soviet Union collapsed. At the time, all of these non-governmental organizations received the bulk of their funding from government sources.[70] Indirectly, therefore, the U.S. government was using a dual-track strategy to promote democratization within the Soviet Union and Russia. The degree of engagement or level of resources devoted to aiding the democrats was minuscule, and this assistance began only a few years and sometimes just a few months before the Soviet collapse and the perceived victory of the "democrats." The assistance that did flow into the Soviet Union at the time could only have occurred during a period of close relations between Washington and Moscow. During the Cold War, Soviet internal suppression of dissidents escalated when conflicts with the U.S. intensified. The same pattern emerged in other communist countries.[71] A similar dynamic has unfolded over the past 30 years regarding U.S. relations with Iran.

In rethinking the U.S. strategy for supporting democracy in these kinds of countries, the first step must be the expansion of the agenda for government-to-government relations. With Iran, for instance, this means an offer of direct talks with the theocrats in Tehran. Everything must be on the agenda: the prospect of formal diplomatic relations and the lifting of sanctions; the potential supply and disposal of nuclear fuel (from a third-party organization or state); suspension of nuclear enrichment; an end to aid to Hezbollah and Hamas; and a serious discussion about stopping the arrests of students and human rights advocates and the persecution of union leaders and religious minorities. Establishment of new regional security institutions in the region also should be on the table.

With Cuba, a new initiative to engage the regime would have to include the restoration of diplomatic relations, lifting of sanctions, as well as discussion about political prisoners and repression of political activities.

With an increasingly autocratic Russia, a new strategy of engagement to support democratic development would require a more comprehensive bilateral agenda that raises issues of mutual concern: preventing weapons of mass destruction from falling into the hands of terrorists, addressing Iran's nuclear ambitions, reducing nuclear arsenals, securing stable supplies of oil and gas from Russia and Eurasia, discussing European security issues, expanding connections between our societies, and increasing investment opportunities.

With China, a comprehensive and mostly positive bilateral agenda already does exist. Without question, U.S.-Chinese relations today are a vast improvement over the 22-year period when no contacts existed. Greater state-to-state engagement has facilitated increased societal contacts between Americans and Chinese, including even some contacts between Chinese democratic leaders, independent journalists, and civil society activists. These interactions were much more constrained when the United States did not have diplomatic relations with China. Obviously, as the case of China illustrates, engagement of authoritarian regimes alone does little to promote democratic change. For the strategy to work, American diplomats must practice dual track diplomacy of the sort practiced by Shultz in dealing with the Soviet Union: engaging autocratic leaders in charge of the state and democratic leaders in society in parallel and at the same time.[72]

Historical analogies only go so far, but the general principles of Shultz's dual track diplomacy still apply today. When engaging Russians to reduce our respective nuclear arsenals or Iranians to end their nuclear enrichment program, Americans must not check their values at the door. Nor should they allow their interlocutors to narrow the scope of bilateral relations to only arms control issues. If developed carefully, a more substantive, less confrontational relationship with these autocratic regimes can fulfill a necessary condition for beginning a more meaningful dialogue about issues of democracy and human rights. A more substantial government-to-government agenda also will create a more favorable environment for engaging societal forces in these countries pushing for democratic change. American NGOs involved in democracy promotion do not have offices in Tehran or Havana. Democratic activists in Iran, Syria, Cuba, and North Korea face severe constraints in making contacts with their counterparts in democracies in large measure because of their regime's activities, but also because of real difficulties of obtaining American visas. In Iran, even the opening of an interests section if not a full-blown embassy would greatly facilitate contacts between Iranian democrats and their American supporters. The public relations value of a giant line of Iranians waiting outside a U.S. embassy in Tehran to get visas should not be underestimated. Greater contact between Iranian and American societies in turn would further undermine the regimes' legitimacy, strengthen the independence of Iranian economic and political groups, and perhaps even compel some regime members to cash out and exchange their diminishing political power for enduring property rights.

Fostering Democratic Breakthroughs in Semi-Autocracies: The Color Revolutions

As discussed earlier, most regimes in the developing world today are neither liberal democracies nor totalitarian dictatorships, but something in between, teetering between electoral democracy and semi-autocracy. More often than not, these regimes do not inch gradually towards greater democratic development, but instead devolve towards some form of soft authoritarian rule. By the end of the 1990s, the expectation that countries making an initial transition to democracy would continue along a path to liberal democracy faded considerably.[73]

Starting in Serbia in 2000, however, a series of breakthrough elections jump-started a new wave of democratic change in the post-communist world. In October 2000, Serbian democratic forces ousted dictator Slobodan Milošević. Three years later, Georgia's far less odious but still semi-autocratic president Eduard Shevardnadze fell before mobilized societal forces. The following year, in 2004, Ukrainian democrats staged a two-week-long mobilization dubbed the Orange Revolution that toppled Viktor Yanukovych, the handpicked successor to corrupt, outgoing president Leonid Kuchma.[74] In all three cases, these democratic breakthroughs were sparked by fraudulent national elections followed by mass demonstrations to reverse the falsified results.

The factors for success in these cases included (1) a semi-autocratic regime, (2) an unpopular incumbent; (3) a united and organized opposition; (4) an ability by the opposition to expose electoral fraud; (5) enough independent media to inform citizens about the falsified vote; (6) a political opposition capable of mobilizing tens of thousands of demonstrators to protest electoral fraud; and (7) divisions among the regime's coercive forces.[75] Of these seven factors, the United States played a role in only a few. Given the extremely precarious distribution of power, however, these inputs from the United States, and the West more generally, were consequential in tipping the balance in favor of the democratic challengers.

In contrast to Saudi Arabia, Uzbekistan, or Syria, none of these regimes was a full-blown autocracy, but instead each allowed for some pockets of pluralism, independent media, political opposition, and perhaps most importantly, elections. They did so in part because they sought legitimacy in the West. Earning respect from the West, and the United States in particular, was especially important for Shevardnadze and Kuchma, but even Milošević desired the same. The Clinton administration eventually led a NATO bombing campaign against Serbia in response to Milošević's brutal treatment of Kosovars, an action that hardly could be described as constructive engagement. Yet just a few years before, Clinton administration official Richard Holbrooke negotiated directly with Milošević during the Dayton peace accords. Though strained at times, American engagement with the Georgian and Ukrainian regimes persisted until right up to and during the Rose and Orange revolutions. These state-to-state relationships helped to dissuade Kuchma and Shevardnadze from cracking down on their opposition movements and also facilitated the work of American non-governmental organizations, which worked with civil society and opposition groups inside both countries.

In the margins, U.S. policy also weakened the power and popularity of these autocratic regimes in each of these countries, though the American impact varied considerably. In Serbia, economic sanctions and the subsequent NATO bombing campaign weakened Milošević's grip on power, even if NATO's attack initially undermined the legitimacy and popularity of Serbia's democratic opposition. Eventually, however, Serbian citizens began to blame Milošević for their declining economic welfare. In Georgia, the United States government gradually redirected assistance away from the state and towards civil society. In the fall of 2003, numerous American envoys tried to convince President Shevardnadze to hold free and fair elections. When he did not, the Bush administration did not immediately denounce the election results, but gradually signaled support for the opposition until they seized power. In the run up to the Orange Revolution in Ukraine, Bush administration officials also encouraged President Kuchma to hold free and fair elections, and by denying visas to prominent Ukrainian businessmen, signaled to the regime the consequences of a fraudulent vote. These threats did not prevent Kuchma from trying to steal the vote, but they may have helped to constrain the president and his entourage from using force against the demonstrators. Indirectly, American-supported media outlets' reports on Kuchma's involvement in the killing of Ukrainian journalist Georgiy Gongadze and the vast corruption of Shevard-nadze's Georgian government also helped to undermine the popularity and power of these leaders.

Regarding unity among the opposition, NDI and IRI played active roles in encouraging cooperation among the democratic groups in Serbia and Ukraine, though less so in Georgia. They did so by collecting and then sharing survey data, which underscored the electoral advantage of a single candidate. In both countries, this data pointed to the need to back particular candidates—Voijislav Kostunica in Serbia and Viktor Yushchenko in Ukraine rather than the more charismatic opposition leaders in both countries at the time (Zoran Djinjic in Serbia and Yulia Timoshenko in Ukraine).

American (and European) assistance also played a crucial role in exposing electoral fraud in all three countries. The ideas and technology for exposing fraud—exit polls, parallel vote tabulation, and poll monitors—were imported from the United States. Funding for these activities in all three countries came largely from American and other Western sources, and the presence of international monitors in Ukraine provided moral support for local monitors.[76] American sources provided technical assistance and funding to the main domestic monitoring organizations in all three countries.[77] U.S. sources also supported exit polls in Georgia and Ukraine. Most innovatively, NDI and Freedom House cooperated to bring to Ukraine the European Network of Election Monitoring Organizations (ENEMO), which was comprised of 1,000 observers from 17 electoral monitoring organizations in formerly communist countries. The ENEMO brought trained electoral monitors, experienced in exposing post-communist vote rigging (many observers also spoke Russian) at a fraction of the cost required to bring in Americans or Western Europeans. All of these international teams released critical reports about the election process, which were instrumental in generating a unified international condemnation of the voting procedures.[78] President Bush dispatched a personal envoy, Senator Lugar, to observe the election in Ukraine on behalf of the White House. Lugar's very tough, critical statement about the election prompted other governments to offer criticism of their own, which in turn emboldened the Ukrainian opposition and its supporters to protest on the streets until the fraudulent results were overturned. The U.S. also contributed directly to the development of independent media in all three "color revolutions."

Imported ideas and resources from the United States also strengthened electoral mobilization, both before and after the vote. Youth groups in all three countries played roles in voter mobilization before and after the elections. They received direct and indirect financial assistance from American and other Western sources.[79]

In the aftermath of these revolutions, all three countries have struggled to consolidate democracy. Internal disagreements about the borders of the states have impeded democratic development in Georgia and Serbia, while conflicts between the president and prime minister have stymied effective governance in Ukraine. Still, the regimes in all three governments are far more democratic today than they were before the revolutions. Though democratization is far from complete, American diplomacy and assistance played a role in nudging the process along. Since these kinds of semi-autocracies now constitute the majority of non-democratic regimes in the world today, the complex mix of engagement of regime and society in these cases might provide guidance for how to foster democratic breakthroughs in many other countries in the world.

Nurturing Democratic Consolidation

The vast majority of funds dedicated to democracy assistance by the United States government support programs that seek to help nurture democratic institutions in new democracies. As already mentioned above, channeling democracy assistance into countries ruled by authoritarian regimes is difficult and sometimes impossible. The real opportunity for aiding democratic development usually begins after a democratic breakthrough. The more recent proliferation of illiberal, partial, or poor-performing democracies has provided fertile terrain for the American democracy assistance business to operate. In places like Pakistan, Russia, or the Philippines, American NGOs dedicated to promoting democratic institutions have been operating for decades.

As discussed in earlier chapters, those working in the democracy assistance sector do not have blueprints or well-defined theories for how to consolidate democracy after a democratic transition. Instead, they usually start by supporting the kinds of democratic institutions found in older, liberal democracies. Models of institutional design from older democracies are much needed, and American NGOs have the means to ship in experts on constitutions, electoral laws, and legal structures. American organizations and their counterparts abroad also have advanced technologies and programs to facilitate free and fair elections, including those that support exit polls, parallel vote tabulations, and qualitative election monitoring. These techniques have not only helped to facilitate democratic breakthroughs, but also have strengthened the integrity of elections in new democracies. Because new democracies often spring up in poor, developing countries, American organizations have intervened to underwrite the birth and development of civil society organizations, trade unions, and independent media.[80] The U.S. frequently channels its direct financial assistance through advocacy NGOs, which are easiest for the U.S. government to aid, in part because of their small size and independence, and in part because they profess to have no religious or partisan agendas.[81] U.S. democracy assistance providers also offer technical assistance for the development of more complex institutions such as political parties, courts systems, parliaments, and election administrations. The United States government has tried to nurture the growth of democratic practices and values indirectly by funding scholarships, exchanges, and society-to-society interactions between citizens in new democracies and the American people. U.S. government-funded media outlets also aim to nurture democratic ideas in new democracies (as well as in old autocracies) by fostering the flow of ideas about democracy.

Measuring the impact of these programs on democratic development is extremely difficult. Steven Finkel, Anibal Perez-Linan, and Mitchel Seligson conducted an ambitious quantitative study in which they surveyed all AID democracy assistance programs around the world undertaken from 1990 to 2003.[82] They found a statistical relationship between AID expenditures on democracy and governance on the one hand and democratic development around the world on the other.[83] They estimate that $10 million in democracy and governance spending will raise a country's Freedom House score by a quarter of a point.[84] Most qualitative studies of individual sectors are less positive.

Elections

During the 1980s and 1990s, U.S. direct assistance to election monitoring and campaign-related activities in semi-autocratic regimes became a familiar formula for democracy promotion. American (and Western) assistance for strengthening election processes has been most successful, in part because the activity—an election—is well defined and the mechanisms for controlling fraud are highly developed.[85] The international norms legitimating foreign interventions to support free and fair elections are also robust, making this kind of democracy assistance easier to deliver and execute than other forms of democracy promotion. While leaders can lambast aid to political parties as meddling in their internal affairs, they find it more difficult politically to reject aid for free and fair elections.

Civil Society

Programs that support civil society and trade unions can trace a fairly straight causal arrow between funding and NGO proliferation. The more supporters spend, the more NGOs emerge. The impact of these NGOs on democratic consolidation is much harder to evaluate. American civil society promoters struggle to identify and interact with those groups most closely connected to society. Almost by definition, the groups closest to the people are also furthest from AID and other Western donors. Geography, language barriers, and cultural differences get in the way, but missions and priorities are often different as well. NGOs working in poorer countries tend to focus on local social and economic welfare issues, and less on advocacy in the capital. Even among the narrow band of advocacy NGOs, donors can distort democratic development by defining goals and recommending activities for NGOs that may have more to do with American tastes than the needs of local communities.[86] More generally, American donors bring with them several implicit assumptions about the role of civil society in rich societies that do not translate well into poorer contexts. As Tom Carothers has observed, "The professionalized NGO model comes out of a society that has wealthy, private grant-making foundations, a large middle class with considerable discretionary income, and a corporate world with a tradition of philanthropy. The model does not do well in societies with none of those characteristics.[87] The scale of the resources involved in grant-making also distorts the labor market in poor societies, making it more lucrative to work for a Western-funded NGO than to head a local NGO or government agency without external support.

Despite these obstacles, many important activities regarding human rights and democracy simply would not occur without this kind of assistance. Especially in autocratic regimes, small grant programs that provide direct assistance to pro-democratic NGOs provide a vital lifeline to organizations that could not survive without external assistance. Although the direct link to democratic development may sometimes be hard to trace, the very existence of civil society organizations brings benefits to countries no matter what their democratic trajectory.

Political Parties

Supporting the emergence of effective political parties poses similar problems, in a more politicized context. All democratic theorists agree that functioning political parties are an essential ingredient of liberal democracy.[88] Yet parties are among the most loathed political actors in most countries around the world. Carothers summarizes the "standard lament" about parties with five indictments: parties are (1) "corrupt, self-interested organizations dominated by power-hungry elites . . ."; (2) "do not stand for anything"; (3) "waste too much time squabbling with each other . . ."; (4) "only become active at election time" and (5) "are ill-prepared for governing the country."[89] None of these complaints is unique to new democracies, but they make the work of the two principal American organizations that support political party development abroad—the International Republican Institute and the National Democratic Institute—much harder. Nevertheless, IRI and NDI have developed effective techniques for transferring knowledge about basic party functions, including campaign methods such as conducting focus groups for message development, producing television advertisements, undertaking mass leafleting and direct mail, and organizing door-to-door and get-out-the-vote campaigns. They also have techniques to transfer basic knowledge about internal party organization, developing relations with constituencies and NGOs, and working effectively in parliaments. NDI and IRI have also helped transfer campaign technologies throughout the new democratic world. The United States is one of the oldest and richest democracies in the world, and the American campaign industry is large, highly developed, and eager to export its expertise. Evidence of this technology transfer is everywhere, including most strikingly in the proliferation of public relations, polling, and consulting firms in new democracies. Measuring the American impact on other party functions is much harder, especially when so many local factors— over which foreigners have little control—are so much more influential in shaping party development.[90]

Rule of Law

On the check-list of institutions that citizens want most after a democratic transition (or before, for that matter), the "rule of law" trumps all others. Citizens want police who protect them rather than extort bribes; courts that defend rather than steal their property; equality before the law; and a government that is not above the law. The most desired democratic institution, however, is also the hardest to promote. Why rule of law emerges in one country and struggles in another is still poorly understood. Without a theory to explain the rule of law's development, external actors are seriously constrained in crafting strategies or blueprints for promoting it. As Carothers reports,

> Aid providers know what endpoint they would like to help countries achieve—the Western-style, rule oriented systems they know from their own countries. Yet, they do not really know how countries that do not have such systems attain them.[91]

Moreover, U.S. rule of law promoters are not working with blank legal slates, but must attempt to promote rule of law in countries where legal institutions have traditionally served the government rather than the people.[92] More generally, legal institutions are complex, large, and powerful. Even understanding how they work is challenging. Designing programs to nudge them to change is even more difficult. In the estimation of Frank Fukuyama, "Putting such a system in place is one of the most complex administrative tasks that state-builders need to accomplish."[93]

No comprehensive evaluation of American rule of law promotion around the world since 1990 has ever been attempted.[94] Studies of individual countries are few, while few of the internally-financed evaluations commissioned by AID and other U.S. government agencies are available to the public.[95] There are some successes. Most obviously, the intellectual imprint of American consultants and organizations on the drafting of new laws can be documented. Whether these laws actually improve the rule of law is another question. For instance, American advisors have played central roles in revising commercial codes throughout the developing world, but with limited spillover to democracy and human rights. American experts also have played observable roles in crafting new criminal procedure codes, though their impact in increasing law and order, protecting the rights of defendants, or defending human rights more generally is always difficult to discern.[96] In Latin America, American assistance programs also helped to transform courts from human rights abusers to human rights defenders.[97] Another example of success is the introduction of jury trials in Russia after the collapse of communism. The practice is still very novel, but acquittal rates for defendants appearing before juries are much higher than those appearing only before judges.[98]

These anecdotes of success do not offset the more general negative assessment in the academic literature on the futility of American rule of law assistance programs.[99] The overwhelming reason for rule of law promotion failures is the scale of the challenge compared to the level of the American effort. Because the number of ministries, agencies, and actors involved in a legal system is so immense, almost all interventions by outsiders—even multi-million-dollar interventions—are small and marginal. Expecting returns from such investments is unrealistic. American pathologies, however, are also to blame. The focus on writing good laws and strengthening legal institutions has pushed rule of law assistance programs towards technocratic outcomes at the expense of thinking of law and its emergence as part of a political or social system.[100] Rule of law promoters assume that their work is apolitical, that law can be insulated from politics, and that best practices in one political setting can be transferred to a country with an entirely different balance of political forces.[101] Rarely is this the case. As one comprehensive study of rule of law programs in Latin America concluded, "Projects that do not address political and systematic obstacles will have limited impact."[102] This technocratic approach also means that state employees rather than non-governmental actors become the partners in rule of law promotion. The strategy is top-down, not bottom up.

Independent Media

Tracing the independent contributions of media assistance is extremely difficult, since the broader political and economic environment plays such a central role.[103] For instance, if the state owns all national television stations, then how can the unique contribution of a U.S.-funded regional magazine be measured? If a country's economy lacks the resources to sustain an advertising industry, then only mammoth subsidies from the U.S. or other donors will keep independent media outlets alive. Any time direct transfers of cash or equipment are involved, the potential for corruption increases, especially in volatile political settings.[104] Like grants to NGOs, direct grants to media organizations—especially less expensive outlets such as Web-based publications or even radio—produce very tangible, measurable increases in the presence of independent media. Given market conditions, many pro-democracy, watchdog publications would simply not exist without American funding. Especially when the sums involved are small, it is hard to argue that media subsidies do not advance democracy. Almost by definition, any objective information provided to citizens about the actions of government officials increases government accountability. Compared with the complexities of rule of law reform or party building, subsidizing a newspaper or radio station is much more straightforward.

Getting Better at Supporting Democratic Consolidation

As a first step toward improving political development assistance for new democracies, the U.S. government simply must invest more resources in evaluation and accumulating and disseminating lessons learned.[105] Some lessons, however, are already clear.

First, the moment of transition is when democracy assistance has the greatest impact.[106] Consequently, U.S. policymakers should expand resources for organizations capable of deploying quickly, such as AID's Office of Transition Initiatives. The U.S. government also should establish a network of civilian democracy and state-building specialists, similar to the National Guard, who could be deployed to transitional settings. In addition, a special fund—a democracy dividend—should be set aside to provide rapid financial aid to those governments making the transition to democracy.

Second, American actors rarely have the power to dictate the sequence of political changes, but in the rare cases when they do have options for sequencing, they should follow certain guidelines. Peace must be secured before genuine democratization can occur. Some minimal state capacity must be present before the first elections. Whenever possible, regional elections should be held before national elections. And the more institutions involved in assuring checks and balances—an independent judiciary, an independent media, non-governmental watch dog organizations—that are in place before the first elections, the better.

Third, regarding institutional design, no single size fits all countries. On average, however, some designs have produced more durable democratic outcomes than others. Parliamentary systems tend to sustain democracy better than presidential systems. Electoral systems that incorporate some degree of proportional representation tend to facilitate party development and more cohesive parliaments better than first-past-the-post systems. Institutions of federalism and decentralization tend to facilitate more democratic development, especially in large countries, than do unitary systems.

Fourth, regarding the choice of aiding state reform or civil society development, the evidence is clear that the former is much harder, more complex, and less susceptible to outside interventions. Aid to non-governmental organizations has more immediate and traceable impact regarding the emergence of civil society, but also has less direct impact on government policy and behavior. Given the limited resources available, American support for civil society also must be targeted to those programs and organizations that directly foster democratic development. The best bang for the buck is support for independent media. Similarly, support for the development of independent think tanks on political issues also strengthens the public debate about policy generally and democracy in particular. Human rights organizations need financial assistance because their activities often cannot be sustained by domestic constituencies in poor countries. More generally, the U.S. should devote more resources to fostering the transfer of Web-based and email-based network technologies to NGOs. Subsidizing these tools for organizing and disseminating information generates real multiplier effects to more traditional training programs. Expanding all tools and mechanisms—radio, television, Web sites, or exchanges—that facilitate the transfer of ideas about democracy and human rights must be the organizing principle of all civil society assistance programs.

Fifth, the United States must be more strategic in seeking to assist the consolidation of liberal institutions in new democracies. Political development aid providers cannot offer the same checklist of assistance programs to all new democracies. Nor does the U.S. have the capacity to promote democracy in all places at all times at the same level of intensity. Instead of providing a little support to all new democracies, the strategic priority must be to fortify new democracies, especially in those strategic countries such as Pakistan, Georgia, Ukraine, Colombia, and South Africa, where democratic backsliding will have negative implications for other American strategic objectives.

Sixth, the consolidation of liberal democracy takes time. American aid providers must not be afraid (and Congressional funders must enable them not to be afraid) to develop and implement programs that will take several if not dozens of years to produce results. For instance, civic education programs, university courses on democratic theory and practice, and educational exchanges nurture specialists on democratic issues and democratic values in a society as a whole. But a new university course on democracy might only yield results on the governance of a country 20 years later, when college students assume positions of authority in the state and society. Often only generational change allows a society to usher in new political and social values.

Integrating Democracy, Development, and State Building

In reaction to George W. Bush's Freedom Agenda, many foreign assistance specialists as well as aid advocates in the United States have pressed for more emphasis on providing basic economic and security needs and less emphasis on democracy. The politics and morality behind these impulses are understandable. Who would argue that clean water is not more important to people in poor countries than the right to vote? Who would disagree that freedom from death in a combat zone is more valuable than the right to free assembly? Empirically, however, as discussed in chapter 2, we are learning that democracy, development, and state-building are intertwined. Governments not beholden to their citizens are less likely to invest in clean water projects than those that must win votes to stay in office. Countries with no functioning state institutions have little capacity to absorb international development assistance.

American foreign economic assistance must address these governance issues more directly. Aid to corrupt regimes or ineffective states reinforces bad behavior rather than fostering economic development. As Larry Diamond has argued, "If, as the facts suggest, aid is actually making things worse by sustaining abusive governments, then it is the West's fault, and doubling aid uncritically and unconditionally will make it doubly so."[107] To better integrate economic and political development aid, the United States needs to make economic assistance conditional upon a country making progress on governance reforms, including democratic reforms. By requiring governments to make progress on governance reforms (as well as meeting standards regarding more traditional measures of sound economic policy) before they receive aid, the Millennium Challenge Corporation has established an effective new mechanism for providing economic aid. Currently, however, the corporation only targets middle income countries that already have crossed rather high thresholds of state capacity, economic development and good governance. The same corporation principles should now be applied to development aid to all countries.

When autocratic governments fail to commit to political reforms, their people should not be punished. Poor people living in autocracies deserve American assistance just as much as poor people living in democracies. Instead, economic assistance in these situations should be delivered only through non-governmental organizations, not state institutions.[108]

Reorganizing the U.S. Government to More Effectively Support Democracy

It has become a cliché for American politicians and military commanders to argue that the effort needed to fight the "global war on terrorism" is 10 percent military and 90 percent non-military.[109] Yet, the organization of the American government in no way reflects these percentages. The Secretary of Defense is a powerful cabinet-level official in charge of the financial resources, know-how, staff, and authority to destroy autocratic regimes hostile to the United States once the political decision to do so has been made. Yet, there is no equivalent position in the U.S. government to mobilize the necessary intellectual and physical resources to help construct democratic regimes friendly to the United States in the wake of autocratic collapse or destruction. For FY 2008, the U.S. military budget hovered around $500 billion, not including supplements for Iraq and Afghanistan that brought the total to about $696 billion.[110] For the same year, U.S. spending on democracy promotion was estimated to be only $1.5 billion,[111] while total spending on foreign assistance as a whole amounted to roughly $20 billion.[112] By comparison, under the Marshall Plan, the United State spent roughly $110 billion a year for European reconstruction in equivalent 2007 dollars.[113]

The asymmetries go well beyond budgets and include imbalances in prestige and career advancement. The Secretary of Defense administers a vast bureaucracy of civilian appointees, generals, other military officers, and new recruits. The Pentagon's military leaders have risen through the ranks of a meritocracy with very clear metrics for promotion. Conversely, the equivalent head of non-military assistance is the Administrator of AID. This Administrator is not a member of the cabinet and does not oversee an organization filled with dozens of political appointees and talented subordinates who have risen through a merit-based hierarchy equivalent to that of the military. Even the title "administrator" underscores the lack of prestige assigned to the job.

Moreover, few believe that the current aid structure works. As Congressman Howard Berman, chairman of the House Committee on Foreign Affairs, declared,

It is painfully obvious to Congress, the administration,
foreign aid experts, and NGOs alike that our foreign
assistance program is fragmented and broken and in
critical need of overhaul. I strongly believe that America's foreign assistance program is not in need of some
minor changes, but, rather, it needs to be reinvented
and retooled . . . .[114]

Without reform of the aid system, budget increases will not
achieve better results.

Secretary of State Condoleezza Rice attempted to add bureaucratic heft to development assistance programs within the
U.S. government by creating a new position in the State Department, the Director of Foreign Assistance, whose responsibilities
included heading up AID. In rank, the job is supposed to be the
equivalent of a deputy Secretary of State, but only de facto, not
de jure.[115] This was one of many Rice reforms aimed at reconfig-
uring the State Department to conduct "transformational diplomacy." The objective, she explained, was "to work with our many
partners around the world to build and sustain democratic, well-
governed states that will respond to the needs of their people—
and conduct themselves responsibly in the international
system."[116] Another Rice reform, the Foreign Assistance reform
process, or "F" process, for devising aid strategy, also aimed to
make the promotion of development and democracy issues of
greater concern for State Department officials.[117]

Although nobly seeking to address the inadequacies of the
status quo, Rice's reforms deliberately tied democracy assistance
more closely to American foreign policy goals. Problems, however, arise when U.S. short-term strategic interests clash with
longer-term goals of promoting democracy and development.
Another problem occurs when democratic activists working in

countries with strained relations with the United States do not want to receive assistance directly from the State Department for fear of being labeled traitors. Concentrating greater levels of democracy assistance funding within the State Department and increasing the role of diplomats in writing strategy on democracy promotion politicized democracy promotion at precisely the historical moment when much of the world had become suspicious of American intentions.[118] The more separation there can be between transformational policies and the U.S. State Department, the more effective these policies will be.

Indeed, what the United States needs is a new Department of Development and Democracy. All foreign assistance resources currently funneled through other agencies and departments, with the exception of military training and assistance, should be transferred to this new department. This new department would largely absorb AID, Pentagon and State Department post-war reconstruction operations, rule of law training programs currently housed in the Department of Justice, agricultural aid now located in the Department of Agriculture, Treasury technical assistance programs, the Millennium Challenge Corporation, and the President's Emergency Plan for AIDS Relief (PEPFAR).[119]

The mandate of the new department would be very different from the traditional missions of the military or of diplomats. It would include state construction, nurturing improved governance, economic development, and democratic consolidation. This separation of departments to fulfill different missions would help each to deepen expertise in their respective fields, and also clarify to the outside world which arm of the U.S. government does what. Soldiers should not kill terrorists one day and teach Jeffersonian democracy the next. Diplomats should not negotiate a basing agreement with a government one day and then turn around the next and approve funding for an opposition leader to that same government.

The Department of Development and Democracy should direct and administer all assistance designed to foster development and democracy and delivered directly to foreign governments. Such assistance must be firmly conditioned on pursuit of development objectives. There will be situations in which the United States has a national security interest in providing an autocratic regime with military aid or antiterrorist assistance, but this aid must not be called democracy assistance or development aid.

At the same time, the new department should not be responsible for providing democracy assistance (or other forms of assistance) to NGOs. To the extent possible, the U.S. government should get out of the business of directly funding NGOs in other countries. Even if a new Department of Development and Democracy is not established, this firewall between state-to-state assistance and the aid given to non-governmental actors should become a guiding principle for reform of democracy assistance. For instance, it is appropriate for AID or some other part of the U.S. executive branch to fund a technical assistance program for a justice ministry in a foreign country under the rubric of a bilateral government-to-government agreement. It is much less appropriate for the U.S. government to provide technical assistance to political parties or opposition groups in other countries. This kind of assistance, when appropriate, is better provided by American non-governmental organizations with as much separation from the State Department and White House as possible.

Inevitably, conflicts of interest and misinterpretations of motives arise when the State Department provides direct financial support to an NGO in another country. Is this money provided to aid democracy? Or is it given to advance a concrete U.S. economic or strategic interest? Non-American NGOs—especially those working in autocratic societies—are increasingly reluctant to accept U.S. assistance for fear of being labeled agents or spies for the United States.[120] Such concerns come up regardless of the exact origin of U.S. funding. Increased separation between the U.S. government and American funders of non-governmental actors thus can only be for the better. Money for direct assistance to NGOs also must be protected from any sanctions directed against authoritarian governments. When the White House decides to cut foreign assistance to a country to pressure it to change its behavior at home or abroad, U.S. funds earmarked to support democracy through non-governmental actors must not be interrupted.

A vastly expanded NED would be one model to provide this greater separation. To assume this role, NED would have to provide direct grants to all U.S. providers of technical and financial assistance for the non-governmental sector, which would loosen its close connection with its four main grantees. The NED also would need to open at least some regional offices around the world.

Because both of these changes might dilute NED's current mission, an alternative model would be the creation of a new Civil Society Foundation, modeled after NED, but with a wider mandate and a different mechanism for providing grants both to U.S. organizations in the democracy assistance business and to local NGOs around the world. Major portions of AID's offices of Democracy and Governance could be reincorporated as an independent foundation, located outside embassy walls, more integrated into the societies they seek to change, and less connected with or constrained by the immediate foreign policy goals of the United States. Obviously, this assistance would still be U.S. government money, but the new structure would increase the distance between the U.S. government and the assistance recipients. While these kinds of organizations would have financial support from the government, they would have their own boards, staffs, and decision-making capacity—all devoted fully to supporting democratic development. Thus their decisions would not be tied up in trade negotiations, arms control agreements, or other more immediate American security and economic interests. Over time, this new foundation could attract private funds as well as support from other democratic governments.

Until a Department of Development and Democracy is created, AID would continue to manage all direct assistance to government institutions, including parliaments, election commissions, courts, and presidential administrations. Having this separation would eliminate the strange circumstance of having the same AID Democracy and Governance (D&G) office funding a foreign government office that is at odds with a civil society organization also funded by the D&G office (i.e., providing technical assistance to a central election commission while also providing funding to a civil society organization trying to monitor elections).

Another strategy for accomplishing the objective of greater separation between the U.S. government and democracy promotion would be to create more regional and functional foundations. For instance, the Middle East Partnership Initiative, currently located within the State Department's Bureau of New Eastern Affairs, could be privatized as a new Middle East Foundation modeled after the Asia Foundation or Eurasia Foundation.[121] The Human Rights Democracy Fund, currently controlled by the Bureau of Democracy, Human Rights, and Labor, also could become an independent foundation for civil society development. A new foundation might be established to focus exclusively on anti-corruption. Pluralism of funding sources stimulates competition both among American NGOs seeking financial support to execute democracy promotion programs and among NGOs in autocratic or democratizing countries seeking direct financial assistance.[122]

Less ambitiously, within AID, the prominence of democracy and governance could be higher. Currently, AID's Office of Democracy and Governance is housed inappropriately within the Bureau for Democracy, Conflict, and Humanitarian Assistance (DCHA). The AID should create a new Bureau for Democratic Governance (DG), with a designated assistant administrator supervising an expanded cadre of professional staff. Given the centrality of governance to other development sectors, the new DG bureau would follow the model of other functional bureaus like Global Health and work integrally with the rest of AID to ensure that democracy assistance strategies are integrated with other development efforts.

Also in the less ambitious category of reforms, all AID assistance earmarked for civil society support could be provided through "assistance mechanisms" (grants and cooperative agreements) and not "acquisitions mechanisms" (contracts).[123] The latter, in essence, makes the contracting organization or company an implementer of U.S. government policy. The NGO or company receiving these funds is executing an AID plan and not providing any strategic input. In some sensitive political situations, this form of direct assistance can make the recipients of AID assistance look like collaborators or agents of the U.S. government. The assistance mechanism provides greater autonomy from the U.S. government. At the same time, for-profit companies should not be allowed to bid to do civil society assistance work, and former AID employees should not be allowed to bid on or execute AID contracts for two years after leaving the U.S. government. The revolving door between AID and contractors must be broken.

Finally, no matter what the final institutional architecture is for promoting democracy more effectively, a new independent institute for evaluation must be established, either as a freestanding organization in Washington or as part of a university. The creation of a new independent institution dedicated solely to evalu-ation would help to end the practice of AID contractors being hired to evaluate AID programs. As discussed in chapter 1, inde-pendent scholars have conducted remarkably few systematic analyses or comprehensive assessments of how U.S. foreign pol-icy, including democracy assistance programs, has helped advance the development of democracy worldwide. Instead, we continue to reinvent the wheel, sometimes with tragic consequences.

Policy Prescriptions That Indirectly Foster Democratic Development

The recommendations discussed so far address U.S. policies that deal directly with democracy promotion. A truly strategic approach to this issue must look beyond AID technical assistance programs for election commissions or presidential meetings with human rights leaders. Several American security and energy poli-cies also shape the prospects for democratic development in other countries. Some changes in these arenas could have indirect, pos-itive effects on democracy promotion.

Expand Trade

In the midst of an international economic recession, few have the courage to advocate greater trade liberalization. On the contrary, the financial meltdown that jolted the world economy in September 2008 could ricochet throughout other sectors and trigger a deep depression. The last world depression wiped out many fragile democracies, and some already worry that the cur-rent economic crisis could do the same.

Over time, past historical trends suggest that trade liberal-ization and subsequent trade expansion facilitate democratization.[124] To foster democracy over the long haul, therefore, the United States must maintain a commitment to trade liberalization.

Reduce American Dependence on Energy Imports

It is more than coincidence that dictators rule in most of the major oil and gas exporting countries in the world.[125] The "resource curse" makes it possible for autocrats to finance their regimes without having to respond to the preferences of their people: no representation without taxation. Major oil and gas consumers, including first and foremost the United States, subsidize the maintenance of autocracy in countries such as Saudi Arabia, Kuwait, Iran, and Angola. If the price of oil and gas decreased, these autocratic regimes would be under greater pressure to change. If American dependence on these countries decreased, U.S. diplomats would be less obliged to coddle these authoritarian regimes. In the long run, therefore, both an American campaign and an international effort to develop alternative energy sources would have a positive influence on democratic development.

Strengthen the Extractive Industry Transparency Initiative

Building on the "Publish What You Pay" campaign, the United Kingdom launched the Extractive Industry Transparency Initiative (EITI) in 2002. This initiative sets out to strengthen good governance in resource-rich countries through the verification and full publication of company payments and government revenues from oil, gas, and mining. The United States is an official supporter but thus far has been on the sidelines of this effort, despite the direct, positive implications of this program for transparent and accountable government in countries Americans depend on for energy imports. By committing to enforce the standards set out by the EITI—as proposed, for instance, in the House of Representatives' Extractive Industries Transparency Disclosure Act (H.R. 6066)[126]—the United States could lead by example and help establish public disclosure of resource payments as a global best practice standard.

Help to Negotiate a Peace Treaty between Israel and Palestine

Reviving the Middle East peace process and resolving the Israeli-Palestinian conflict could spark lots of positive indirect consequences for democracy in the Middle East. A truly democratic Palestine would be the worst nightmare of the September 11 terrorists and their supporters. Autocratic Arab governments could no longer hide behind and use this conflict to avoid pressures for democratic change at home. The West would no longer have to coddle dictators in Syria or back away from reformers in Egypt because of those countries' key role in peace negotiations. American leverage and legitimacy would be enhanced in the Arab world and anger would be reduced, depriving terrorist groups of the tools they manipulate to fuel the fires of the global jihadist movement against the West.[127]

Strengthen Peacemaking

Scholars disagree about the relationship between war and democracy. According to Nancy Bermeo,

> Of the 385 armed conflicts that ended between 1946 and 1991, only 23 percent produced a change of regime and only 10 percent produced an electoral

democracy. Of these new electoral democracies, approximately 30 percent failed within five years.[128]

Conversely, Leonard Wantchekon has found that "forty percent of all civil wars that took place from 1945 to 1993 resulted in an improvement in the level of democracy."[129] Both sides in this debate agree, however, that wars must end before democratization can have a chance to take hold. New elections almost always constitute a condition of the peace settlement, and if organized properly, can jump-start democratic development.[130] Consequently, helping to negotiate peace settlements either directly, by supplying American mediators, or indirectly, by supporting United Nations efforts, can facilitate democratic development.

Towards a Smarter Democracy Promotion Strategy

As a country, we know very little about the most autocratic region of the world, the greater Middle East. To fight the decades-long battle against communism, the United States invested billions of dollars in education and intelligence. The U.S. government sponsored centers of Soviet studies, provided foreign-language scholarships in Russian and Eastern European languages, and offered dual-competency grants to get graduate students to acquire expertise both in security issues and in Russian culture. We need a similar effort today to help us better understand our friends and foes in the wider Middle East. While some scholars today do study Islam and the languages and countries of the people who profess it, we suffer from severe shortages of linguists, academic scholars, and senior policymakers trained in the languages, cultures, politics, and economics of the wider Middle East. Universities, with government support, should encourage the study of Islam from within the social sciences and humanities, the better to promote truly interdisciplinary conversation. Universities need to make a priority of the teaching of Arabic, Persian, and Turkish, and it should be done not by part-time adjunct faculty but by tenured professors. Better knowledge of the local context in its historical, cultural, political, and sociological dimensions is especially critical for assisting democratic development in post-conflict situations.

Major U.S. Military Interventions and Democracy

Country	Time Period	Regime Type 10 Years After Intervention[131]
Philippines	1898-1936	Autocracy
Cuba	1898-1902	Autocracy
China **	1900-1927	Autocracy
Panama	1903-1936	Autocracy
Cuba	1906-1909	Autocracy
Nicaragua	1909-1933	Autocracy
Haiti	1915-1934	Autocracy
Dominican Republic	1916-1924	Autocracy
Russia	1918-1920	Autocracy
Italy	1943-1948	Democracy
China	1945-1949	Autocracy
West Germany	1945-1949	Democracy
South Korea ***	1945-1949	Autocracy
Austria	1945-1950	Democracy
Japan	1945-1952	Democracy
South Korea	1950-1953	Autocracy
South Vietnam	1964-1975	Autocracy
Dominican Republic	1965-1966	Autocracy
Cambodia	1969-1973	Autocracy
Lebanon	1982-1984	Autocracy
Grenada	1983	Democracy
Panama	1989-1992	Democracy

Country	Time Period	Regime Type 10 Years After Intervention[131]
Iraq	1990-1992	Autocracy
Kuwait	1990-1992	Autocracy
Somalia	1993-1994	Autocracy
Haiti	1994-1996	Autocracy
Bosnia	1995-present	Partial Democracy*
Yugoslavia (Kosovo)	1999-present	Democracy*
Afghanistan	2001-present	Partial Democracy*
Iraq	2003-present	Autocracy*

* Freedom House scores are used to determine regime classification.

** China. In 1900, the United States, along with Britain, Germany, Russia, Japan, Italy, Austria-Hungary, and France, took control of the Chinese capital, Peking, and spread into the Chinese country side putting down the Boxer Rebellion. (The Boxer Society was a rapidly growing anti-Western secret society.) After several months, Chinese authorities agreed to officially abolish the Boxer Society. Between 1922 and 1949, the U.S. military deployed forces to China multiple times prior to and during the Chinese civil war to protect Americans in the country and American interests. There is some speculation about how much support the United States gave to the Nationalist party during this time, but according to the Department of the Navy, U.S. involvement was aimed only at protecting U.S. citizens. Also during this time the United States sent 50,000 troops to Northern China to disarm and repatriate the Japanese in China.

*** South Korea (1945–1950). Liberation of Korea from the Japanese and the establishment of the 38th parallel/U.S. Army Military Government (USAMGIK) was the official ruling body of South Korea.

Covert U.S. Military Intervention and Democracy

Country	Time Period	Regime Type 10 Years After Intervention[132]
Greece	1947-1949	Democracy
Syria	1949	Autocracy
Philippines	1949-1952	Democracy
Albania	1949-1953	Autocracy
Puerto Rico	1950	Democracy
Yugoslavia	1951	Autocracy
Guyana	1953-1964	Democracy
Iran	1953	Autocracy
Guatemala	1954	Autocracy
Costa Rica	1955	Democracy
China (Tibet)	1956-1973	Autocracy
Syria	1957	Autocracy
Lebanon	1957	Democracy
Laos	1957-1975	Autocracy
Lebanon	1958	Democracy
Haiti	1959	Autocracy
Cuba	1959-1960	Autocracy
Peru	1960	Autocracy
Ecuador	1960	Autocracy
Congo/Zaire	1960-1961	Autocracy
Cuba	1961	Autocracy
Dominican Rep.	1961	Autocracy
Brazil	1962	Autocracy
Thailand	1962	Democracy
India	1962	Autocracy
Dominican Rep.	1963	Democracy
Guatemala	1963	Autocracy
Haiti	1963	Autocracy
Congo/Zaire	1964	Autocracy
Dominican Rep.	1965-1966	Autocracy
Indonesia	1965-1967	Autocracy
Ghana	1966	Autocracy
Guatemala	1966	Autocracy

Country	Time Period	Regime Type 10 Years After Intervention[132]
Bolivia	1966	Autocracy
Cyprus	1967	Democracy
Cambodia	1970-1973	Autocracy
Bolivia	1971	Autocracy
Uruguay	1972	Autocracy
Iraq	1972-1975	Autocracy
Chile	1973	Autocracy
Cyprus	1974	Autocracy
Angola	1975-1978	Autocracy
Congo/Zaire	1978	Autocracy
Iran	1980	Autocracy
Afghanistan	1980-1991	Autocracy
Nicaragua	1981-1990	Democracy
El Salvador	1981-1991	Democracy
Guatemala	1982	Democracy
Cambodia	1982-1991	Democracy
Honduras	1982-1990	Democracy
Chad	1983	Autocracy
Sudan	1984	Autocracy
Lebanon	1985	Autocracy
Angola	1985-1991	Autocracy
Peru	1992	Democracy
Venezuela	2002	Partial Democracy*
Haiti	2004	Partial Democracy*

6

Encouraging the Internationalization of Democracy Promotion

If President Obama and his administration seek to improve American methods for supporting democratic development around the world, then a crucial strategic move will be simply to get out of the way and let others take the lead. More helpfully, the Obama administration should develop policies that will enable other governments, non-American NGOs, and international institutions to play a leading role in supporting democratic development. Contributing to the codification of international norms about democracy, human rights, and democracy promotion itself also would also help to nurture democratic ideas and practices in the world.

The Role of Multilateral Institutions in Supporting Democracy

The United Nations

The United States has played a pivotal role in creating several multilateral organizations that, although often overlooked as a method for supporting democratic development, have directly and indirectly defended and promoted democracy.[1] The United States can continue to look for new opportunities to strengthen older international institutions and develop new ones to meet the specific challenges of the contemporary world.

President Wilson's first attempt to help create international institutions to promote democracy failed miserably. Even his own Senate would not ratify his idea of creating a League of Nations. The devastation of the Second World War created new American enthusiasm for international institutions that would defend both American values and interests. President Roosevelt did not support the formation of the United Nations to promote democracy worldwide, but Roosevelt did see the U.N. as an organization to help preserve international peace, a condition that in turn protected older democracies and facilitated the emergence of new ones. The Universal Declaration of Human Rights, adopted in 1948, also launched a gradual reframing of the responsibilities of states to defend individual human rights. Over time, and especially after the Cold War's end, the U.N. has increased its commitment to defending human rights at the expense of state sovereignty, a normative shift that gradually has facilitated the international commitment to democratic governance.[2] General Secretary of the United Nations Kofi Annan underscored this change while accepting his Nobel Peace Prize in 2001, arguing that "today's real borders are not between states, but between powerful and powerless, free and fettered, privileged and humiliated."[3]

The U.N.'s role in democracy promotion has extended well beyond speeches and resolutions.[4] The United Nations frequently has taken the lead in peacekeeping operations, and peace is a precondition for democracy in countries recovering from civil war. The idea that elections should occur soon after a civil war's end has become an international norm, most certainly in play when the United Nations gets involved in a peacekeeping operation.[5] Since sending its first election-monitoring mission to Nicaragua in 1990, the U.N. increasingly has played the chief institutional role in providing election assistance and monitoring in post-conflict countries, including the very difficult cases of Afghanistan, Palestine, and Iraq.[6] The United Nations Development Fund now devotes nearly half of its annual budget to institution-building for democratic governance. A separate U.N. Democracy Fund, created in 2005, also provides direct grants to NGOs around the world seeking to strengthen democracy. In 2004, the United States worked with other leading democracies to establish the United Nations Democracy Caucus.

NATO and Other Military Alliances

During the Cold War, American leaders helped create the North Atlantic Treaty Organization (NATO), a military alliance to protect the liberal West from communist encroachment. The American military presence on the continent played an essential role in protecting wobbly democracies in France and Italy, containing Soviet military expansion in Europe (which surely would have undermined democracies in the West otherwise, as it did in Czechoslovakia in 1948), and keeping the peace between formerly hostile countries within the alliance. During the Cold War,

NATO tolerated autocratic regimes in the alliance. However, when these countries—Portugal, Greece, and Turkey—eventually made transitions to democracy, the alliance helped to smooth the process by eliminating the potential for external communist interference. The prospect of NATO membership also helped empower Spanish democrats to establish firm civilian control over the military during the democratic transition after ruler Francisco Franco's death.[7] More generally, the stable security environment in Western Europe provided the permissive conditions for democracy to deepen within member states and encouraged economic and later political cooperation, culminating in the creation of the European Union.

After the collapse of communism in Europe, the Clinton administration explicitly called for NATO enlargement as a mechanism for expanding the democratic community of states.[8] The promise of NATO membership helped accelerate democratic consolidation in East Central Europe and provided real incentives for the democratic laggards in the region, such as Bulgaria and Romania, to embrace political reform. NATO enlargement also helped to bridge the gap for these countries as they prepared to make bids to join the European Union.[9]

In Asia, the United States established alliances with Japan and South Korea, and provided security guarantees to Taiwan. Obviously, American leaders created and maintained these military agreements to contain communism and thereby defend American national security interests. At the same time, the American security umbrella allowed these countries to spend less on defense and more on developing their economies, which in turn nurtured the middle classes that drove democratization, especially in South Korea and Taiwan. And remember the counterfactual. Had the United States not defended these countries and others in the region, the People's Republic of China or the

Soviet Union would have tried to exercise their influence over domestic politics in all of them.

International Financial Institutions

In addition to helping create the United Nations and establishing military alliances, American presidents and diplomats spearheaded the creation of the international economic architecture that bound the West together against a common enemy.[10] Most importantly, American leaders launched the Bretton Woods agreements and their institutions, the International Monetary Fund and the World Bank, to help maintain an open, liberal capitalist order, and avoid the protectionist-driven meltdown of the 1930s. These economic institutions were not designed to promote democracy; democratic government was not a prerequisite for membership. Nonetheless, these international financial institutions helped to preserve capitalism, promote market reforms, and aid economies in distress. Economic stability and growth in turn have played a positive role in sustaining new democracies in the developing world.[11] In the 1990s and especially in this decade, the World Bank has recognized the importance of political institutions for sustaining economic development, and placed much greater emphasis on promoting "good governance."

Helsinki and the OSCE

In the 1970s, American diplomats also played a role in making human rights a component of the Helsinki Final Act. Signed in 1975 by most European countries, the United States, Canada, and the Soviet Union, the Helsinki Final Act and the new multilateral organization it founded—the Conference on Security and Cooperation in Europe (CSCE), which later evolved into the Organization on Security and Cooperation in Europe (OSCE)—helped to defuse tensions between East and West by acknowledging the inviolability of borders between states. The accords also recognized the sanctity of individual human rights for those living within these borders, a recognition pushed by West European and American diplomats as a condition for acquiescing to norms of the "territorial integrity of states," and "non-intervention in internal affairs." Because the accords recognized Soviet military conquests in exchange for abstract language about human rights, many initially dismissed them as a diplomatic coup for the Soviets. President Richard Nixon and Secretary of State Henry Kissinger themselves saw defending human rights as ancillary to the Helsinki process, not least because the United States had three allies at the time—Portugal, Greece, and Spain—that were ruled by dictators. But over time, the Helsinki Accords emboldened human rights activists in Eastern Europe to press for the rights codified in the document that was signed by their governments. The Helsinki watchdog organizations, which sprouted throughout the region, helped to bring down communism just a decade later.[12] After the collapse of communism, the OSCE assumed a central role in consolidating democracy in the region, most critically by establishing the Office for Democratic Institutions and Human Rights (ODIHR)—"the specialized institution of the OSCE dealing with elections, human rights, and democratization."[13] Beginning in the 1990s, OSCE delegations monitored elections throughout the region, sometimes playing a pivotal role in exposing fraud and legitimating free and fair elections.[14]

The United States is not a member of the most successful regional organization for democracy promotion: the European Union. The accession process to the European Union has offered countries in Eastern Europe and the former Soviet Union concrete economic incentives to undertake a comprehensive package of reforms, including democratic changes.[15] This mechanism for promoting democracy may have reached its limits—EU members are uneasy regarding expansion to Turkey and Ukraine—but the results to date have been remarkable.[16] Obviously, the United States played no direct role in the creation or expansion of the EU, but it is hard to imagine the EU having succeeded without NATO and American military power on the continent beforehand. Just as internal peace and security facilitate democratic development within a country, peace and security between states also create a fertile environment for democratization.

Other Regional Organizations

Other regional organizations also have elevated the attention given to democratic governance among member states. The Organization of American States (OAS), of which the United States is a founding member, adopted the Santiago Commitment to Democracy in 1991, which explicitly committed the organization to act collectively to help sustain fragile democracies in the region.[17] A decade later, the general assembly of the OAS adopted the "Inter-American Democratic Charter," which states that "the people of the Americas have a right to democracy, and their governments have an obligation to promote and defend it."[18] The OAS condemned democratic reversals in Peru in 1992 and in Venezuela in 2001, supported democracies under duress in Paraguay and Guatemala, and even provided multilateral support for American military intervention in Panama and Haiti to restore democracy.[19]

Given the colonial legacy, the Organization of African Unity (OAU)—later re-chartered as the African Union (AU)—not surprisingly championed sovereignty, territorial integrity, and non-intervention in the internal affairs of other states as paramount norms for the African continent. After the end of the Cold War, however, human rights issues seeped into the AU's agenda, including most strikingly in June 2008, when the AU took the unprecedented step of denouncing fraudulent elections in Zimbabwe. A similar slow, evolutionary process of norms development on behalf of human rights and democracy is unfolding within the Association of Southeast Asian Nations (ASEAN).[20] The United States is not a member of the AU or ASEAN, but these regional organizations are reacting in part to norms established by the OSCE and the OAS, regional organizations the U.S. did help to create.

Given the small number of democratic member states, it is not surprising that the Organization of Islamic Conference (OIC) has devoted much less attention to promoting and defending democracy compared to the EU or OAS. The OIC instead places greater emphasis on respecting

> the right of self-determination and non-interference in the domestic affairs and to respect sovereignty, independence and territorial integrity of each Member State.[21]

Other regional organizations dominated by non-democracies such as the Commonwealth of Independent States (CIS), the Eurasian Economic Commonwealth, the Collective Security Treaty Organization (CSTO), and the Shanghai Cooperation Organization (SCO) also do not promote democracy. On the contrary, a resurgent and increasingly autocratic Russia has attempted to reinvigorate these regional institutions to counterpose Western democratic clubs. Russia, China, and other members of the SCO explicitly endorse the idea of "sovereign democracy," with a heavier emphasis on the adjective than on the noun. Russia also has wielded its clout within the OSCE to try to weaken the organization's democracy promotion efforts, both by trying to decrease funding for ODIHR and by questioning the legitimacy of OSCE election observation missions.

The Community of Democracies

At the end of his second term, President Clinton and his administration spearheaded the creation of a new international organization, the Community of Democracies, dedicated to defending and promoting democracy.[22] In June 2000, this new organization convened its founding conference in Warsaw, and has continued to meet every two years. The Community of Democracies has provided another international voice for democracy issues, such as lobbying for the creation of the U.N.'s Democracy Caucus and Democracy Fund, or publishing a *Diplomat's Handbook for Democracy Development Support*.[23]

The Community of Democracies has faced a major development obstacle because several founding signatories of its Warsaw Declaration—including Algeria, Egypt, Morocco, and Tunisia—were not democracies at the time. Several more have become considerably less democratic over the last decade, calling into question the normative basis of the organization. During the eight years of the Bush administration, this "Clinton project" also received very little attention from the United States government.[24]

The Bush Era of Anti-Multilateralism

The Bush administration expressed little enthusiasm for the Community of Democracies and for most multilateral forums or institutions. Most striking was the way President Bush ignored the United Nations Security Council after it failed to support his invasion of Iraq. This decision created a serious impasse between the White House and all other international organizations, which subsequently tried to steer clear of associating with Bush policies, including his freedom agenda. Bush, however, never seemed very interested in trying to mobilize these organizations to advance democracy. Bush officials did support the creation of the United Nations Democracy Fund and Democracy Caucus, and Bush also used his chairmanship of the G8 in 2004 to launch the Broader Middle East and North Africa (BMENA) initiative, the Forum of the Future, and Foundation for the Future, a new international fund dedicated to promoting democracy and human rights in the broader Middle East and North Africa.[25] Bush also called upon Europeans to encourage democratic transformations in the broader Middle East "by taking up the duties of great democracies" and renewing "our great alliance of freedom."[26] With less fanfare, the Bush administration initiated the Partnership for Democratic Governance (PDG) under the auspices of the Organization for Economic Co-operation and Development (OECD), a new association dedicated to

> looking into how the international community can effectively support service delivery and provide expertise to help developing countries and emerging democracies strengthen their core government institutions and services.[27]

By the beginning of Bush's second term, however, most European and other world leaders wanted to disassociate themselves from his approach to democracy promotion. Europeans in particular wanted to pursue their own instruments for encouraging democracy in North Africa and the Middle East through their Barcelona Process and the European Neighborhood Policy. As many Europeans found themselves in vehement disagreement with the Bush administration's position on Iraq, world trade, the Kyoto Protocol on Global Warming and the International Criminal Court (ICC), they found it difficult to separate their displeasure from the more specific focus on democracy promotion. In some European quarters, agreeing with President Bush on anything became a politically unfashionable *faux pas*.[28] A similar anti-Bush dynamic created divisions within the OAS, especially after the Bush administration appeared to support a coup attempt against Venezuelan president Hugo Chavez in 2002.[29]

Building New and More Effective Multilateral Institutions to Support Democracy

In learning from these historical experiences, American diplomats must seek to strengthen those multilateral organizations committed to democratic norms. In Europe and Eurasia, this means providing the OSCE's democracy promotion arm, the ODIHR, with greater resources and diplomatic clout. In the Americas, the United States should work with OAS partners to establish a foundation for democracy support, with headquarters in Lima or Santiago, not Washington. In dealing with other regional organizations with fewer democratic members and no U.S. membership, the American objective should be to promote the adoption of international treaties and doctrines that privilege the rights of individuals over the rights of states.

In the Middle East, improving existing institutions is not enough. To promote security, development, and democracy, the Middle East desperately needs its own Helsinki process, including a permanent, multilateral security organization. The impetus for creating such a regional structure must come from within the region, but outsiders, including the United States, the European

Union, and perhaps Russia and Canada, also could support the initiative, just as the United States and Canada are members of the OSCE today.

The first challenge is to decide on membership. A new security organization in the Middle East would add no value if it comprised only Arab states or U.S. allies. Rather, in addition to the Arab countries, Israel, Iran, Turkey, and perhaps even Afghanistan and Pakistan, should be invited to join. (Though not technically in the region, the latter two countries' security is closely intertwined with that of the rest of the Middle East.) External actors also must be included. Many Arab states and Israel will want U.S. participation to counter Iranian involvement; others will want a similar external check to the United States.

The second challenge is to define the agenda. The original Helsinki process is instructive. Although politicians and analysts now fondly remember the role the Helsinki process played in fostering human rights inside the Warsaw Pact, the first priority in drafting the original accords—Basket One—was security, territorial integrity, and a recognition of the borders, a long-standing Soviet demand. A similar focus on borders and security must be the starting point of a Middle East security conference. Of course, the Israeli-Palestinian conflict, like the "German question" in Europe during the Cold War, will not be resolved by the creation of a new international organization. But the basic security guarantees in the Helsinki accords—that all signatories will respect the territorial integrity of states and refrain from the use of force or internal intervention in other states (including an end to support for terrorist organizations)—must constitute the core of a new organization.

Enhancing security may sound like the roundabout way to foster regional democracy. But the great lesson of Helsinki was that improved security among states can facilitate internal democratic change. A multilateral security organization also would provide a forum for countries without developed bilateral relations to meet: Iran and the United States, for instance, might find it easier to interact first in a multilateral setting than a bilateral one. Moreover, an ongoing Middle East security conference would compel politicians to develop an agenda in preparation for each summit. Institutionalized meetings, rather than ad hoc encounters, have the advantage of set dates and the same actors. A permanent organization also would create bureaucracies and expertise.

Starting a Helsinki-like process or creating an OSCE-like organization in the Middle East would not be easy. But compared to the Middle East today, Europe in the first half of the twentieth century had much deeper ideological divisions, ethnic tensions, and territorial disputes. Creating a security organization, which included former antagonists France and Germany or contemporary enemies such as the Soviet Union and the United States, was as difficult as any set of security, religious, ethnic, and ideological issues that now divide the Middle East. And, if nothing more, the very process of negotiating a Middle East conference on security and cooperation would create more regular interaction between countries in desperate need of more contact.

Strengthening the capacity of various bureaucracies of the United Nations, while pushing for internal U.N. reforms to make the institution work more effectively, could indirectly improve American democracy promotion efforts abroad.[30] Because peace is often a precondition to democratization in warring and war-torn countries, the United States should provide greater financial support to the U.N.'s peacekeeping operations, which today are overstretched and underfunded.[31] The U.S. also should strengthen the election-monitoring capacities of the United Nations. In many parts of the world today, the U.N. has a better brand name than

American election-monitoring NGOs. Most Americans (68 percent) also support the idea of promoting democracy "by working through the UN because such efforts will be more legitimate."[32] American support for the United Nations Development Programme and the U.N. Democracy Fund also should increase. President Obama also could use the bully pulpit of his new presidency to encourage other countries as well as private individuals to donate funds to these U.N. agencies.

Within the World Bank, American officials must use their influence to encourage greater attention to governance and anticorruption issues. Much progress has been made toward this reorientation within the bank, but much more could be done.[33] The data on foreign assistance now show conclusively that functioning state institutions are necessary for the effective use of economic aid, while the provision of foreign aid without a competent state in place produces waste and corruption. Consequently, the World Bank and other development banks must devote a greater fraction of their resources to programs that help to build state institutions, including democratic institutions. As the largest shareholder in the World Bank, the United States must exercise its "property rights" to press for this reorientation. A first signal of credible commitment to the effort would be the introduction of the word "democracy" into the bank's lexicon.

Even the World Trade Organization and other trade treaties must be understood as mechanisms for opening up economies, which in turn foster democratic development. Leaving countries such as Iran out of the WTO only hurts the democratic forces inside Iran that favor more integration of their country, not less, into the world system.

In addition, American sources of democracy assistance such as AID, MEPI, DRL, and even NED, must consider giving greater levels of direct financial support to non-American democracy promotion organizations. At a time when the American trademark is damaged, Canadian, Ghanaian, Slovak, Czech, and Hungarian democracy promotion organizations should take the lead, especially when working in countries such as Cuba or Iran, where American NGOs cannot operate.[34] The counterproductive practice of requiring the AID label to appear on AID-funded projects must end. The push to encourage other democracies to establish NED-like democracy promotion foundations also should continue. Some day, the center of gravity for democracy promotion should move from Washington to New Delhi or from Brussels to Santiago.

Transnational, Non-Governmental Cooperation

Government-to-government disagreements during the George W. Bush era did not trickle down to relations between American and non-American NGOs. On the contrary, before, during, and after the Bush administration, American NGOs continued to work with their counterparts in other countries to create international networks and norms to promote and defend democracy. For instance, in 1999 the National Endowment for Democracy helped to convene the first meeting of the World Movement for Democracy in New Delhi, India. This organization brings together leaders from NGOs, political parties, trade unions, and governments working to advance democracy around the world.[35] Less formally, NDI and IRI also interact with political party foundations in Europe to transfer knowledge about party development and to demonstrate solidarity with parties working in difficult, non-democratic settings. Trade unions have a long history of international organization and affiliation through the International Trade Union Confederation (ITUC, formerly the ICFTU) and the Global Union Federations. Although these international labor organizations focus primarily on workers' rights, wages, and workplace conditions, they also place a priority on member participation in union decisionmaking and member involvement in civil society more generally. Labor activists have expressed their solidarity with democratic movements in a variety of ways, from direct financial support to Solidarity in the 1980s to the refusal of unionized dock workers in South Africa in 2008 to unload Chinese arms shipments destined for Zimbabwe. In addition, international NGOs, especially in the human rights field, have built informal networks with local NGOs to pressure bad governments into performing better.[36]

Likewise, political activists—including youth movements, women's rights campaigners, and even antiwar groups using non-violent civic resistance—have formed networks for exchanging information and learning from each other about their techniques. Some have even spawned professional NGOs such as the Centre for Applied Nonviolent Action and Strategies (CANVAS) in Serbia, which is dedicated to exporting successful ideas and methods for democratic change. The American-based International Center on Nonviolent Conflict (ICNC) also has provided learning tools and resources to activists and NGOs in these networks, teaching resistance strategies and tactics through field workshops, university curricula, and the production of films and a video game. But the main impetus for this widespread adoption of nonviolent strategies has come from people involved in local struggles against the suppression of political and social rights, giving these networks a distinctly transnational and non-American profile.[37] Of course, a non-American, Mahatma Gandhi, was the chief inspiration for the spread of these methods throughout the world.

The United States government has no direct role to play in the development of these transnational, non-government networks. In the margins, though, the Obama administration could do more to facilitate such interaction. For instance, the Obama administration could increase college scholarships and international exchanges to bring more students into contact with each other or subsidize platforms that could facilitate interaction, be they web technologies, conferences, or more traditional media outlets.

International Norms of Democracy and Democracy Promotion

Since the Treaty of Westphalia, state leaders have recognized state sovereignty as the most important norm in international affairs, even if powerful countries have violated this norm recurrently.[38] At the end of World War II, the newly formed United Nations became an institutional ally for state sovereignty, helping to destroy empires and undermine the legitimacy of colonization. Eventually, empire became an illegitimate and near-extinct form of government. During this period, many hoped that acquiring state sovereignty would be the first step toward popular sovereignty. People living in colonies could choose their rulers only after shedding their colonial masters. Decolonization, self-determination, and democratization were to go hand in hand. They did not. Instead, new leaders in many former colonies trumpeted the importance of state sovereignty as a way to deny popular sovereignty to their citizens. During the Cold War, the specter of Soviet and American "neo-imperialism" armed autocrats with an additional rationale for the defense of state sovereignty. In their respective orbits, both superpowers also invoked state sovereignty to suppress internal agents of regime change ("socialists" in Chile or "anti-communists" in Czechoslovakia) and limit the activities of external allies who supported these internal changes.

Since the end of the Cold War, new normative doctrines have evolved that privilege individual rights over states' rights. This normative realignment has in turn opened space for considering democracy to be a human right.[39] Democracy, therefore, would be a system of government that other democratic states and international institutions should promote. The 1948 Universal Declaration of Human Rights established a set of principles placing individual rights over state sovereignty, and a few important treaties and documents adopted during the Cold War further codified the normative shift. Norms, however, do not always influence behavior. During the Cold War, the balance of power between the USSR and the U.S. severely constrained real actions to defend human rights in both the communist and capitalist camps. Since the end of the Cold War, both the normative arguments and actions of states in defense of human rights have expanded considerably. A new doctrine called the Responsibility to Protect provides the most ambitious justification for external intervention in defense of human rights. If governments fail to provide basic security to their citizens, including stopping genocide, then this doctrine contends that the international community has a responsibility to protect threatened citizens by any means necessary, even military force.[40] Responsibility to Protect is a norm, not a law, but many states, multilateral organizations, and civil society networks have adopted and pursued policies in accordance with this idea.

Military intervention in defense of individual human rights has sometimes occurred, even if serious debates remain about which international body has the legitimacy to authorize such missions. The U.S. initiated or led some of these interventions, including those in Somalia, Haiti, and Kosovo in the 1990s.[41] Although the United Nations usually provides the authority for peacekeeping operations, it is striking how other regional actors and their armed forces have undertaken humanitarian interventions without American participation: Australia in East Timor, the Military Observer Group (ECOMOG) of the Economic Community of West Africa States (ECOWAS) and then its U.N. reincarnation, the United Nations Observer Mission in Sierra Leone (UNAMSIL), or the European Union in Eastern Congo. As Martha Finnemore has concluded, "Humanitarian activity in the 1990s suggests that certain claims, particularly human rights claims, now trump sovereignty and legitimize intervention in ways previously not accepted."[42]

National and international courts also have expanded their reach into the sovereign affairs of individual states to defend human rights. Under the doctrine of universal jurisdiction, domestic courts can try foreign defendants accused of slavery, genocide, torture, and war crimes.[43] The International Court of Justice, the International Criminal Tribunal, and the International Criminal Court represent institutions designed to centralize and further legitimate the exercise of universal jurisdiction for war crimes and crimes against humanity. Most boldly, in July 2008, the International Criminal Court's prosecutor sought to charge a sitting leader, Sudanese President Omar al-Bashir, with crimes against humanity for his support for genocide in Sudan's Darfur region.[44]

Obviously, the international institutions, states, and NGOs dedicated to defending human rights do not act consistently or uniformly. Powerful states such as China, Russia, Iran, and the United States exercise their sovereignty regarding internal human rights violations more effectively than do weak states. And many calls for forceful intervention to stop suffering—be it in Darfur, North Korea, or Burma—go unanswered.[45] The application of universal jurisdiction by different national courts also has not been uniform or always consistent with other normative goals, such as national reconciliation in war-torn states.[46] American reluctance to join the International Criminal Court is not only an expression of American power, but also a statement about the flaws that must be addressed in order for the Court to be effective. Nonetheless, it is a radical and growing idea that individuals have rights, no matter where they live, and that rulers face constraints in how they exercise sovereignty, no matter what challenges they face.

The right to freedom and democratic government has nowhere near the international standing afforded to the right to avoid genocide, but the norm has developed along several dimensions since the 1990s. Rhetorically, international organizations comprised primarily of democratic states and non-governmental networks that promote democracy and human rights have gone beyond theoretical discussions to assert democracy and democracy promotion as a universal value. In Europe, democracy promotion abroad made its first cursory appearance in European Community (EC) documents with the 1986 Statement on Human Rights, in which the EC foreign ministers affirmed "their commitment to promote and protect human rights and fundamental freedoms and emphasize the importance in this context of the principles of parliamentary democracy and the rule of law."[47] After the end of the Cold War, the right to political participation was strengthened through pronouncements and newly crafted monitoring mechanisms by international actors, including the U.N. General Assembly, the International Covenant on Civil and Political Rights (ICCPR) Human Rights Committee, the European and Inter-American Commissions on Human Rights, the OAS, the OSCE and the Council of Europe. By 2003, the first European Security Strategy, unanimously endorsed by the European Council in Brussels, declared,

> The quality of international society depends on the quality of the governments that are its foundation. The

best protection for our society is a world of well-governed democratic states. Spreading good governance,
supporting social and political reform, dealing with
corruption and abuse of power, establishing the rule
of law and protecting human rights are the best means
of strengthening the international order.[48]

The Community of Democracies' Warsaw Declaration, adopted
on June 27, 2000, may be the boldest doctrinal statement affirming
the "right" to democracy, while also stating unequivocally that
democracy is the only legitimate form of government for the world
today. International norms also have been codified around the legitimacy of domestic and international election monitoring, the
freedom of assembly, basic standards for political party behavior,
and the rights and responsibilities of NGOs.[49] Perhaps most amazingly, the U.N. Security Council has authorized the use of force to
restore democracy after military coups against elected governments in Haiti (1991–1994) and Sierra Leone (1997–1998).[50]

These norms about democracy shape and constrain the behavior of governments and NGOs even less profoundly than
human rights norms. Obviously, the norm of democracy promotion is not universal; many autocrats still control major chunks
of the world. While few of these dictators would argue against
democracy as a value or system of government, they do rail
against exporters of democracy as illegitimate, illegal, and imperial. A norm can coexist side by side with enduring violations of
that same norm. In international affairs, anti-slavery norms enjoyed widespread recognition hundreds of years before the practice of slavery finally ended. Norms about self-determination and
decolonization also garnered international legitimacy well before
the last great empire collapsed. Still today, slavery and colonization have not been fully eradicated. Nonetheless, new norms

against slavery and decolonization eventually played a pivotal role in changing actual practices.

Might dictatorship follow the same path to extinction as slavery and empire? It is still too early to tell. It is clear, however, that the normative basis for pushing history in this direction already has been constructed, while the normative framework in support of autocracy is fading fast. Since the 1990s, democrats fighting apartheid in South Africa, communism in Poland, or dictatorship in the Philippines have invoked this international normative framework as a means to access resources and win legitimacy, while at the same time weakening the power and prestige of their autocratic enemies. Influenced by this same set of values, democratic governments in turn have come to aid these democratic movements.

Periodically, the United States played a central role in prodding this normative evolution. As discussed above, the U.S. role internationalizing human and democratic rights has waned as leaders of democratic countries and democratic activists have criticized American foreign policy and questioned America's commitment to democratic values. However, these same critics have rarely challenged the value of democracy or the morality of democracy promotion. A country, organization, or individual can be anti-American and pro-democracy at the same time. The very possibility of this distinction strengthens the international norm of democracy and the legitimacy of democracy promotion.

Codifying a Code of Conduct for Democracy Promotion

The collapse of communism ushered in a giddy era for democracy promoters. Because so many autocratic regimes disappeared at the same time, new post-communist regimes welcomed Western democracy promoters into their countries with open arms and few restrictions. Today, the atmosphere for democracy promotion is markedly different. The supposedly "easy" cases of democratic transition in East Central Europe have consolidated and require no further assistance from democracy promoters. Autocratic regimes, originally weak after communism's collapse, have themselves consolidated and now have the means to push back. The war in Iraq has tainted the idea of democracy promotion. Finally, as discussed earlier, some autocracies such as Russia, Iran, and Venezuela are devoting more resources to exporting their forms of governments.

This more challenging international environment requires a new strategy for bolstering the legitimacy of democracy promotion and the defense of human rights. Governments must come together and draft a code of conduct for democratic interventions in the same way that governments and the international human rights community have specified conditions in which external actors have the responsibility to protect threatened populations. A "right to help" doctrine is needed.[51] As mentioned above, international norms concerning the right to free and fair elections are most advanced, including the idea that international organizations as well as nonpartisan local organizations have the right to monitor elections. This normative framework needs to be expanded to include other forms of democracy assistance.[52] Perhaps most urgently, the international community needs to develop the normative framework to defend the right of local nongovernment organizations to received foreign assistance.

It is commonly assumed that the flow of these funds goes only from the rich (and some would say imperial) "core" to the poor "periphery" as a means to meddle in the internal affairs of weaker states. Yet in fact these flows move in all directions. The Japanese Hitachi Foundation gives grants to the American-based

Family Violence Prevention Fund; the AFL-CIO works out of Paris; the British BBC broadcasts all over the world (including in the U.S.) as does Al Jazeera, Al-Manar, and virtually every national television station from a major country; Russian oligarchs provide financial assistance to American think tanks; Venezuelan foundations provide social assistance to poor families in the Bronx; the German party institutes have offices and programs in Washington; Saudi princes endow chairs at American universities, and other Saudi foundations support mosques and schools around the world; the Taiwanese government offers grants to research institutes; and foreign firms and governments from all around the world hire public relations specialists in Washington, London, and New York to lobby for their causes. This vast network of foreign interventions in the domestic affairs of other countries needs to be regulated; some of it should be stopped, but most of it is beneficial and should be legitimated. For instance, countries might agree to prohibit the direct funding of political parties or candidates, but protect the legality of foreign assistance to nonpartisan NGOs. Norms about transparency are also desperately needed, regarding both the donors and recipients of NGO funding. It is hard for the democratic governments and Western NGOs to call for transparency in autocratic governments when they themselves do not operate transparently.

Once these rules of the road for democracy promotion are codified, signatories to such a covenant would be obligated to respect them. If they did not, their violation would serve as a license for further intrusive behavior from external actors.

An internationally agreed-upon code of conduct for democracy assistance might constrain the activities of some U.S. actors. But such a legal and normative framework also would enable other kinds of activities and interventions. In the long run, the United States and other democracies will only be effective in promoting freedom abroad if they develop international institutions that enhance mutually beneficial cooperation and then abide by the rules of these institutions in the conduct of foreign policy.

Conclusion

The American record of achievement in promoting democracy abroad in the twenty-first century is underwhelming. Since President Bush made the promotion of freedom a major tenet of his foreign policy, it is not clear that more people live in freedom in 2009 than they did a decade ago. The use of military force in the name of freedom's advance has not only produced limited results for democracy in Afghanistan and Iraq, but tainted all efforts—especially American efforts—to promote democracy around the world.

The Bush record, however, cannot be cited as a reason to abandon the project altogether. Democratic and Republican foreign policymakers with America's long-term national interests at stake must come together to recommit the United States to the noble and prudent purpose of advancing freedom around the world. As chapters 2, 3, and 4 of this book have attempted to demonstrate, it is both the right thing to do on behalf of others and the pragmatic thing to do in pursuit of our own economic and security interests.

Reaffirming our commitment to democracy's advance does not mean continuing to pursue our recent strategies. In fact, only a new course—a radically new course as outlined in the last two chapters of this book—will rebuild the international legitimacy and domestic support needed to sustain democracy promotion until the right to live under democratic government is accepted around the globe and autocracy becomes as antiquated as imperialism and slavery.

Acknowledgements

My first debt goes to my editors, Peter Berkowitz and Tod Lindberg, for originally asking me to write this book and then being so patient in waiting for its delivery. I also am indebted to Kathy Goldgeier for her terrific editing work on the final manuscript. I also would like to thank John Raisian, the director of the Hoover Institution, for his support of this project and of all the work I do. I also want to thank the Smith-Richardson Foundation for supporting another major research project of mine on the external dimensions of democratization that has contributed to many of the ideas in this book.

I am also deeply indebted to the army of research assistants who contributed significantly to this book. Kate Berglund, Jonathan Gatto, Sherri Hanson, Tatyana Krasnopevsteva, Erin Mark, Whitney Ping, Rokas Salasevicius, Jessica Schaffer, and Rachel Silverman all did terrific work. Laura Mottaz stands out for the number of years she has helped me with the research for this book, but also for her intellectual contributions to this project.

The idea for this book germinated during my two years in the Hoover Institution's Washington office and then came to fruition during my time as director of the Center on Democracy, Development, and Rule of Law (CDDRL) at Stanford University. I value few things in life more than smart, engaging, congenial, and fun colleagues. I had/have them in abundance in both places. For helping to develop the themes in this book, I am especially grateful for conversations, debates, and arguments with Rachel Abrams, Peter Berkowitz, and Tod Lindberg in Washington, and Larry Diamond, Gerhard Caspar, Eric Jensen, Steve Krasner, Amichai Magen, Kathryn Stoner-Weiss, and Jeremy Weinstein at CDDRL. The staff at CDDRL always kept my spirits up, and Tram Dinh in particular was instrumental in providing the administrative and editorial support needed to get this project done.

Finally, I thank Donna, Cole, and Luke, for enduring all the distractions and strains this project imposed on our family life. To them, I promise never again to write a book under deadline.

I dedicate this book to Cole and Luke, with the hope that whatever they eventually do in their lives, they will continue to think about the struggles of the many democratic activists we have been privileged to host at our home over the years. In some small way, I hope they too will join the world movements for democracy.

Michael McFaul wrote this book before joining the Obama Administration in January 2009. The views reflected in this publication are his alone and do not necessarily represent or reflect U.S. Government policy."

Notes

Chapter 1

1. On other components of this new grand strategy, see: Ivo Daalder and James Lindsay, *America Unbound: The Bush Revolution in Foreign Policy* (Washington: Brookings Institution Press, 2003).
2. President George W. Bush, "Address to the Nation," aboard the U.S.S. Abraham Lincoln, May 1, 2003.
3. George W. Bush, "President Sworn-In to Second Term," http://www.white house.gov/news/releases/2005/01/20050120-1.html.
4. The White House, "The National Security Strategy of the United States," http://www.whitehouse.gov/nsc/nss/2006/.
5. Freedom House, "Meeting our Commitment to Democracy and Human Rights: An Analysis of the U.S. Congressional FY2008 Appropriations," http://www.freedomhouse.org/uploads/special_report /64.pdf.
6. Anatol Lieven and John Hulsman, *Ethical Realism: A Vision for America's Role in the World* (New York: Pantheon Books, 2006). Fred Kaplan, *Daydream Believers: How a Few Grand Ideas Wrecked American Power* (Hoboken: John Wiley & Sons, 2008). Robert Merry, *Sands of Empire: Missionary Zeal, American Foreign Policy and the Hazards of Global Ambition* (New York: Simon and Shuster, 2005).

7. Americans and the World, "US Role in the World: Promoting Democracy and Human Rights," http://www.americans-world.org/digest/overview/us_role/democracy.cfm.

8. Program on International Policy Studies (PIPA), the Chicago Council on Foreign Relations, and Knowledge Networks, "Americans on Promoting Democracy," 5, http://www.pipa.org/OnlineReports/AmRole_World/Democratization_Sep0 5/Democratization_Sep09_rpt_revised.pdf.

9. Quoted here from Karlyn Bowman, "The Federal Government: Losing Public Support," *Roll Call*, http://www.rollcall.com/issues/52_36/bowman/15317-1.html.

10. Larry Diamond rightly dates the beginning of this democratic recession to the 1999 military coup in Pakistan. For his comprehensive overview, see chapter 3 of his *The Spirit of Democracy: The Struggle to Build Free Societies throughout the World* (New York: Times Books, 2008).

11. Arch Puddington, "Freedom in Retreat? Is the Tide Turning? Finding of Freedom in the World 2008" (mimeo, 2008), 1.

12. Freedom House, *Freedom in the World 2008: The Annual Survey of Political Rights and Civil Liberties* (New York: Rowman and Littlefield, 2008), 879.

13. Andrew J. Bacevich, "Picking Up after Failed War on Terror," Los Angeles Times, November 6, 2007, http://www.latimes.com/news/opinion/la-oebacevich 6nov06,0,7058482.story?coll=la-opinion-rightrail.

14. The White House, "President Bush and Russian President Putin Participate in Press Availability," http://www.whitehouse.gov/news/releases/2006/07/20060715-1.html.

15. Ibid.

16. "Prominent Iranian Dissident and Former Political Prisoner Akbar Ganji on Why He Refused to Meet President Bush and the Dangers of a US Invasion of Iran," www.democracynow.org/2006/ 7/25/prominent_iranian_dissident_and_former_political.

17. The Syrian withdrawal from Lebanon—the main achievement of the Cedar Revolution in 2005—has not been reversed. Lebanese democracy, however, was no stronger in 2008 than it was in 2005.

18. Steven Heydemann, "Upgrading Authoritarianism in the Arab World" (Washington: Saban Center for Middle East Policy at the Brookings Institution, 2007). Barry Rubin, "Pushback or Progress? Arab Regimes Respond to Democracy Challenge Policy Focus" (Washington: Washington Institute for Near East Policy, 2007).

19. Tom Carothers, "The Backlash against Democracy Promotion," *Foreign Affairs* 85:2 (2006), 55-68. Carl Gershman and Michael Allen, "The Assault on Democracy Assistance," *Journal of Democracy* 17:2 (2006), 36-51.

20. Regine Spector and Michael McFaul, "External Sources and Consequences of Russia's 'Sovereign Democracy,'" in *New Challenges to Democratization?* ed. Peter Burnell and Richard Youngs (forthcoming).

21. For details, see: Diamond, *Spirit of Democracy*, chapter 3.

22. PIPA, "Americans on Promoting Democracy."

23. See in particular: James Traub, *The Freedom Agenda:Why America Must Spread Democracy [Just not the Way George Bush Did]* (New York: Farrar, Straus and Giroux, 2008). Frank Fukuyama, *America at the Crossroads: Democracy, Power, and the Neoconservative Legacy* (New Haven: Yale University Press, 2006). Diamond, *Spirit of Democracy*. Jennifer Windsor, "Advancing the Freedom Agenda: Time for a Recalibration?" *The Washington Quarterly* 29:3 (2006), 21-34. Radwan Masmoudi and Joseph Loconte, "A Faltering Freedom Agenda: The Disillusion of Muslim Reformers," The *Weekly Standard*, April 9, 2008, http://weeklystandard.com/Content/Public/Articles/000/000/ 014/960lvsno.asp.

24. It also reflects the fact that democracy assistance in the 1990s focused on countries that had already made the transition to electoral democracy and were then consolidating liberal democracy. Most American NGOs in the democracy promotion business showed up in the post-communist world and Africa after 1989.

25. Stefan Halper and Jonathan Clarke, *America Alone: The Neo-Conservatives and the Global Order* (Cambridge, UK: Cambridge University Press, 2004).

26. Joanna Gowa, *Ballots and Bullets:The Elusive Democratic Peace* (Princeton: Princeton University Press, 1999), 4.

27. Edward Mansfield and Jack Snyder, "Prone to Violence: The Paradox of the Democratic Peace," *The National Interest*, December 1, 2005, http://www.nationalinterest.org/Article.aspx?id=10876.

28. Dimitri Simes, "America's Imperial Dilemma," *Foreign Affairs* 82:6 (2003), 91.

29. Stephen Walt, *Taming American Power:The Global Response to U.S. Primacy* (New York: Norton & Norton, 2005).

30. Peter Baker and Thomas Ricks, "Old Hands from the Family Business," *The Washington Post*, November 10, 2006, A1.

31. See in particular Bush's speech on the Middle East at the Brookings Institution on December 5, 2008 at http://www.whitehouse.gov/news/releases/2008/12/20081205-8.html.

32. Richard Haass, *The Opportunity: America's Moment to Alter History's Course* (New York: Public Affairs, 2005), 27.

33. David Brooks, "For 2008: An American Themistocles," *The New York Times*, March 25, 2008, WK13.

34. Robert Kaplan, "Hostage to Fortune," *The Wall Street Journal*, September 6, 2006, A20.

35. On the proliferation of weak states, see: Susan Rice and Stewart Patrick, *Index of Weak States in the Developing World* (Washington: Brookings Institution, 2008).

36. Nancy Soderberg and Brian Katulis, *The Prosperity Agenda:What the World Wants from America—and What We Need in Return* (New York: Wiley, 2008).

37. Thomas Friedman, "Anxious in America," *The New York Times*, June 29, 2008, 10, http://www.nytimes.com/2008/06/29/opinion/29friedman.html?scp=1&sq=thomas%20friedman%20anxious&st=cse.

38. Patrick Buchanan, "Who's in Charge of Russia Policy?" Antiwar.com, December 29, 2004, http://www.antiwar.com/pat/?articleid=4224. Anatol Lieven, "Liberal Hawk Down," *The Nation*, October 25, 2004, 3.

39. Anne Norton, *Leo Strauss and the Politics of American Empire* (New Haven: Yale University Press, 2004).

40. Walter Russell Mead has called this perspective the "Jeffersonian tradition." Mead writes, "The Jeffersonian view of the United States as a revolutionary nation with a revolutionary mission runs deep. The Jeffersonian party looks at the American Revolution with something of the same emotion with which good Bolsheviks once viewed Lenin's October revolution. In Jeffersonian eyes, the American Revolution was more than a break with a blundering king and a usurping Parliament; it was the start of a new era in the world." Walter Russell Mead, *Special Providence: American Foreign Policy and How It Changed the World* (New York: Knopf, 2001), 180.

41. Anne R. Pierce, *Woodrow Wilson and Harry Truman: Mission and Power in American Foreign Policy* (Westport: Praeger, 1996).

42. President Woodrow Wilson's Fourteen Points, delivered to a joint session of Congress, January 8, 1918.

43. Classic realist statements include: E. H. Carr, *The Twenty Years' Crisis, 1919-1939* (London: Macmillan, 1962). Hans Morgenthau, *Politics among Nations: The Struggle for Power and Peace* (New York: Alfred Knopf, 1967). Kenneth Waltz, *Theory of International Politics* (Reading: Addison-Wesley, 1979). John Mearsheimer, *The Tragedy of Great Power Politics* (New York: W.W. Norton, 2001).

44. William Burr, ed., *The Kissinger Transcripts: The Top Secret Talks with Beijing and Moscow* (New York: New Press, 1999), 64.

45. George Shultz, *Turmoil and Triumph: Diplomacy, Power, and the Victory of the American Ideal* (New York: Simon and Shuster, 1993). Peter Schweizer, *Reagan's War* (New York: Doubleday, 2002).

46. David Adesnik and Michael McFaul, "Engaging Autocratic Allies to Promote Democracy," *The Washington Quarterly* 29:2 (2006), 7-26.

47. James Goldgeier and Michael McFaul, *Power and Purpose: American Policy toward Russia after the Cold War* (Washington: Brookings Institution Press, 2003).

48. *A National Security Strategy of Engagement and Enlargement* (Washington: Government Printing Office, 1994). Thomas Carothers, "The Democracy Nostrum," *World Policy Journal* 11 (1994), 47-53.

49. The main arguments of this debate in the academic literature are outlined in: Michael Brown, Sean Lynn-Jones, and Steven Miller, eds., *Debating the Democratic Peace* (Cambridge, US: MIT Press, 1996). Strobe Talbott cites this academic literature in his essay: "Democracy and the National Interest," *Foreign Affairs* 75:6 (1996), 47-63.

50. President Bill Clinton, "A Strategic Alliance with Russian Reform," U.S. Department of State Dispatch, vol. 4, April 1, 1993, 3-4.

51. President Bill Clinton, "State of the Union," January 25, 1994, http://www.let. rug.nl/usa/P/bc42/ speeches/sup94wjc.htm.

52. Anthony Lake, "From Containment to Enlargement," U.S. Department of State Dispatch, vol. 4, September 27, 1993, 658-64.

53. Kissinger lamented this kind of influence on foreign policymaking. See: Paula Stern, *Water's Edge: Domestic Politics and the Making of Foreign Policy* (Westport: Greenwood Press, 1979).

54. John Arquilla, *The Reagan Imprint: Ideas in American Foreign Policy from the Collapse of Communism to the War on Terror* (Chicago: Ivan R. Dee, 2006), 117.

55. James Mann, *Rise of the Vulcans: The History of Bush's War Cabinet* (New York: Viking Press, 2004).

56. Barbara Geddes, "What Do We Know about Democratization after Twenty Years?" *Annual Review of Political Science* 2:1 (2008), 115-144.

57. On economic modernization as a cause for democratic change, see: Seymour Martin Lipset, *Political Man: The Social Basis of Politics* (Garden City: Doubleday, 1960). On economic crisis as a trigger for democratic change, see: Stephan Haggard and Robert R. Kaufman, *The Political Economy of Democratic Transitions* (Princeton: Princeton University Press, 1995).

58. Those emphasizing elites and the benefits of pacts include: Guillermo O'Donnell and Philippe Schmitter, *Transitions from Authoritarian Rule: Tentative Conclusions about Uncertain Democracies, v.4*, (Baltimore: Johns Hopkins University Press, 1986). Terry Lynn Karl, "Dilemmas of Democratization in Latin America," *Comparative Politics* 23 (1990), 1-21. Those downplaying pacts and giving greater attention to masses include: Nancy Bermeo, "Myths of Moderation: Confrontation and Conflict during the Democratic Transitions," *Comparative Politics* 29:3 (1996), 305-22. Ruth Collier, *Paths towards Democracy: The Working Class and Elites in Western Europe and South America* (New York: Cambridge University Press, 1999). Elisabeth Jean Wood, *Forging Democracy from Below: Insurgent Below: Insurgent Transitions in South Africa and El Salvador* (New York: Cambridge University Press, 2000). Michael McFaul, "The Fourth Wave of Democracy and Dictatorship: Noncooperative Transitions in the Postcommunist World," *World Politics* 54:2 (2002), 212-44.

59. Nonetheless, important work has been done already. No one has contributed more to this literature than Thomas Carothers, whose books and articles on democracy promotion essentially created this field of inquiry and defined several of the major themes and disputes in this literature. His books include: *In the Name of Democracy: U.S. Policy Toward Latin America in the Reagan Years* (Berkeley: University of California Press, 1991). *Assessing Democracy Assistance: The Case of Romania* (Washington: Carnegie Endowment for International Peace, 1996). *Aiding Democracy Abroad: The Learning Curve* (Washington: Carnegie Endowment for International Peace, 1999). *Critical Mission: Essays on Democracy Promotion* (Washington: Carnegie Endowment for International Peace, 2004). *Promoting the Rule of Law Abroad: In Search of Knowledge* (Washington: Carnegie Endowment for International Peace,

2006). *Confronting theWeakest Link:Aiding Political Parties in New Democracies* (Washington: Carnegie Endowment for International Peace, 2006). Other important studies include: Sarah Mendelson and John Glenn, *The Power and Limits of NGOs* (NewYork: Columbia University Press, 2002). Laurence Whitehead, ed., *The International Dimensions of Democratization* (Oxford: Oxford University Press, 1996). RichardYoungs, *International Democracy and theWest:The Role of Governments, Civil Society, and Multinational Business* (Oxford: Oxford University Press, 2004). Michael Cox, John Ikenberry, andTakashi Inoguchi, eds., *American Democracy Promotion: Impulses, Strategies, and Impacts* (Oxford: Oxford University Press, 2000). Francis Fukuyama, *State-Building: Governance andWorld Order in the 21st Century* (Baltimore: Johns Hopkins Press, 2004). Edward Newmann and Roland Rich, *The UN Role in Promoting Democracy: Between Ideals and Reality* (New York: United Nations University Press, 2004), 135-66. Jon Pevehouse, *Democracy from Above: Regional Organizations and Democratization* (Cambridge, UK: Cambridge University Press, 2005). Gordon Crawford, "Promoting Democracy from Without—Learning from Within (Part1), *Democratization* 10:1 (2003), 77-98. Gordon Crawford, *Foreign Aid and Political Reform:A Comparative Analysis of Political Conditionality and Democracy Assistance* (Basingstoke: Palgrave Macmillan, 2001). Peter Burnell, ed., *Democracy Assistance: International Co-operation for Democratization* (London: Frank Cass, 2000). On assessments of AID programs as well as instructive proposals for how to improve evaluations more generally, see: Steven Finkel, Anibal Perez-Linan, and Mitchel Seligson, "Effects of U.S. Foreign Assistance on Democracy Building: Results of a Cross-National Quantitative Study,"Vanderbilt University, January 12, 2006, version #34, http://pdf.usaid.gov/pdf_docs/Pnade694.pdf; Steven Finkel, Anibal Perez-Linan, and Mitchell Seligson. "The Effects of U.S. Foreign Assistance on Democracy Building: 1990-2003," *World Politics* 59 (2007), 404-39. Committee on Evaluation of USAID Democracy Assistance Programs, *Improving Democracy Assistance: Building Knowledge Through Evaluations and Research* (Washington: National Academy of Sciences, 2008). See also the set of case studies on external sources of domestic change at http://cddrl.stanford.edu/research/evaluating_international_influences_on_democratic_development/

60. Philippe Schmitter asserted that: "[O]ne of the firmest conclusions that emerged . . . was that transitions from authoritarian rule and immediate prospects for political democracy were largely to be explained in terms of national forces and calculations. External actors tended to play an indirect and usually marginal role. . . ." in "An Introduction to Southern EuropeanTransitions," O'Donnell and Schmitter, *Transitions from Authoritarian Rule.*

61. In 1991, Geoffrey Pridham pointed out that the role of international structures and actors was "the forgotten dimension in the study of democratic transition." Geoffrey Pridham, ed. *Encouraging Democracy:The International Context of Regime Transition in Southern Europe* (New York: St. Martin's Press, 1991), 18.

62. On representative works, see footnote 52.

63. As a field representative for the National Democratic Institute in Moscow at the time, the author participated in these debates.

64. On the deleterious consequences of presidentialism for Afghan democracy, see: Amin Saikal and William Maley, "The President Who Would Be King," *The New York Times*, February 6, 2008, A21.

65. Thomas Carothers, *Aiding Democracy Abroad: The Learning Curve* (Washington: Carnegie Endowment for International Peace, 1999).

66. U.S. Department of State, Office of the Coordinator for Reconstruction and Stabilization, http://www.state.gov/s/crs.

67. In 1971, the Board for International Broadcasting took over responsibility for the two radio stations from the CIA. In 1994, the governmental Broadcasting Board of Governors took control of Radio Free Europe/Radio Liberty as well as all other non-military U.S. government-funded international media.

68. The AFL-CIO had several regional institutes before the creation of NED. The Democratic Party, the Republican Party, and the Chamber of Commerce did not.

69. The original authorized level for NED in 1983 was $31.3 million, however its actual appropriation was set much lower, at $18 million. NED's appropriation was not to reach the original authorized level for another ten years. From 1983 to 1993, Congressional funding for NED slowly increased to $30 million. In 1993, under the new Clinton administration, the House Foreign Affairs committee approved an increase in NED's authorization level from $30 million to $48 million, however Congress approved a slightly scaled down increase of $35 million. In 1994, the Appropriations Committee recommended a small decrease in NED's budget to $33 million. In 1993, 1994, 1997, and 1999, amendments seeking to cut off all Congressional funding to NED were defeated.

70. The Freedom Support Act also established a new position in the State Department called Coordinator of U.S. Assistance to the NIS. President Clinton symbolically elevated the position by giving the officeholder the added title of "special adviser to the President and to the Secretary of State on assistance to the new independent states" and ambassadorial rank.

71. AID's list of implementing partners for democracy and governance programs includes Abt Associates, the Academy for Education Development, Associates in Rural Development, Casals & Associates, Manila Consulting, Chemonics International, Creative Associates International, DPK Consulting, Development Alternatives, Development Associates, Financial Markets International, International City Management, International Development Law, Management Sciences for Development, MSI, National Center for State Courts, Pact, Inc., PADCO, Research Foundation of SUNY, Research Triangle Institute, The Urban Institute, Women's Campaign International, and World Learning.

72. USAID, *Foreign Aid in the National Interest* (Washington: United States Agency for International Development, 2002). "Promoting Democratic Governance" is chapter 1 of this book.

73. National Endowment for Democracy, http://www.ned.org/about/ned history.html#congressionalSupport. While NED's overall budget has increased, NED's budget for grant-making actually decreased in 2008 as more of its funds were earmarked for specific countries and financial support for its four core institutions.

74. U.S. Department of State, Bureau of Democracy, Human Rights, and Labor, http://www.state.gov/g/drl/p/.

75. For details, see: Tamara Cofman Wittes and Sarah Yerkes, "The Middle East Partnership Initiative: Progress, Problems, and Prospects," Saban Center for Middle East Policy, Brookings Institution, November 29, 2004, http://www.brookings.edu/papers/2004/1129middleeast_wittes.aspx.

76. Foundation for the Future, "Mission Statement," http://www.foundationfor-future.org/index.php?q= en/node/43/menu_id=113.

77. USAID Fact Sheet, "Institutionalizing the Freedom Agenda: President Bush Calls On Future President and Congresses To Continue Leading The Cause of Freedom Worldwide," October 9, 2008, at http://www.usaid.gov/press/fact-sheets/2008/fs081009.html.

78. In the jargon of the foreign assistance business, MCC aims to enforce ex ante conditionality rather than ex post conditionality.

79. This said, some MCC decisions seemed to reflect American geopolitical concerns. For instance, many believe Morocco made the first list of threshold countries because the Bush administration officials wanted to have an Arab country appear in the list.

80. George W. Bush, March 15, 2002. Quoted in "U.S. Millennium Challenge Corporation Overview," Millennium Challenge Corporation, May 31, 2007, http://www.america.gov/st/texttrans-english/2007/May/20070531132811xjsnommis0.9933893.html.

81. The White House, "Department of Defense," Office of Management and Budget, http://www.whitehouse.gov/omb/budget/fy2008/defense.html.

Chapter 2

1. Samuel Huntington, *The Third Wave: Democratization in the Late Twentieth Century* (Norman: University of Oklahoma, 1991), 26.

2. Edward Mansfield and Jack Snyder, *Electing to Fight: Why Emerging Democracies Go to War* (Cambridge, US: MIT Press, 2005).

3. Seymour Martin Lipset and Jason Lakin, *The Democratic Century* (Norman: University of Oklahoma, 2004), 19.

4. Joseph Schumpeter, *Capitalism, Socialism and Democracy, third ed.* (New York: Harper & Row, 1950), 269.

5. Adam Przeworski, *Democracy and the Market: Political and Economic Reforms in Eastern Europe and Latin America* (Cambridge, UK: Cambridge University Press, 1991), 10.

6. Kinds of autocracies include monarchies, theocracies, military juntas, totalitarian systems, hegemonic-party autocracies. On the distinctions, see: Juan Linz, *Totalitarian and Authoritarian Regimes* (Boulder: Lynn Reinner, 2000).

7. For a more precise definition of the "selectorate" in all polities, see: Bruce Bueno de Mesquita et al., *The Logic of Political Survival* (Cambridge, UK: MIT Press, 2003), 41-51.

8. For a more complete list of traits that constitute electoral authoritarianism, see: Steven Levitsky and Lucan Way, "The Rise of Competitive Authoritarianism," *Journal of Democracy* 13:2 (2002), 51-65. Andreas Schedler, ed., *Electoral Authoritarianism: The Dynamics of Unfree Competition* (Boulder: Lynn Reinner, 2006), especially the chapters by Andreas Schedler and Geraldo Munck.

9. Thomas Carothers, "The End of the Transition Paradigm," *Journal of Democracy* 13:1 (2002), 5-21.

10. On the distinction between liberal and electoral democracy, see: Larry Diamond, *Developing Democracy Toward Consolidation* (Baltimore: Johns Hopkins University Press, 1999). On forms of autocracy, see: Larry Diamond, "Thinking About Hybrid Regimes," *Journal of Democracy* 13:2 (2002), 21-35. Levitsky and Way, "The Rise of Competitive Authoritarianism." Philip Roeder, "Varieties of Post-Soviet Authoritarian Regimes," *Post-Soviet Affairs* 10:1 (1994), 61-101.

11. Terry Lynn Karl, "Imposing Consent? Electoralism Versus Democratization in El Salvador," in *Elections and Democratization in Latin America*, 1980–1985, eds. Paul Drake and Eduardo Silva (San Diego: Center for Iberian and Latin American Studies, 1986), 9-36. Terry Lynn Karl, "The Hybrid Regimes of Central America," *Journal of Democracy* 6:3 (1995), 72-86.

12. Diamond, *Developing Democracy*.

13. Robert Dahl, *On Democracy* (New Haven: Yale University Press, 1998), 31.

14. For a review and evaluation of these different metrics, see: Gerardo Munck, *Measuring Democracy: A Bridge between Scholarship and Politics* (Baltimore: Johns Hopkins University Press, 2008).

15. On the pluses and minuses of presidentialism, see: Juan Linz and Arturo Valenzuela, eds., *The Failure of Presidential Democracy: Comparative Perspectives*, vol. 1 (Baltimore: Johns Hopkins University Press, 1994). Donald Horowitz, "Comparing Democratic Systems," in *The Global Resurgence of Democracy*, eds. Larry Diamond and Marc Plattner (Baltimore: Johns Hopkins University Press, 1996). Scott Mainwarning and Matthew Soberg Shugart, *Presidential Democracy in Latin America* (New York: Cambridge University press, 1997).

16. Adam Przeworski et al., *Democracy and Development: Political Institutions and the Well Being in the World*, 1950-1990 (Cambridge, UK: Cambridge University Press, 2000), 129.

17. Guillermo O'Donnell, "Delegative Democracy," *Journal of Democracy* 5:1 (1994), 59. Ethan Kapstein and Nathan Converse have pressed for a more nuanced measure of institutional design. Instead of focusing on presidential versus parliamentary

institutions, they show that institutional arrangements with "weak constraints on executive power" are more likely to fail than democracies with "strong constrains on executive power." See: Ethan Kapstein and Nathan Converse, "Why Democracies Fail," *Journal of Democracy* 19:4 (2008), 64. In contrast to others who have invoked his definition, however, O'Donnell believes, "Delegative democracy is not alien to the democratic tradition. It is more democratic, but less liberal, than representative democracy" (60).

18. M. Steven Fish, "Stronger Legislatures, Stronger Democracies," *Journal of Democracy* 17:1 (2006), 5.

19. State legislatures originally selected senators, not the voters directly.

20. On the advantages of federalism for democracy, see: Diamond, *Developing Democracy*, chapter four, written with Svetlana Tsalik.

21. The regime did and has continued to violate Singaporean citizens' human rights.

22. Bueno de Mesquita et al., *The Logic of Political Survival*, 50.

23. Morton Halperin, Joseph Siegle, and Michael Weinstein, *The Democracy Advantage: How Democracies Promote Prosperity and Peace* (New York: Routledge, 2003), 43. The authors compare measures of the Human Development Index for autocracies and democracies at similar levels of income.

24. Dahl, *On Democracy*.

25. William Easterly, Roberta Gatti, and Sergio Kurlat, "Development, Democracy, and Mass Killings," Working Paper no. 93, Center for Global Development, August 2006.

26. Anne Applebaum, *The Gulag: A History* (New York: Doubleday, 2003), 581, 583.

27. Robert Conquest, *Stalin: Breaker of Nations* (New York: Viking, 1991).

28. These figures come from: Jung Chang and Jon Halliday, *Mao: The Unknown Story* (New York: Anchor Books, 2005).

29. Amartya Sen, "Democracy as a Universal Value," *Journal of Democracy* 10:3 (1999), 7.

30. These are near exact quotes that the author has encountered when debating this issue in public presentations and in the media.

31. Dahl, *On Democracy*.

32. Edward C. Banfield, *The Moral Basis of a Backward Society* (Chicago: University of Chicago, 1958).

33. Other important Islamist theoreticians, including Abo Al-A'laa Maududi of Pakistan and Imam Khomeini of Iran, are more equivocal in their denunciations of democracy.

34. Vladislav Surkov, "Nationalizing the Future: Excerpts from speech," *Ekspert* 43 (2006), 102-8.

35. Joseph Kahn, "In China, Talk of Democracy Is Simply That," *New York Times*, April 20, 2007, 1. David Shambaugh, "Let a thousand democracies bloom," *International Herald Tribune*, July 6, 2007, 4.

36. "Full text of Hu Jintao's report to the 17th Party Congress," Xinhua News Agency, http://news.xinhuanet.com/english/2007-10/24/content_6938749.htm.

37. Fareed Zakaria, "We Should Join Hands," *Newsweek*, October 6, 2008, 23.

38. Some refer to his ideology as Islamic fundamentalism, but in fact, many Muslims around the world practice a form of Islamic fundamentalism without endorsing, much less pursuing, bin Laden's anti-systemic objectives and violent means.

39. Quoted from an interview with bin Laden in November 1996, reprinted in: Bruce Lawrence, ed., *Messages to the World: The Statement of Osama Bin Laden* (New York: Verso Press, 2005), 39.

40. Interview with bin Laden on October 21, 2001 reprinted in: Lawrence, ed., *Messages to the World*, 121.

41. Zawahari, as quoted in: Moataz Fattah, *Democratic Values in the Muslim World* (Boulder: Lynne Reinner, 2006), 14.

42. Fattah, *Democratic Values in the Muslim World*, p. 12. Fattah draws this conclusion from a series of focus groups he conducted in the Muslim world with, among others, societal leaders who identified themselves as traditionalist Islamists.

43. On this ideological decline, see: Gilles Kepel, *Jihad: The Trail of Political Islam* (Cambridge, US: Harvard University Press, 2002).

44. Shibley Telhami and Zogby International, "Arab Attitudes toward Political and Social Issues, Foreign Policy and the Media," unpublished manuscript, November 2005.

45. United Nations Development Programme and Arab Human Fund for Economic and Social Development, *Arab Human Development Report 2002: Creating Opportunities for Future Generations* (New York: United Nations Publication, 2002).

46. Amr Hamzawy, Marina Ottaway, and Nathan Brown, "Islamist Movements and the Democratic Process in the Arab World: Exploring the Gray Zones," *Carnegie Papers, no. 67* (Washington: Carnegie Endowment for International Peace, March 2006). Marina Ottaway, "Morocco: From Top-down to Democratic Transition?" *Carnegie Papers, no. 71* (Washington: Carnegie Endowment for International Peace, September 2006). Fattah, *Democratic Values in the Muslim World*, 138-9.

47. For evidence of the latter, see: Hamzawy, Ottaway, and Brown, "Islamist Movements and the Democratic Process in the Arab World."

48. Martin Kramer, "The Mismeasure of Political Islam," in *The Islamist Debate*, ed. Martin Kramer (Tel Aviv: The Moshe Dayan Center for Middle Eastern and African Studies, 1997), 161-73.

49. Adam Garfinkle, "The Impossible Imperative? Conjuring Arab Democracy," *The National Interest* (2002), 162.

50. Fareed Zakaria, "A Conversation with Lee Kuan Yew," *Foreign Affairs 73:2* (1994), 122-3.

51. Garfinkle, "The Impossible Imperative?" 162.

52. Vali Nasr, "The Rise of 'Muslim Democracy,'" *Journal of Democracy* 16 (2005), 13-27. M. Steven Fish, "Islam and Authoritarianism," *World Politics* 55:1 (2002), 3-37. In Africa, there also is no correlation between Islam and autocracy. See: Staffan I. Lindberg, *Democracy and Elections in Africa* (Baltimore: John Hopkins University, 2006), 19.

53. Steven Kull et al., *World Public Opinion on Governance and Democracy* (Washington: PIPA, 2008). The cluster of articles under the rubric, "How People View Democracy" in *Journal of Democracy* 12:1 (2001), 93-145. The cluster in comprised of four articles based on surveys in post-communist Europe, Africa, Asia, and Latin America. On attitudes in the Middle East, see: James Zogby, *What Arabs Think:Values Beliefs and Concerns* (Washington: Zogby International, 2002).

54. For a detailed discussion, see: Larry Diamond, *The Spirit of Democracy:The Struggle to Build Free Societies throughout theWorld* (NewYork:Times Book, 2008).

55. Mark Tessler, "Do Islamic Orientations Influence Attitudes toward Democracy in the ArabWorld? Evidence from Egypt, Jordan, Morocco, and Algeria," *International Journal of Comparative Sociology* 43:3-5 (2002), 229-49.

56. See: Ronald Inglehart and Pippa Norris, "TheTrue Clash of Civilizations," *Foreign Policy* 135 (2003), 63-69. For more detail: Ronald Inglehart and Pippa Norris, *Rising Tide: Gender Equality and Cultural Change Around theWorld* (Cambridge, UK: Cambridge University Press, 2003).

57. Diamond, *The Spirit of Democracy*, 39.

58. Francis Fukuyama, *The End of History and the Last Man* (NewYork: Free Press, 1992).

59. As Senator John Edwards stated, "Freedom is meaningless if your children are dying of preventable diseases like Malaria. Freedom is meaningless to a child that shows up at a school but is turned away because that child can't pay for a uniform. And freedom is meaningless when 1 billion people live on less than a dollar a day." Full text of Edwards' speech at the London School of Economics, May 25, 2005, http://johnedwards.com/news/speeches/lse20050525/.

60. Just how fast Stalin's Soviet Union grew is the subject of considerable debate. See chapter two of: R.W. Davies, Mark Harrison, and S.G. Wheatcroft, *The Economic Transformation of the Soviet Union, 1913-1945* (Cambridge, UK: Cambridge University Press, 1994). Moreover, it was not only the democraticWest that suffered during the depression, but also the autocraticWest.

61. World Bank, *The East Asian Miracle: Economic Growth and Public Policy* (Washington: World Bank, 1993), 402.

62. Bruce Bueno de Mesquita and Hilton L. Root, eds., *Governing for Prosperity* (New Haven:Yale University Press: 2000), 6.

63. Halperin, Siegle, andWeinstein, *The Democracy Advantage*, 17.

64. Jan Fidrmuc, "Economic reform, Democracy and Growth During Post-Communist Transition," *European Journal of Political Economy* 19:3 (2003), 583-604.

65. Jose Tavares and RomainWacziarg, "How democracy Affects Growth," *European Economic Review* 45:8 (2001), 1341-78.

66. Gilles Saint-Paul andThierryVerdier, "Education, Democracy and Growth," *Journal of Development Economics* 42:2 (1993), 399-407.

67. Douglas North, *Institutions, Institutional Change, and Economic Performance* (Cambridge, UK: Cambridge University Press, 1990).

68. Mancur Olson, "Dictatorship, Democracy, and Development," *American Political Science Review* 87:3 (1993), 567-76.

69. Douglass North, *Structure and Change in Economic History* (New York: W. W. Norton & Co, 1981). Avner Greif, *Institutions and the Path to the Modern Economy: Lessons from Medieval Trade* (Cambridge, UK: Cambridge University Press, 2006).

70. Douglass North and Barry Weingast, "Constitutions and Commitment: The Evolution of Institutions Governing Public Choice in Seventeenth-Century England," *Journal of Economic History* 49:4 (1989), 803-32.

71. Douglass North, William Summerhill, and Barry Weingast, "Order, Disorder, and Economic Change: Latin America Versus North America," in Bueno de Mesquita and Root, eds., Governing for Prosperity, pp. 17-58.

72. Ibid, p. 39. Of course, economic policy, especially in the last half century, also played a role. See: Francis Fukuyama, ed., *Falling Behind: Explaining the Development Gap Between Latin America and the United States* (Oxford, UK: Oxford University Press, 2008).

73. Stephen Knack and Philip Keefer, "Does Inequality Harm Growth Only in Democracies? A Replication and Extension," *American Journal of Political Science* 41:1 (1997), 323-32.

74. Robert Barro, "Determinants of Economic Growth: A Cross-Country Empirical Study," *NBER Working Papers 5698*, National Bureau of Economic Research, 1996. Olson, "Dictatorship, Democracy, and Development," 567-76. Christopher Clague et al., "Property and Contract Rights in Autocracies and Democracies," *Journal of Economic Growth* 1:2 (1996), 243-76. Ross Levine and David Renelt, "A Sensitivity Analysis of Cross Country Growth Regressions," *American Economic Review* 82:4 (1992), 942-63. North, *Institutions, Institutional Changes, and Economic Performance*.

75. Gerhard Schwartz, "Democracy and Market-Oriented Reform—a Love-Hate Relationship?" *Economic Education Bulletin* 32:5 (1992).

76. Seymour Martin Lipset, *Political Man: The Social Basis of Politics* (London: Heinemann, 1983), 31.

77. Przeworski et al., *Democracy and Development*, 103.

78. Barro, "Determinants of Economic Growth." Aymo Brunetti, "Political Variables in Cross-Country Growth Analysis," *Journal of Economic Surveys* 11:2 (1997), 163-90. Jenny A. Minier, "Democracy and Growth: Alternative Approaches," *Journal of Economic Growth* 3:3 (1998), 241-66. G. Williams Dick, "Authoritarian versus Nonauthoritarian Approaches to Economic Development," *Journal of Political Economy* 82:4 (1974), 817-27. Roger C. Kormendi and Philip G. Meguire, "Macroeconomic Determinants of Growth: Cross-Country Evidence," *Journal of Monetary Economic* 16:2 (1985), 141-63. Karen L. Remmer, "Democracy and Economic Crisis: the Latin American Experience," *World Politics* 42:3 (1990), 315-35. John Sloan and Kent L. Tedin, "The Consequences of Regime Type for Public Policy Outputs," *Comparative Political Studies* 20:1 (1987), 98-124. Timothy R. Scully, *Re-*

thinking the Center: Party Politics in Nineteenth- and Twentieth-Century Chile (Stanford: Stanford University Press. 1992).

79. John F. Helliwell, "Empirical Linkages Between Democracy and Economic Growth," *British Journal of Political Science* 24:2 (1994), 225-48. Tavares and Wacziarg, "How Democracy Affects Growth," 1341-78. Michael P. Croizier, Samual P. Huntington, and Joji Watanuki, *The Crisis of Democracy: Report on the Governability of Democracies at the Trilateral Commission* (New York: New York University Press, 1975). Erich Weede, "Extended Deterrence by Superpower Alliance," *Journal of Conflict Resolution* 27:2 (1983), 231-53. Daniel Landau, "Government and Economic Growth in the Less-Developed Countries: An Empirical Study for 1960-1980," *Economic Development and Cultural Change* 35:1 (1986). Robert M. Marsh, "Does Democracy Hinder Economic Development in the Latecomer Developing Nations," *Comparative Social Research* 2 (1979), 215-48.

80. Alberto Alesina et al., "Political Instability and Economic Growth," *Journal of Economic Growth* 1:2 (1996), 189-211. Jakob de Haan and Clements L.J. Siermann, "A Sensitivity Analysis of the Impact of Democracy on Economic Growth," *Empirical Economics* 20:2 (1995), 197-215. Przeworski and Limongi, "Political Regimes and Economic Growth," *Journal of Economic Perspectives* 7:3 (1997), 51-69.

81. Przeworski et al., *Democracy and Development*, 178.

82. Barro, "Determinants of Economics Growth," 58.

83. Helliwell, "Empirical Linkages," 235.

84. Fred Bergsten, Bates Gill, Nicholas Lardy, and Derek Mitchell, eds., *China: The Balance Sheet:What the World Needs to Know About the Emerging Superpower* (New York: Public Affairs, 2006), 18.

85. Paul Collier, *The Bottom Billion:Why the Poorest Countries Are Falling Behind and What Can Be Done about It* (Oxford, UK: Oxford University Press, 2007), 43.

86. As Minxin Pei writes, "An important—if not inevitable—by-product of economic reform was the significant decline of the state's role in the economy. In terms of industrial output, the share of state-owned enterprises fell from nearly 78 to 41 percent from 1978 to 2002, while the share of the private sector (including foreign-invested firms) rose from 0.2 to 4.1 percent." Minxin Pei, *China's Trapped Transition:The Limits of Developmental Autocracy* (Cambridge, US: Harvard University Press, 2006), 2-3.

87. Yasheng Huang, "The Next Asian Miracle," *Foreign Policy* 167 (2008), 36.

88. Barro, "Determinants of Economics Growth," 59.

89. Robert Kaplan, *The Coming Anarchy: Shattering the Dreams of Post Cold War* (New York: Random House, 2000), 62.

90. Gerard Roland, *Transition and Economics, Politics, Markets, and Firms* (Cambridge, US: MIT Press, 2000).

91. Democracy can present a risk to growth since it is open to pressures from interest groups [Mancur Olson, *The Rise and Decline of Nations* (New Haven:Yale University

Press, 1982)], and suffers from lobbying, which is wasteful and causes dead-weight loss by transferring income [Gary Becker, "A Theory of Competition Among Pressure Groups for Political Influence," *The Quarterly Journal of Economics* 98:3 (1983), 675-700.

92. Vaman Rao, "Democracy and Economic Development," *Studies in Comparative International Development* 19:4 (1984), 67-81. Stephan M. Haggard, Pathways from the Periphery: *The Politics of Growth in the Newly Industrializing Countries* (Ithaca: Cornell University Press, 1990).

93. Samuel Huntington and Joan Nelson, *No Easy Choice: Political Participation in Developing Countries* (Cambridge, US: Harvard University Press, 1976).

94. Dani Rodrik and Roman Wacziarg, "Do Democratic Transitions produce Bad Economic Outcomes?" CDDRL Working Paper 29, 1-2. To generate their results, Rodrik and Wacziarg compared Polity IV scores with growth data from Penn World Tables for 154 countries between 1950 and 2000.

95. Ibid.

96. Amy Chua, *World on Fire: How Exporting Free Market Democracy Breeds Ethnic Hatred and Global Instability* (New York: Anchor Books, 2003), 124. See also: Michael Mann, *The Dark Side of Democracy: Explaining Ethnic Cleansing* (Cambridge, UK: Cambridge University Press, 2005).

97. Fareed Zakaria, *The Future of Freedom: Illiberal Democracy at Home and Abroad* (New York: W. W. Norton and Company, 2003).

98. Edward Mansfield and Jack Snyder, *Electing to Fight: Why Emerging Democracies Go to War* (Cambridge, US: MIT Press, 2005), 2.

99. Ibid.

100. In earlier times, monarchies relied on heredity to establish the rules for orderly succession and in many countries, this mechanism worked quite well for long periods of times. Only a small numbers of regimes in the world today are genuine monarchies.

101. The survival rates of autocracies are highest in the very poorest and the very richest countries. Middle income countries that are growing economically are the most unstable places for dictatorships. See: Przeworksi et al., Democracy and Development, 92.

102. Ibid., 98.

103. Ibid., 109. These averages, however, hide some important anomalies. For instance, countries that made the transition from communist to democratic rule in Eastern Europe endured severe economic depressions that—contrary to predictions—did not undermine democratic rule in the region. Conversely, economic growth in Russia in the last decade has contributed to democratic erosion.

104. Kapstein and Converse, "Why Democracies Fail," 60.

105. Hein Goemans and Nikoay Marinov, "What Happened to the Coup d'Etat? The International Community and the Seizure of Executive Power," unpublished manuscript, October 23, 2008.

106. Bruce Russett, *Grasping the Democratic Peace: Principles of a Post-Cold War World* (Princeton: Princeton University Press, 1993), 11. In this book, Russett examines the entire range of cases over the last 200 years and discusses all of the near misses, including the War of 1812 and the Spanish-America War of 1898, which are frequently cited as refutations of the "democratic peace" thesis.

107. Jack Levy, "Domestic Politics and War," in T*he Origins and Prevention of Major Wars*, eds. Robert Rotberg and Theodore Rabb (New York: Cambridge University Press, 1989), 88. For other empirical validations of the democratic peace, see: Zeev Moaz and Nasrin Abdolali, "The Regime Types and International Conflict, 1816-1976," *Journal of Conflict Resolution* 33:1 (1989), 3-35. John Oneal and Bruce Russett, "The Classical Liberals Were Right: Democracy, Interdependence, and Conflict, 1950-1985," *International Studies Quarterly* 41:2 (1997), 267-94.

108. Conversely, leaders in authoritarian regimes can pursue belligerent foreign policies that go against the preferences of society more easily than can their counterparts in democratic states. See: Michael Howard, *War and the Liberal Conscience* (New Brunswick: Rutgers University Press, 1978).

109. For the Kant quotation, see: Michael Doyle, "Kant Liberal Legacies and Foreign Affairs," in *Debating the Democratic Peace*, eds. Brown, Lynn-Jones, and Miller, (Cambridge, US: The MIT Press, 1996), 24-25. Frivolous or un-winnable wars rarely will be fought. Doyle goes even farther to assert that "liberal wars are only fought for popular, liberal purposes."

110. Political scientist James Fearon has taken this argument one step further by arguing that commitments by democratic governments tend to be more credible than those by authoritarian regimes, because policy makers care more about how their audiences, that is their constituents, respond to them. Simply put, reputation matters more for those who have to face reelection. See: James Fearon, "Signaling Foreign Policy Interests," *Journal of Conflict Resolution* 41:1 (1997), 68-90.

111. The phenomenon known as the "security dilemma," where one state is inclined to increase its security by building arms, thereby making the other state less secure and prompting a costly and dangerous arms race, does not occur among "like-minded" democratic states. On the security dilemma, see: Robert Jervis, "Cooperation Under the Security Dilemma," *World Politics* 30 (1978), 186-214.

112. Bruce Russett, "Why Democratic Peace," in *Debating the Democratic Peace*, eds. Brown, Lynn-Jones, and Miller, (Cambridge, US: The MIT Press, 1996), 82-115.

113. Oneal and Russett, "The Classical Liberals Were Right," 267-94.

114. Randall Calvert, "Rational Actors, Equilibrium, and Social Institutions," in *Explaining Social Institutions*, eds. Jack Knight and Itai Sened (Ann Arbor: Michigan University Press, 1995), 57-94.

115. International institutionalists have gone even farther to argue that these institutions actually make the peace. The evidence for this proposition, however, is mixed. See: Russett, "Why Democratic Peace?" 84-85.

116. For the conditions under which conquest can pay, see: Peter Liberman, *Does Conquest Pay? The Exploitation of Occupied Industrial Societies* (Princeton: Princeton University Press, 1996).

117. Hedley Bull, *The Anarchical Society: A Study of Order in World Politics* (London: Macmillan, 1977).

118. Russett, "Why Democratic Peace?" 97.

119. Mansfield and Snyder, *Electing to Fight*, 101.

120. This set of cases includes countries that experienced democratization more than once, after regressing from democracy earlier during this period.

121. The data set for political violence use here comes from the Center for Systemic Peace, http://members.aol.com/cspmgm/warlist.htm.

122. These are cases that move away from autocracy but fail to consolidate democracy. In the numerical language of Polity III, which is the coding system used in their book, these are countries stuck between a score of six and minus six, while regimes with scores greater than six are coded as coherent democracies and regimes with scores less than minus are coded as coherent autocracies. Remember, successful cases of democratization are not war-prone.

123. For a more detailed discussion of these cases, see: Michael McFaul, "Are New Democracies War-Prone?" *Journal of Democracy* 18:2 (2007), 160-67.

124. Zakaria, *The Future of Freedom*, 31.

125. Juan Linz and Alfred Stepan, *Problems of Democratic Transition and Consolidation* (Baltimore: Johns Hopkins University Press, 1996), 17. See also: Francis Fukuyama, "'Stateness' First," *Journal of Democracy* 16:1 (2005), 84-88.

126. Dankwart A. Rustow, "Transitions to Democracy," *Comparative Politics* 2:3 (1970), 350-51. Linz and Stepan, *Problems of Democratic Transition and Consolidation*, 17.

127. Przeworski et al., *Democracy and Development*, 178.

128. Ibid.

129. Michael McFaul and Kathryn Stoner-Weiss, "The Myth of the Authoritarian Model: How Putin's Crackdown Holds Russia Back," *Foreign Affairs* 87:1 (2008), 68-84. Georgy Egorov, Sergei Guriev, and Konstantin Sonin, "Media Freedom, Bureaucratic Incentives, and the Resource Curse," CDDRL Working Papers, 2006.

130. Thomas Carothers, "The End of the Transition Paradigm," *Journal of Democracy* 13:1 (2002), 5-21.

131. On the positive effect in the Soviet case, see: Michael McFaul, *Russia's Unfinished Revolution: Political Change from Gorbachev to Putin* (Ithaca: Cornell University Press, 2001). On the negative effects of elections on liberalization in the Middle East, see: Daniel Brumberg, "Liberalization versus Democracy," in *Uncharted Journey: Promoting Democracy in the Middle East*, eds. Thomas Carothers and Marina Ottaway (Washington: Carnegie Endowment for International Peace, 2005), 15-36. Eva Bellin, "The Robustness of Authoritarianism in the Middle East," *Comparative Politics* 36:2 (2004), 139-57.

132. Barro, "Determinants of Economics Growth," 49-50.
133. Michael McFaul, "Transitions from Postcommunism," *Journal of Democracy* 16:3 (2005), 5-19.
134. Staffan Lindberg, *Democracy and Elections in Africa* (Baltimore: Johns Hopkins University Press, 2006).
135. Nikolay Marinov, "Is the Globalization of Elections Good for Democracy?" APSA paper, August 27, 2006.
136. Barrington Moore, *Social Origins of Dictatorship and Democracy: Lord and Peasant in the Making of the Modern World* (Boston: Beacon Press, 1966), chapter 1.
137. Charles Tilly, *Coercion, Capital, and European States, A.D. 990-1990* (Cambridge, UK: Blackwell, 1990).
138. Rustow, "Transitions to Democracy."
139. Lindberg, *Democracy and Elections in Africa*, 155.

Chapter 3

1. The argument that aid to Hosni Mubarak is necessary to prevent another Egyptian-Israeli war is not made on the normative grounds that lives would be saved but rather on the grounds of insurance for U.S. material interests. See: Leslie Gelb, "Dual Loyalties," *New York Times*, September 23, 2007, Book Review, where he states, "It's true, for instance, that the lobby has made America's longstanding $3 billion annual aid program to Israel untouchable and indiscussible. By the same token, there isn't much discussion about the $2 billion yearly aid package for Egypt. The United States regards this $5 billion as insurance against an Egyptian-Israeli war, and it's cheap at double the price."
2. Some claimed at the time that these autocratic regimes were better than the dictatorships that were likely to replace them should these friends of the United States fall. As discussed below in detail, few of these dire predictions became true.
3. See: Robert Kagan, *Dangerous Nation: America's Place in the World from Its Earliest Days to the Dawn of the Twentieth Century* (New York, Knopf, 2006). Walter Russell Mead, *Special Providence: American Foreign Policy and How It Changed the World* (New York: Knopf, 2001). Walter McDougall, *Promised Land, Crusader State: The American Encounter with the World Since 1776* (New York: Mariner Books, 1997).
4. Grover Cleveland, quoted in McDougall, *Promised Land, Crusader State*, 101.
5. Formally, the United States was not an "ally" of Great Britain, France, and Russia but an "associated power."
6. The term *realist* implies that policies informed by this perspective are realistic (and others would add pragmatic) yet in fact, as explained later in the chapter, many policies pursued in the name of realism were very unrealistic if not downright naïve. The term *liberal* is even more disorienting since the policies suggested by

this analytic tradition have little or nothing to do with the set of domestic policies in the U.S. typically associated with liberals.

7. On liberalism as a theory of international relations, see: Immanuel Kant, "Perpetual Peace" (1795) in *The Philosophy of Kant*, ed. Carl Friedrich (New York: Modern Library, 1949). Joseph S. Nye Jr. and Robert O. Keohane, *Power and Interdependence, third ed.* (New York: Longman, 2000). Richard Rosecrance, *The Rise of the Trading State: Commerce and Conquest in the Modern World* (New York: Basic Books, 1986). Michael Doyle, Bruce Russett, and John Owen IV in *Debating the Democratic Peace*, eds. Michael Brown, Sean Lynn-Jones, and Steven Miller (Cambridge, US: MIT Press, 1996). John Ikenberry, *After Victory: Institutions, Strategic Restraint, and the Rebuilding of Order After Major Wars* (Princeton: Princeton University Press, 2001). In academia, however, liberal theorists have focused on the liberalizing role of international institutions on domestic policies. They have paid less attention to the role of states in fostering domestic change within other states.

8. Kant, to be accurate, focused on liberal states, not democratic states. Subsequent academic analysis of the "democratic peace" has not accentuated the differences between the two since our indices of liberalism and democracy highly correlate.

9. President Woodrow Wilson's Fourteen Points, delivered to a joint session of Congress, January 8, 1918.

10. On the Wilsonian tradition in American foreign policy, see: Alexander George and Juliette George, *Woodrow Wilson and Colonel House* (Mineola: Dover Publications, 1956). Tony Smith, *America's Mission: The United States and the Worldwide Struggle for Democracy in the Twentieth Century* (Princeton: Princeton University Press, 1994). Kagan, *Dangerous Nation*. Mead, *Special Providence*, chapter 5. Of course, the practice of Wilsonianism preceded Wilson himself, and some of Wilson's views on foreign policy are hotly rejected by neo-conservative thinkers. On the fundamental debate as to whether regime type matters, however, Wilsonian liberals and neo-conservatives agree.

11. Classic realist statements include: E. H. Carr, *The Twenty Years' Crisis, 1919-1939* (London: Macmillan, 1962). Hans Morgenthau, *Politics among Nations: The Struggle for Power and Peace* (New York: Knopf, 1973). Kenneth Waltz, *Theory of International Politics* (Boston: Addison-Wesley, 1979). John Mearsheimer, *The Tragedy of Great Power Politics* (New York: W.W. Norton, 2001).

12. This list of assumptions and the summary of the different branches of realism are based on "Introduction: Realism vs. Liberalism" in *Tragedy of Great Power Politics*, Mearsheimer. Realist theorists in academia would contest this simplified characterization of their theories, as several schools of realist thinking exist, including classical realism, offensive realism, and defensive realism. In the policy world, self-described realists rarely identify themselves with one of these sub-schools, while the main cleavage in foreign policy debates remains between liberalism and realism, especially when discussing the topic of this book, democracy promotion. On the various realist schools, see: Mearsheimer, *Tragedy of Great Power Politics*.

13. Mearsheimer, *Tragedy of Great Power Politics*, 18.

14. William Burr, ed., *The Kissinger Transcripts:The Top Secret Talks with Beijing and Moscow* (NewYork: New Press, 1999), 64.

15. PatrickTyler, *A Great Wall: Six Presidents and China* (NewYork: Public Affairs, 2000).

16. David Hendrickson and Robert Tucker, "The Freedom Crusade," *The National Interest* (2005), 18.

17. For a chronicle of these realists and liberal swings, see: Smith, *America's Mission*.

18. Republican realists also have reacted against George W. Bush. See, for instance: Pat Buchanan, *State of Emergency: The Emergency: The Third World Invasion and Conquest of America* (New York: St. Martin's Press, 2006). Steve Clemons's blog, http://www.thewashingtonnote.com. In 2008, Clemons hosted an event entitled, "Ending the Nonsense in American Foreign Policy: Senator Chuck Hagel on a Realist Internationalism for the 21st Century," at the New America Foundation, April 30, 2008. Self-described liberal Anatol Lieven and self-described conservative John Hulsman make the case for bi-partisan realism In their book, *Ethical Realism: A Vision for America's Role in the World* (New York: Pantheon Books, 2006).

19. The end of the Cold War undermined realism's hegemony in the academy, but this school remains a core theory of international relations against which all other theories are still judged.

20. Kenneth Waltz, "The Origins and Prevention of Major Wars," *Journal of Interdisciplinary History* 18:4 (1988), 624-25.

21. John Lewis Gaddis, "Grand Strategy in the Second Term," *Foreign Affairs* 84:1 (2005), 2.

22. Kagan, *Dangerous Nation*, 18.

23. Douglass North, *Institutional Change and American Economic Growth* (Cambridge, UK: Cambridge University Press, 1971).

24. Steven Solnick, *Stealing the State: Control and Collapse in Soviet Institutions* (Cambridge, US: Harvard University Press, 1998).

25. Quoted in: Kagan, *Dangerous Nation*, 374.

26. See: Henry Kissinger, *A World Restored: The Politics of Conservatism in a Revolutionary Age* (NewYork: Grosset and Dunlop, 1964).

27. The Concert of Europe actually did not last throughout the entire century but functioned most effectively from 1815 to 1848. Compared to the scale of conflict in Europe in the twentieth century, the second half of the nineteenth century also looked peaceful and balance of power politics played a role in preserving this relative peace.

28. The word relative must be emphasized because it took a great deal of war and repression of democratic or liberal movements to maintain the status quo. See: Alexis de Tocqueville, *Recollections: The French Revolution of 1848* (Garden City: Doubleday, 1970). Charles Breunig, *The Age of Revolution and Reaction, 1789-1850* (NewYork: Norton, 1970).

29. Quoted in: Kagan, *Dangerous Nation*, 159.

30. This paragraph draws heavily from: Kagan, *Dangerous Nation*.

31. Washington, quoted in: Kagan, *Dangerous Nation*, 44.

32. This political divide pitted the pacifist Whigs against the bellicose Jacksonian Democrats.

33. Arthur Balfour, Tory Leader in the House of Commons, January 1896, as quoted in: Kagan, *Dangerous Nation*, 373.

34. Smith, *America's Mission*, chapter 2.

35. John Judis, *The Folly of Empire: What Empire: What George W. Bush Could Learn from Theodore Roosevelt and Woodrow Wilson* (Oxford: Oxford Univeristy Press, 2004), 2. Smith, *America's Mission*, 42.

36. Anne R. Pierce, *Woodrow Wilson and Harry Truman: Mission and Power in American Foreign Policy* (Westport: Praeger, 2003).

37. After World War II, many world leaders and analysts labeled the exercise of American power as "neo-imperialism," an issue that will be discussed at length in chapter 4. During this era, however, the United States never tried to annex new territory, transplant settlers, or establish new colonies.

38. Woodrow Wilson's Message to the Provisional Government of Russia, May 22, 1917, as quoted in: Pierce, *Woodrow Wilson and Harry Truman*, 43, emphasis added.

39. Tsarism in Russia crumbled in February 1917, two months before the United States entered the war. The emergence of a liberal government in Russia after the February revolution made it easier for Wilson to justify American involvement. See: Margaret MacMillan, Paris 1919 (New York: Random House, 2003), 4.

40. Woodrow Wilson, War Message to Congress, April 2, 1917.

41. Pierce, Woodrow Wilson and Harry Truman, 44.

42. Mark Haas, *The Ideological Origins of Great Power Politics, 1789-1989* (Ithaca: Cornell University Press, 2005), chapter 4.

43. During the inter-war period, strategies of balancing against German power failed miserably in large measure because regime type and the intentions of the Nazi regime did not figure prominently enough into these realist strategies of deterrence.

44. Before the U.S. entered World War II, Roosevelt championed the idea of an American "arsenal of democracy," which meant supplying American technology and economic power to the war effort, but not military manpower.

45. Catherine Merridale, *Ivan's War: Life and Death in the Red Army, 1939-1945* (New York: Metropolitan Books, 2006), 4.

46. John Lewis Gaddis, *Strategies of Containment: A Critical Appraisal of Postwar American National Security Policy* (New York: Oxford University Press, 1982), 8.

47. In contrast, there have been other periods in which both the norms of behavior between states and the internal organization of states more closely correlated. See for instance: Edward Gulik, *Europe's Classical Balance of Power* (Ithaca: Cornell University Press, 1955). Kissinger, *A World Restored*. Robert Jervis, "From Balance to Concert: A Study of International Security Cooperation," *World Politics* 38:1 (1985).

48. The Western powers, including two American expeditions of 8,000 and 5,000 men, invaded Russia in 1918 in an attempt to undermine the Bolshevik Revolution. See: David Foglesong, *The American Mission and the "Evil Empire"* (Cambridge, UK: Cambridge University Press, 2007), 55-56.

49. On the general tendency of great powers to export their domestic institutions, see: John Owen IV, "The Foreign Imposition of Domestic Institutions," *International Organization* 56:2 (2002), 375-410.

50. See for example: John J. Mearsheimer, "Why We Will Soon Miss the Cold War," *The Atlantic*, August 1990, 35-50.

51. David Holloway and Stephen Stedman, "Civil Wars and State-Building in Africa and Eurasia," in *Beyond State Crisis: Postcolonial Africa and Post-Soviet Eurasia in Comparative Perspective*, eds. Mark Beissinger and Croawford Young (Washington: Woodrow Wilson Center Press, 2002), 161. Most of these deaths—16 million by one conservative estimate—occurred in civil wars, not interstate conflicts. See: James Fearon and David Laitin, "Ethnicity, Insurgency, and Civil War," *American Political Science Review* 97:1 (2003), 75-90.

52. William Blum, *The CIA: A Forgotten History* (London: Zed Books, 1986). Robert M. Gates, *From the Shadows: The Ultimate Insider's Story of Five Presidents and How They Won the Cold War* (New York: Simon & Schuster 1997). John Prados, *Presidents' Secret Wars: CIA and Pentagon Covert Operations Since World War II* (New York: William Morrow, 1986). William Blum, *Killing Hope: U.S. Military and CIA Interventions Since World War II-Updated Through 2003* (Monroe, Maine: Common Courage Press, 2004).

53. The strategy became known as the Reagan Doctrine. See: U.S. State Department, "Reagan Doctrine 1985," http://www.state.gov/r/pa/ho/time/rd/17741.htm.

54. Whether U.S. military assistance to anti-communist forces in Nicaragua, the contras, helped or delayed democratization is disputed. For a compelling case that U.S. military assistance to the contras helped to pressure the Sandinistas to hold elections, see: Robert Kagan, *A Twilight Struggle: American Power and Nicaragua, 1977-1990* (New York: Free Press, 1996).

55. Michael McFaul, "Rethinking the `Reagan Doctrine' in Angola," *International Security* 14:3 (1989), 99-135.

56. Steve Coll, *Ghost Wars: The Secret History of the CIA, Afghanistan, and bin Laden, from the Soviet Invasion to September 10, 2001* (New York: Penguin Press, 2004).

57. Autocrats and their policies—not ethnic hatred—caused these Balkan wars. See: V.P. Gagnon, *The Myth of Ethnic War: Serbia and Croatia in the 1990s* (Ithaca: Cornell University Press, 2004).

58. "Table I: military expenditures, armed forces, GNP, CGE, population, and their ratios, by group and country, 1989-1999," in *Bureau of Verification and Compliance, World Military Expenditures and Arms Transfers: 1999—2000* (June 2002), 51-101. Data on Afghanistan were not available.

59. See: Tim Kane, "Troop Deployment Dataset, 1950–2003," The Heritage Foundation, Center for Data Analysis, October 2004: "Only 510 servicemen were

based in South Korea in 1950, prior to the attack. U.S. Department of Defense (DOD) records show that 326,863 troops were deployed in South Korea in 1953, a number that stabilized between 50,000 and 60,000 in the 1960s and 1970s. A slow draw-down continued as troops averaged 40,000 in the 1980s and 35,000 in the 1990s." U.S. economic assistance ended by the early 1970s, and U.S. military assistance ended in 1986.

60. See: "U.S. Military Spending vs. the World," Center for Arms Control and Non-Proliferation, February 5, 2007. The U.S. spent more than $420 billion in FY 2005, while Iran spent $4.9 billion.

61. John Mearsheimer and Stephen Walt, "An Unnecessary War," *Foreign Policy* 134 (2003), 50-59.

62. The Cuban-American community that helps to maintain this belligerent U.S. policy exists only because of the Cuban autocratic regime. If Cuba democratized, the Cuban-American lobby would either dissolve or adopt a different policy.

63. On China's potential as a military and economic superpower, see: Fred Bergsten et al., *China: The Balance Sheet* (New York: Public Affairs, 2006). Susan Shirk, *China: Fragile Superpower* (Oxford, UK: Oxford University Press, 2007).

64. The reversal in relations between Libya and the United States is another recent example.

65. Gary Schmitt, "The Power China Is Building," *Washington Post*, June 14, 2007. Shirk, *China*, 9.

66. Interview with bin Laden on October 21, 2001 reprinted in: Bruce Lawrence, ed., *Messages to the World: The Statement of Osama Bin Laden* (New York: Verso Press, 2005), 121.

67. Lawrence Wright, *The Looming Tower: Al-Qaeda and the Road to 9/11* (New York: Knopf, 2006).

68. Political movements in Chechnya, Kashmir, and Sri Lanka also use terrorist methods to pursue their goals of independence. Although perceived by some as freedom fighters and national liberation movements, these groups have dubious commitments to democracy. They do not threaten the United States directly, but their struggles do not advance U.S. security interests.

69. Mead, *Special Providence*, 162-63.

70. Barry Rubin, "America and the Egyptian Revolution, 1950-1957," *Political Science Quarterly* 97:1 (1982), 73-90.

71. On Karimov's misperceptions, see: Fiona Hill and Kevin Jones, "Fear of Democracy or Revolutions: The Reaction to Andijon," *The Washington Quarterly* 29:3 (2006), 111-25.

72. Helen Cooper, Mark Mazzetti, and Jim Rutenberg, "U.S. Officials Voice Frustrations With Saudis, Citing Role in Iraq," *New York Times*, July 27, 2007, A1. These tensions predate September 11. See: Rachel Bronson, *Thicker than Oil: America's Uneasy Partnership with Saudi Arabia* (Oxford, UK: Oxford University Press, 2006).

73. Richard Oppel, "Foreign Fighters in Iraq Are Tied to Allies of U.S.," *New York Times*, November 22, 2007, A1.

74. Coll, *Ghost Wars*. Carlotta Gall, "Musharraf Vows to Aid Afghanistan in Fighting Taliban," *New York Times*, September 7, 2006, A8. David Rhode, "Al Qaeda Finds Its Center of Gravity," *New York Times*, September 10, 2005, 3. Ismail Khan and Carlotta Gall, "Pakistan Lets Tribal Chiefs Keep Control Along Border," *New York Times*, September 6, 2006, A8.

75. See: GlobalSecurity.org, "Iran-Iraq War: 1980-1988," http://www.globalsecurity.org/military/world/war/iran-iraq.htm.

76. For details, see: Christopher Layne, "Kant or Cant: The Myth of the Democratic Peace," *International Security* 19:2 (1994), 5-49.

77. See: John Mearsheimer, "Back to the Future: Instability in Europe after the Cold war," *International Security* 15 (1990), 5-55. Charles Kupchan, *The End of the American Era: U.S. Foreign Policy and the Geopolitics of the Twenty-first Century* (New York: Knopf, 2002).

78. Waltz, *Theory of International Politics*.

79. For elaboration of this argument see: James M. Goldgeier and Michael McFaul, "A Tale of Two Worlds: Core and Periphery in the Post-Cold War Era," *International Organization* 46:2 (1992), 467-91.

80. For predictions of NATO's demise, see: Mearsheimer, "Back to the Future," and Kenneth N. Waltz, "The Emerging Structure of International Politics," *International Security* 18:2 (1993), 44-79.

81. This divide was between what U.S. Secretary of Defense Donald Rumsfeld termed "Old Europe" and "New Europe."

82. Nikolas Sarkozy, as quoted in: Tabassum Zakaria, "Bush, Sarkozy promote ties over burgers, hot dogs," *Reuters*, August 11, 2007.

83. John Mearsheimer and Stephen Walt, *The Israel Lobby and US Foreign Policy* (New York: Farrar, Straus and Giroux, 2007).

84. For an insider's account of the transformation of this relationship from estrangement to engagement, see: Strobe Talbott, *Engaging India* (Washington: Brookings Institution Press, 2004).

85. Sharon Squassoni, "The India Nuclear Deal: The Top Rule-Maker Bends the Rules," *International Herald Tribune*, August 16, 2007.

86. The overthrow of Nazi puppet regimes in France, Austria, Belgium and the Netherlands also produced new allies for the United States. For a history of the post-World War II U.S.-Europe alliance, see: Philip Gordon and Jeremy Shapiro, *Allies at War: America, Europe, and the Crisis over Iraq* (New York: McGraw-Hill, 2004).

87. Joanna Gowa, *Ballots and Bullets: The Elusive Democratic Peace* (Princeton: Princeton University Press, 1999).

88. Several of the signatories to this letter, published on January 30, 2003, were actually from "old" Europe, including Britain, Spain, Italy, Portugal, and Denmark. The three East Central European signatories were Hungary, the Czech Republic,

and Poland. Another declaration of support was signed on February 18, 2003, and included Albania, Bulgaria, Croatia, Estonia, Latvia, Lithuania, Macedonia, Romania, Slovakia, and Slovenia.

89. "Poland to Send 1,000 More troops to Afghanistan in 2007," *Reuters*, September 15, 2006.

90. Whether this system will serve American national security interests is debatable. But if American leaders agree with their NATO allies that a ballistic missile defense system in Europe is needed, then having new allies in East Central Europe—allies created through the transformation of these regimes from autocracies to democracies—will be of real benefit. For an overview of the debates, see: Steven Hildreth and Carl Ek, *Long-Range Ballistic Missile Defense in Europe, CRS Report for Congress*, Order Code RL34051, June 22, 2007.

91. Realists posit that war is the only event that can change the balance of power in the international system in an abrupt way. Robert Gilpin, *War and Change in World Politics* (Cambridge, UK: Cambridge University Press, 1981), 203.

92. See: Peter Schweizer, *Victory: The Reagan Administration's Secret Strategy that Hastened the Collapse of the Soviet Union* (New York: Atlantic Monthly Press, 1994).

93. Author's interviews with Nikolai Ryzhkov, former prime minister of the USSR and Politburo member of the Communist Party of the Soviet Union, summer 1992. Transcripts of these interviews are deposited in the Hoover Institution Archives.

94. Pavel Podvig, "Did Star Wars Help to End the Cold War? Soviet Response to the SDI Program," unpublished manuscript, March 14, 2007. Twenty-five years later, the United States still lacks a ballistic missile defense system capable of repelling a Russian nuclear attack.

95. For details, see: Michael McFaul, *Russia's Unfinished Revolution: Political Change from Gorbachev to Putin* (Ithaca: Cornell University Press, 2001).

96. Realists, in contrast, posit that war is the only event that can change the balance of power in the international system in an abrupt way. See, for instance: Gilpin, *War and Change*, 203.

97. Reagan, "Address to Members of the British Parliament," in *Administration of Ronald Reagan, 1982* (Washington: Government Printing Office, 1983), 743.

98. Edward Mansfield and Jack Snyder, "Democratization and the Danger of War," *International Security* 20 (1995), 5-38.

99. Stephen E. Hanson and Jeffrey S. Kopstein, "The Weimar/Russia Comparison," *Post-Soviet Affairs* 13:3 (1997), 252-83. Michael McFaul, "Thwarting the Specter of Russian Fascism," *Demokratizatsiya* 1:2 (1993), 1-19. Bill Perry, "Weimar Russia," *Hoover Digest* 1 (1998).

100. Michael McFaul, "The Precarious Peace: Domestic Politics in the Making of Russian Foreign Policy," *International Security* 22:3 (1998), 5-35.

101. On this era, see: Strobe Talbott, *Russia Hand: A Memoir of Presidential Diplomacy* (New York: Random House, 2002).

102. For elaboration, see: James Goldgeier and Michael McFaul, *Power and Purpose: American Policy toward Russia after the Cold War* (Washington: Brookings Institution Press, 2003).

103. As quoted in: Angela Stent, *Russia and Germany Reborn* (Princeton: Princeton University Press, 1999), 223.

104. Goldgeier and McFaul, *Power and Purpose*, chapter 9.

105. Although Yeltsin, and his emissary, Viktor Chernomyrdin, eventually did play a positive role in ending the crisis, there were many precarious moments in U.S.-Russian relations during the conflict, including a standoff between American and Russian forces in Pristina, Kosovo, that almost resulted in armed conflict. See: John Norris, *Collision Course: NATO, Russia, and Kosovo* (Westport: Praeger Press, 2005).

106. Russia, for example, is a member of the G-8, the OSCE, and the Council of Europe. However flawed, Russia developed a formal relationship with NATO in the 1990s through the Permanent Joint Council, which then became the NATO-Russia Council in 2002. See: James M. Goldgeier and Michael McFaul, "Russians as Joiners: Realist and Liberal Conceptions of Post-Communist Europe," in *After the Collapse of Communism: Comparative Lessons of Transition*, eds. Michael McFaul and Kathryn Stoner-Weiss (Cambridge, UK: Cambridge University Press, 2004).

107. Some right-wing radicals in Russia, including Vladimir Zhirinovsky, were threatening to send Russian volunteers into the theater in the Balkans. In 2003, Zhirinovsky also advocated military assistance to Saddam Hussein. After the U.S.-led invasion, it was later revealed that Zhirinovsky had profited handsomely from various schemes associated with the U.N.-administered oil-for-food program in Iraq.

108. Gagnon, *The Myth of Ethnic War*.

109. Edward Mansfield and Jack Snyder, *Electing to Fight: Why Emerging Democracies Go to War* (Cambridge, US: MIT Press, 2005), 206-12.

110. Michael McFaul, "Transitions from Postcommunism," *Journal of Democracy* 16:3 (2005), 5-19.

111. Jeane Kirkpatrick, *Dictatorship and Double Standards: Rationalism and Reason in Politics* (New York: Simon and Schuster, 1982).

112. Gaddis, *Strategies of Containment*, 338-39.

113. David Adesnik and Michael McFaul, "Engaging Autocratic Allies to Promote Democracy," *The Washington Quarterly* 29:2 (2006), 7-26.

114. John Owen IV, "Democracy, Realistically," *The National Interest*, Spring 2006, 35.

115. Stephen Walt, *Revolution and War* (Ithaca: Cornell University Press, 1996). David Armstrong, *Revolution and World Order: The Revolutionary in International Society* (Oxford, UK: Clarendon Press, 1993). Theda Skocpol, *States and Social Revolutions: A Comparative Analysis of France, Russia, and China* (Cambridge, UK: Cambridge University Press, 1979).

116. Juan Linz, *The Breakdown of Democratic Regimes: Crisis, Breakdown and Reequilibrium* (Baltimore: Johns Hopkins University Press, 1978).

117. According to Kenneth Pollack, a more accurate assessment of Mossadeq would reveal that, "By subverting Iran's election process and rallying popular support to depose the shah's Prime Minister, Mohammad Mossadeq, the lifelong constitutional democrat, had effectively made himself dictator of Iran." Kenneth M. Pollack, *The Persian Puzzle: The Conflict between Iran and America* (New York: Random House, 2004), 62.

118. Ahmed Rashid, *Taliban: Militant Islam, Oil & Fundamentalism in Central Asia* (New Haven: Yale University Press, 2000), 18.

119. As Rashid argues, "The US strategic absence allowed all the regional powers, including the newly independent CAR's [Central Asian Republics] to prop up competing warlords, thereby intensifying the civil war and guaranteeing its prolongation." Rashid, *Taliban*, 176.

120. On the possibilities of democracy taking hold if the U.S. adopted a serious and sustained strategy for fostering democratic development, see: Larry Diamond, *Squandered Victory: The American Occupation and the Bungled Effort to Bring Democracy to Iraq* (New York: Times Books, 2005), 19. As the title of his book underscores, Diamond shows how the U.S. failed to promote democracy in Iraq, but the book develops the hypothesis that democracy could have taken hold with a different U.S. strategy.

121. McFaul, *Russia's Unfinished Revolution*.

122. Vladimir Putin, "Speech at the Military Parade in Honor of the 62nd Anniversary of Victory in the Great Motherland War," May 9, 2007.

123. Owen, "Democracy, Realistically," 36.

124. Michael D. Ward and David R. Davis, "Sizing up the Peace Dividend: Economic Growth and Military Spending in the United States, 1948-1996," *The American Political Science Review* 86:3 (1992), 748-55. For further empirical studies on the complexity of the effect of military spending on the U.S. economy see: Alex Mintz, *The Political Economy of Military Spending in the United States* (London: Routledge, 1992), chapters 9-12.

125. See: Travis Sharp, "Tying U.S. Defense Spending to GDP: Bad Logic, Bad Policy," The Center for Arms Control and Non-Proliferation, April 15, 2008, http://www.armscontrolcenter.org/policy/securityspending/articles/tying_sp ending_to_gdp_bad_policy/

126. Alex Mintz and Chi Huang, "Defense Expenditures, Economic Growth, and the 'Peace Dividend'," *The American Political Science Review* 84:4 (1990), 1283-93.

127 Richard Hornik, "The Peace Dividend: Myth and Reality," *Time*, February 12, 1990, 22.

128. Owen, "Democracy, Realistically," 37.

129. For a discussion of the difficulties and proposed solutions for defense conversion in the U.S. see: J. Davidson Alexander, "Military Conversion Policies in the USA:

1940s and 1990s," *Journal of Peace Research* 31:1 (1994), 19-33. Kenneth Adelman and Norman Augustine, "Defense Conversion: Bulldozing the Management," *Foreign Affairs* 71:2 (1992), 26-47. Steve Chan, "Grasping the Peace Dividend: Some Propositions on the Conversion of Swords into Plowshares," *Mershon International Studies Review* 39:1 (1995), 53-95.

130. Anders Aslund, *Building Capitalism: The Transformation of the Former Soviet Bloc* (Cambridge, UK: Cambridge University Press, 2001), 401.

131. http://www.worldbank.org/fandd/english/0397/articles/040397.htm. This article is derived from "Worldwide Military Spending, 1990–95," IMF Working Paper No. 96/64 (June 1996).

132. Joseph Stiglitz and Linda J. Bilmes, *The Three Trillion Dollar War: The True Cost of the Iraq Conflict* (New York: W.W. Norton, 2008). The Congressional Budget Office has estimated that "$1 trillion to $2 trillion is more realistic..." Quoted in: David Herszenhorn, "Estimates of Iraq War Cost Were Not Close to Ballpark," *New York Times*, March 19, 2008, A9.

133. Joseph Stiglitz, "Seven Questions: Joe Stiglitz on How the Iraq War Is Wrecking the Economy," *Foreign Policy* (April 2008). http://www.foreignpolicy.com/story/cms.php?story_id=4246.

134. Edward Mansfield, Helen Milner, and Peter Rosendorff, "Free to Trade: Democracies, Autocracies, and International Trade," *American Political Science Review* 94:2 (2000), 305-21.

135. Helen Milner and Keiko Kubota, "Why the Move to Free Trade? Democracy and Trade Policy in the Developing Countries," *International Organization* 59 (2005), 112-13. Milner and Kubota show empirically that democratization has a greater effect on trade liberalization than do economic crises, the popularity of neoliberal economic policies, or external pressures from the West and international financial institutions such as the IMF and World Bank.

136. Adam Przeworski, *Democracy and the Market: Political and Economic Reforms in Eastern Europe and Latin America* (Cambridge, US: Cambridge University Press, 1991).

137. Joel Hellman, "Winners Take All: The Politics of Partial Reform," *World Politics* 50:2 (1998), 203-34.

138. http://dataweb.usitc.gov/scripts/prepro.asp. U.S. International Trade Commission Data. U.S. exports went from 1,025,199 in 1989 to 18,018,610 (in 1,000 dollars) for these countries. The specific countries investigated were Albania, Armenia, Azerbaijan, Belarus, Bulgaria, Czechoslovakia, Georgia, Germany DR, Hungary, Kazakhstan, Kyrgyzstan, Moldova, Poland, Romania, Russia, Tajikistan, Turkmenistan, Ukraine, and Uzbekistan.

139. Milner and Kubota, "Why the Move to Free Trade?"

140. Ivo Daalder and James Lindsay, "Restore Trust in America's Leadership," Brookings, Fall 2007, http://www.brookings.edu/articles/2007/fall_iraq_daalder.aspx.

Chapter 4

1. U.S. involvement in the Middle East is not driven solely by oil. During the Cold War, containing communism was the central motivation. Since then, worries about ideological threats have also motivated American foreign policy. But the large deposits of oil in the region mean that U.S. will be involved in the Middle East in the foreseeable future irrespective of the ebbs and flows of ideological threats.

2. Mark Mazzetti and Helene Cooper, "U.S. Arms Plan for Middle East Aims to Counter Iranian Power," New York Times, July 31, 2007, A6.

3. Michael McFaul, "Chinese Dreams, Persian Realities," Journal of Democracy 16:4 (2005), 74-82.

4. On why these factors facilitate democracy, see: Dankwart Rustow, "Transitions to Democracy: Towards a Dynamic Model," Comparative Politics 2:3 (1970), 337-63.

5. Adam Przeworski et al., Democracy and Development: Political Institutions and the Well Being in the World, 1950-1990 (Cambridge, UK: Cambridge University Press, 2000).

6. Iran has other motivations for obtaining nuclear weapons. See: Shahram Chubin, Iran's Nuclear Ambitions (Washington: Carnegie Endowment for International Peace, 2006).

7. Scott Sagan, "How to Keep the Bomb from Iran," Foreign Affairs 85:5 (2006), 45-59.

8. Robert Pape, Dying to Win: The Strategic Logic of Suicide Terrorism (New York: Random House, 2005).

9. Alan Kruger and David D. Latin, "Kto Kogo? A Cross-country Study of the Origins and Targets of Terrorism," in Terrorism, Economic Development, and Political Openness, eds. Phil Keefer and Norman Loayza (Cambridge, UK: Cambridge University Press, 2008), 165-66.

10. In its 2005 annual report, Freedom House observed: "Between 1999 and 2003, 70 percent of all deaths from terrorism were caused by terrorists and terrorist groups originating in Not Free societies, while only 8 percent of all fatalities were generated by terrorists and terror movements with origins in Free societies." Adrian Karatnycky, "Civic Power and Electoral Politics," in Freedom House, Freedom in the World 2005: The Annual Survey of Political Rights and Civil Liberties (New York: Freedom House, 2005), 10. See also: Dalia Dassa Kaye et al., More Freedom Less Terror? Liberalization and Political Violence in the Arab World (Santa Monica: RAND Corporation, 2008), xiv.

11. Olivier Roy, Globalized Islam: The Search for a New Ummah (New York: Columbia University Press, 2004). Gilles Kepel, The War for Muslim Minds: Islam and the West (Harvard: Harvard University Press, 2004), chapter 7.

12. The extent to which extremists can remain viable political groups in a democracy also depends heavily on the institutional design of the political system, and especially on the nature of the electoral law. Hamas, for instance, won a majority of

seats in the January 2006 parliamentary election without winning a majority of votes. See: "It's The Election System, Stupid: The Misleading Hamas Majority and the System that Created It," *Fair Vote*, February 3, 2006, http://fairvote.org/.

13. Socialist and communist parties faced a similar dilemma in Europe in the late nineteenth century. An essential component for making the choice of participation in the democratic process stick was an effective state. See: Sheri Berman, "Taming Extremist Parties: Lessons from Europe," *Journal of Democracy* 19:1 (2008), 5-18.

14. On the effects of limited liberalization on terrorism, see: Dassa Kaye et al., *More Freedom Less Terror?*

15. See: Robert Barro, *Determinants of Economic Growth: A Cross-Country Empirical Study* (Cambridge, US: The MIT Press, 1997), part 2. Barro finds that an increase in democracy in highly repressive regimes initially stimulates growth to a much greater degree than does democratization in less repressive regimes.

16. UNDP, *Arab Human Development Report 2004: Towards Freedom in the Arab World* (New York: UNDP, 2005), 2.

17. Paul Collier, *The Bottom Billion: Why the Poorest Countries are Failing and What Can Be Done About It* (New York: Oxford University Press, 2007), 64-79.

18. During both democratic and autocratic periods, Pakistan's Inter-Services Intelligence, or ISI, has supported the Taliban in Afghanistan. It is the lack of civilian control over this organization, however, that has allowed the ISI to support these terrorist groups. More democracy in Pakistan, in parallel with the development of a more capacious state, would presumably weaken if not eliminate this rogue activity by the ISI.

19. Gregory Gause, "Can Democracy Stop Terrorism?" *Foreign Affairs* 84:5 (2005), 62.

20. President George Bush, "National Strategy for Combating Terrorism," White House, July 4, 2006, http://www.whitehouse.gov/infocus/nationalsecurity/index.html.

21. Europe, in fact, has produced a much greater share of radical, violent fundamentalists than the Middle East. See: Roy, *Globalized Islam*.

22. The International Islamic Relief Organization and the Muslim World League are two examples. See: Steve Coll, *Ghost Wars: The Secret History of the CIA, Afghanistan, and Bin Laden, from the Soviet Invasion to September 10, 2001* (New York: Penguin Press, 2004), 278-79.

23. Congressional Research Service, "Saudi Arabia: Terrorist Financing Issues," *CRS Report to Congress*, December 4, 2004, http://www.fas.org/irp/crs/RL32499.pdf.

24. In 2007, Freedom House classified the regime as "unfree," giving it a rating of six out of seven with seven being the most autocratic regime type and one being the most democratic regime type. See: Freedom House, *Country Report 2007*, http://www.freedomhouse.org/template.cfm?page=22&year=2007&country=7197.

25. In 2008, Afghanistan had a Freedom House rating of five, making it a "partly free" country.

26. Martin Kremer, "Inside the Middle East: Now I'm a . . . Neorealist!" *Jerusalem Post*, August 27, 2007.

27. Steve Simon and Ray Takeyh, "We've Lost. Here's How to Handle It," *Washington Post*, June 17, 2007, B1.

28. Gause, "Can Democracy Stop Terrorism?" 62.

29. It is inaccurate, however, to assert that Hitler was elected chancellor in free and fair elections in 1933. Instead, M. Rainer Lepsius describes the undemocratic circumstances which lead to the Nazi electoral victories in the following terms: "The appointments and dismissals of Bruning, Papen, and Scleicher, and finally also the appointment of Hitler, were effected in the influence of Hindenburg on a very small and publicly irresponsible group of people. A process of gradual denaturation took place, covering up even the most obvious violations of constitutional rights. The depossession of the Prussian government by the Papen government on 20 July 1932 could still pretend to be legally justified by a presidential decree. This blurring of the categories of legality and legitimacy also served to make the seizure of power by Hitler look legal. He was appointed by the president but could not win a vote of confidence in Parliament. Therefore, the Reichstag was dissolved once more two days after his appointment, and new elections were scheduled for 5 March 1933. Hitler had five weeks without a constitutional basis to establish his rule and in particular to take over the police in Prussia, suppressing leftist forces and intimidating all opposition . . . The election on 5 March 1933, conducted under the unrestricted impact of Nazi propaganda, using all the suppressive power of the government, brought the Nazis 43.9 percent of the vote. . . . Pseudo-legality was transformed into a normal legitimacy, which in turn was used to destroy constitutional legality and to establish an undemocratic rule." M. Rainer Lepsius, "From Fragmented Party Democracy to Government by Emergency Decree and National Socialist Takeover: Germany," in *The Breakdown of Democratic Regimes: Europe*, eds. Juan Linz and Alfred Stepan (Baltimore: Johns Hopkins University Press, 1994), 49-50.

30. The Nazi party's popularity was already beginning to decline when it seized power and could have fallen even more dramatically had elections continued to occur. As James Sheehan reports, "Between September 1930 and July 1932, their share of the vote grew dramatically, from 18 to 37 percent, and then, in November, two months before taking power, they lost two million voters and declined to 33 percent. Party membership was even more unstable: although it also grew rapidly after 1930, as many as 40 percent of those who joined between 1925 and 1933 eventually left the party." See: James Sheehan "What Was in It for Them?" review of William Brustein's The Logic of Evil: The Social Origins of the Nazi Party, 1925-1933, in the *New York Times*, September 15, 1996, http://query.ny times.com/gst/fullpage.html?res=9E04E3DA1E3BF936A2575AC0A96095826.

For details, see: Richard Hamilton, *Who Voted for Hitler?* (Princeton: Princeton University Press, 1982).

31. Luis Martinez, *The Algerian Civil War: 1990-1998* (New York: Columbia University Press, 1998).

32. Politically constrained, illiberal contexts help the radicals and impede the development of liberal, secular political organizations. See: Tamara Cofman Wittes, *Freedom's Unsteady March: America's Role in Building Arab Democracy* (Washington: Brookings Institution Press, 2008), chapter 7.

33. When these arguments were advanced in negotiations between Palestinian and American leaders over the elections, the Palestinian side rightly countered that an election without Hamas' participation would not be seen as legitimate in the eyes of Palestinian citizens. Palestinian president Mahmoud Abbas was also confident that his Fatah party would win a majority of the seats.

34. Esther Pan, "Lebanon: Election Update," Council on Foreign Relations, June 6, 2005, http://www.cfr.org/publication/8156/#5.

35. Erdogan called for the 2007 elections in response to an effort by Turkey's military leaders to block Turkey's foreign minister and AK member Abdulahh Gul from becoming president. By affirming AK's popularity in free and fair elections, Erdogan made it politically untenable for the military to continue to impede Gul's election by parliament, which occurred on August 28, 2007.

36. For elaboration, see: Michael McFaul and Tamara Cofman Wittes, "Morocco's Elections: The Limits of Limited Reforms," *Journal of Democracy* 19:1 (2008), 19-33.

37. Shadi Hamid, "Islamists and the Failure of Nonviolent Action," in *Civilian Jihad: Popular Struggle, Democratization, and Governance in the Middle East*, ed. Maria J. Stephan (New York: Routledge, forthcoming 2009).

38. Mohammad Suliman Abu Rumman, "The Muslim Brotherhood in the 2007 Jordanian Parliamentary Elections: A Passing 'Political Setback' or Diminished Popularity?" *Friedrich-Ebert-Stiftung*, November 2007.

39. Amr Hamzawy, Marina Ottaway, and Nathan Brown, "What the Islamists Need to be Clear About: The Case of the Egyptian Muslim Brotherhood," *Policy Outlook* (Washington: Carnegie Endowment for International Peace, February 2007), 5.

40. Nathan Brown, Amr Hamzawy, and Marina Ottaway, "Islamist Movements and the Democratic Process in the Arab World: Exploring the Gray Zones," *Carnegie Papers*   67,   March   2006, http://www.carnegieendowment.org/publications/index.cfm?fa=view&id=18 095&prog=zgp.

41. Nathan Brown, *Islamist Movements and the Electoral Process in the Arab World*, unpublished manuscript, chapter 2, 3.

42. Wittes, *Freedom's Unsteady March*, 105.

43. These pressures are documented in: UNDP, *Arab Human Development Report 2002* (New York: UNDP, 2002).

Chapter 5

1. Benjamin Franklin, as cited in: Robert Kagan, *Dangerous Nation: America's Foreign Policy from Its Earliest Days to the Dawn of the Twentieth Century* (New York: Knopf, 2006), 39.

2. See, for instance: Congress of Communist and Workers Parties, *The Tasks of the Struggle Against Imperialism in the Modern Stage and the Unity of Action of the Communist and Workers Parties of All the Anti-Imperialist Forces* (Moscow: Polizdat, 1969). Rostislav Ulyanovsky, *Socialism and the Newly Independent Nations* (Moscow: Progress Publishers, 1974).

3. Tim Wiener, *Legacy of Ashes: The History of the CIA* (New York: Random House, 2007).

4. Joseph Nye, "The Decline of America's Soft Power," *Foreign Affairs* 83:3 (2004).

5. John Lewis Gaddis, *Strategies of Containment: A Critical Appraisal of Postwar American National Security Policy* (Oxford: Oxford University Press, 1982).

6. At the beginning of his administration, President Kennedy tried to move away from supporting NATO ally Portugal, and even provided modest sums of support for Angolan nationalist liberation movements. But he and subsequent presidents gradually moved away from this confrontational policy as Portugal's Azores islands became increasingly useful for NATO activities. A similar drama of conflicting interests played out regarding South Africa and Rhodesia.

7. Mary Dudzniak, *Cold War Civil Rights: Race and the Image of American Democracy* (Princeton: Princeton University Press, 2000), 26-27.

8. Ibid., 82.

9. Ivo Daalder and James Lindsay, *America Unbound: The Bush Revolution in Foreign Policy* (Washington: Brookings Institution Press, 2003).

10. Laura K. Donohue, *The Cost of Counterterrorism: Power, Politics, and Liberty* (New York: Cambridge University Press, 2008), 71-72.

11. Ibid., 80.

12. Freedom House, *Today's American: How Free?* (New York: Freedom House, 2008), 12.

13. Ibid., 8-9. These rendition practices began in the 1990s.

14. This outcome has occurred four times in U.S. history. For details on this electoral irregularity as well as others, see: Ibid., chapter 9.

15. For a comprehensive treatment of the effects of presidential rhetoric for advancing democracy, see: David Adesnik, "Reagan's 'Democratic Crusade': Presidential Rhetoric and the Remaking of American Foreign Policy." Ph.D. dissertation, Oxford University, 2006.

16. Jennifer Windsor, "Advancing Freedom Agenda: Time for a Recalibration," *The Washington Quarterly* 29:3 (2006), 29.

17. All too frequently, there is also a tendency for diplomats working in country or closely over time with a specific country to soften the message of democracy from higher ranks in the government when dealing directly with their counterparts

from other countries. These lower-level officials believe they need good contacts in foreign governments to get more important business done. The unintended consequence of their winks and nods about democracy is to undermine the credibility of their superiors, an especially troubling outcome when the superior in question is the president of the United States.

18. Anthony Lake, "Do the Doable," *Foreign Policy* 54 (1984), 121.

19. Anne-Marie Slaughter, *The Idea That Is America: Keeping Faith with Our Values in a Dangerous World* (New York: Basic Books, 2007).

20. Adam Przeworski et al., *Democracy and Development: Political Institutions and Well-Being in the World, 1950-1990* (Cambridge, UK: Cambridge University Press, 2000).

21. Carles Boix, *Democracy and Redistribution* (Cambridge, UK: Cambridge University Press, 2003), 11-12.

22. Even President Lincoln's call to arms at the beginning of the Civil War was initially motivated by his desire to preserve the Union and not free the slaves. In 1992, President George H. W. Bush sent American soldiers into Panama to restore democracy. In 1994, President Clinton sent American armed forces to Haiti to carry out a United Nations mandate to restore democracy, but this military occupation occurred without an actual military conflict as the ruling military junta simply capitulated.

23. Daalder and Lindsey in *America Unbound* argue that this deployment of military force is new. John Lewis Gaddis argues that it is not new. See: John Lewis Gaddis, *Surprise, Security, and the American Experience* (Cambridge, US: Harvard University Press, 2004).

24. Minxin Pei, Samia Amin, and Seth Garz count 200 cases of the American use of force since 1900, in which "nation-building" was attempted 17 times. Their definition of nation-building—not democracy promotion—includes three restricting criteria: (1) the declared U.S. goal is regime change, (2) large numbers of U.S. ground troops are deployed, and (3) American military and civilian personnel are involved in governing the occupied country for some period of time. See: Minxin Pei, Samia Amin, and Seth Garz, "Building Nations: The American Experience," in *Nation-Building: Beyond Afghanistan and Iraq*, ed. Frank Fukuyama (Baltimore: John Hopkins University Press, 2006), 64-65.

25. Pei, Amin, and Garz, Ibid., 64-85.

26. Jeffrey Pickering and Mark Peceny, "Forcing Democracy at Gunpoint," *International Studies Quarterly* 50:3 (2006), 552. They find a more positive relationship between U.N. intervention and democratization.

27. Ibid., 554.

28. The U.S. covertly supported the assassination of Dominican strongman Rafael Trujillo (a rather undemocratic means to promote democracy!), but then failed to intervene to protect democracy when Juan Bosch was overthrown just four years later, in a 1965 coup. The U.N.-backed restoration of democracy in Haiti

in 1994 marked a watershed moment in American foreign policy in that it was the first time U.S. forces were deployed explicitly and only to promote democracy. A decade later, however, democracy was only weakly rooted in Haiti.

29. Larry Diamond, *Squandered Victory: The American Occupation and the Bungled Effort to Bring Democracy to Iraq* (New York: Times Books, 2005). George Packer, *The Assassin's Gate: America in Iraq* (New York: Farrar, Straus and Giroux, 2005).

30. For a comprehensive and scathing review of the process, see: Nora Bensahel et al., *After Saddam: Prewar Planning and the Occupation of Iraq* (Santa Monica: RAND Corporation, 2008).

31. James Glanz and T. Christian Miller, "Official History Spotlights Iraq Rebuilding Blunders: Poor Planning, Waste and Deception Led to $100 Billion Failure, Report Says," *New York Times*, December 14, 2008, A1.

32. Diamond, *Squandered Victory*.

33. Przeworski et al., *Democracy and Development*.

34. On this list of countries, Zimbabwe may be the one exception where a U.N.-sanctioned military intervention could topple the existing dictatorship and quickly restore democratic rule, because Zimbabwe has had relatively successful democratic institutions in place before and because the situation has become so dire that a change in government could positively affect economic development, which in turn could facilitate democratic consolidation.

35. William Easterly, Shanker Satyanath, and Daniel Berger found that "surprisingly, once endogeneity is addressed, US and Soviet interventions have equally detrimental effects on the subsequent level of democracy; both decrease democracy by about 33%." See: William Easterly, Shanker Satyanath, and Daniel Berger, "Superpower Interventions and the Consequences for Democracy," *Brookings Global Economy and Development*, Working Paper 17 (January 2008).

36. Lance Davis and Stanley Engerman, "History Lesson: Sanctions: Neither War nor Peace," *Journal of Economic Perspectives* 17:2 (2003), 187-97.

37. Nikolay Marinov, "Do Sanctions Help Democracy? The US and EU's Record, 1977-2004," Center on Democracy, Development, and the Rule of Law Working Papers, no. 28 (November 2004), 1-24.

38. Nikolay Marinov, "Do Economic Sanctions Destabilize Country Leaders?" *American Journal of Political Science* 49:3 (2005), 564-76.

39. Marinov, "Do Sanctions Help Democracy?"

40. Neta Crawford and Audie Klotz, *How Sanctions Work: Lesson from South Africa* (London: MacMillan Press, 1999), 10.

41. Sarah Graham-Brown, "Sanctioning Iraq: A Failed Policy," *Middle East Report* 215 (2000), 8-13.

42. Clifton Morgan and Valerie Schwebach, "Fools Suffer Gladly: The Use of Economic Sanctions in International Crises," *International Studies Quarterly* 41 (1997), 28. See also: Robert Pape, "Why Sanctions Do Not Work," *International*

Security 22:2 (1997), 90-136. Morgan and Schewebach confirm the findings of the earlier literature but through a large-N study of sanctions, suggest the conditions under which sanctions can work.

43. Marinov, "Do Sanctions Destabilize Country Leaders?" 564.

44. As a rule of thumb, the world's democratic community should take its cues about sanctions from the democratic opposition in the target country. If those sitting in jail for their democratic beliefs advocate sanctions, then the United States should support them. If democratic leaders argue against sanctions, then American policymakers should not second-guess their thinking. The struggle against apartheid in South Africa is the classic example of a situation in which local democrats supported sanctions. The current situation in Iran is a counter example in which most Iranian human rights leaders do not support sanctions against the Islamic Republic.

45. "With Friends Like These . . . Condoleezza Rice's Inglorious Moment," *Washington Post*, April 18, 2006, A18.

46. Egypt today ranks in the top ten recipients of democracy assistance, yet everyone understands that most of these funds are not targeted to foster real democratic change.

47. David Adesnik and Michael McFaul, "Engaging Autocratic Allies to Promote Democracy," *The Washington Quarterly*, 29:2 (2006), 7-26.

48. Terry Lynn Karl, "Petroleum and Political Pacts: The Transition to Democracy in Venezuela," *Latin American Research Review* 22 (1987), 63-94. Guillermo O'Donnell and Philippe Schmitter, *Transitions from Authoritarian Rule: Tentative Conclusions about Uncertain Democracies* (Baltimore: Johns Hopkins University Press, 1986), chapter 4. A pact is not a necessary condition for a successful democratic transition, but most certainly enhances the probability of success. See: Terry Lynn Karl and Philippe Schmitter, "Democratization around the Globe: Opportunities and Risks," in *World Security*, Michael Klare and Daniel Thomas (New York: St Martin's Press, 1994), 43-62.

49. Ronald Reagan, November 12, 1984, as cited in: A. David Adesnik and Sunyak Kim, "If at First You Don't Succeed: The Puzzle of South Korea's Democratic Transition," CDDRL Working Paper, 2008, 20.

50. Ibid.

51. George Shultz, *Turmoil and Triumph: Diplomacy, Power, and the Victory of the American Ideal* (New York: Simon and Schuster, 1993), 970.

52. The CAAA severely restricted lending to South Africa and imposed import bans on iron, steel, coal, uranium, textiles, and agricultural goods. Strategic materials, diamonds, and most forms of gold were omitted. Philip Levy, "Sanctions on South Africa: What did they do?" *American Economic Review* 89:2 (1999), 415-20.

53. Shultz, *Turmoil and Triumph*, 901.

54. Chester Crocker, *High Noon in Southern Africa: Making Peace in a Rough Neighborhood* (New York: Norton, 1992).

55. In particular the Americans prodded their Chilean counterparts to run positive, upbeat television ads, even if the message was to vote "no." The NDI also worked closely with Chilean pollsters affiliated with the democratic opposition to organize a parallel vote tabulation or quick count similar to the NAMFREL exercise in the Philippines. The NED also provided financial assistance to Chilean and U.S. NGOs for election monitoring training to ensure against fraud. For details of groups supported, see the interview with NED President Carl Gershman in *El Mercurio*, January 10, 1988.

56. National Endowment for Democracy, "NED 20th Anniversary Timeline," http://www.ned.org/about/nedtimeline.html.

57. For typologies and criteria for distinguishing amongst Islamist movements, see: Tamara Cofman Wittes, *Freedom's Unsteady March: America's Role in Building Arab Democracy* (Washington: Brookings Institution Press, 2008). Nathan Brown, Amr Hamzawy, and Marina Ottaway, "Islamist Movements and the Democratic Process in the Arab World: Exploring the Gray Zones," *Carnegie Papers* 61 (Washington: Carnegie Endowment for International Peace, March 2006).

58. Amr Hamzawy, "The Key to Arab Reform: Moderate Islamists," *CEIP Policy Brief* 40 (2005), 1.

59. Joseph Biden, "A New Approach to Pakistan," *The Huffington Post*, November 8, 2007, http://www.huffingtonpost.com/joe-biden/a-new-approach-to-pakista_b_71733.html.

60. U.S. efforts to promote democracy in Poland followed a similar dynamic of sanctions and reengagement of the regime paralleled by direct support to the opposition. See: Greg Domber, "Evaluating International Influence on Democratic Development: Poland 1980-1989," CDDRL Working Paper, 2008.

61. Shultz, Turmoil and Triumph, 159.

62. Ibid, 159.

63. Shultz, *Turmoil and Triumph*, 267. Shultz never saw negotiations or expanding contacts with Soviets and Americans as a concession to Moscow or a signal of legitimacy for the communist dictatorship. In the debate about opening consulates in both countries—a move that some hardliners at the time saw as a sign of weakness—Shultz firmly supported the idea as a change in the American national interest. As he quotes on page 275 from a memorandum he wrote in 1982, "I believe the next step on our part should be to propose the negotiation of a new U.S.-Soviet cultural agreement and the opening of U.S. and Soviet consulates in Kiev and New York. . . . Both of these proposals will sound good to the Soviets, but are unambiguously in our interest when examined from a hard headed American viewpoint."

64. Bush went out of his way to aid the Soviet Union's survival, including most famously in a speech in Kiev in August 1991, when he warned of the dangers of ethnic conflict fueled by state collapse. Bush proclaimed, "We support the struggle in this great country for democracy and economic reform." At the same time, he

warned advocates of Ukrainian independence that "freedom cannot survive if we let despots flourish or permit seemingly minor restrictions to multiply until they form chains, until they form shackles. . . . Yet freedom is not the same as independence. America will not support those who seek independence in order to replace a far-off tyranny with local despotism. They will not aid those who promote a suicidal nationalism based upon ethnic hatred. We will support those who want to build democracy." President George H.W. Bush, "Remarks to the Supreme Soviet of the Republic of the Ukraine in Kiev, Soviet Union," August 1, 1991, http://bushlibrary.tamu.edu/papers/1991/91080102.html.

65. James Goldgeier and Michael McFaul, *Power and Purpose: U.S. Policy toward Russia after the Cold War* (Washington: Brookings Institution Press, 2003).

66. More generally, a more benign international environment anchored by a liberal democratic power rather than threatening autocratic powers in Europe and Asia made it safer for internal reform inside the Soviet Union. This argument is persuasively developed in: Daniel Duedney and G. John Ikenberry, "The International Sources of Soviet Change," *International Security* 16:3 (1991), 74-118. Jack Snyder, "International Leverage on Soviet Domestic Change," *World Politics* 42:1 (1989), 1-30.

67. For an overview, see: Linda Cook, *Labor and Liberalization: Trade Unions in the New Russia* (New York: Twentieth Century Fund Press, 1997), chapter 5.

68. At its May 1988 meeting, the NED board adopted a resolution that considered support to national democratic movements crucial for promoting democracy within the Soviet Union. Board member Zbigniew Brzezinski, elected in 1987, played a central role in pushing NED in this direction. (Interview and email exchange with Nadia Diuk, NED program officer for this region since 1987, March 4, 2003). In 1991, NED approved a major grant to fund a printing press for the Democratic Russia movement. Similarly, NDI initially directed "its efforts towards the institutions which are spearheading democratic reform—the the city soviets and the republics of Russia and Ukraine." NDI, *Report of the Survey Mission to the Soviet Union: July 29-August 3, 1990* (Washington: 1990), 22. For a description of NDI programs in the Soviet Union, see: NDI, *The Commonwealth of Independent States: Democratic Developments Issues and Options* (Washington: January 1992).

69. NDI, *Report of the Survey Mission to the Soviet Union*, 22. For a description of NDI programs in the Soviet Union, see: NDI, *The Commonwealth of Independent States.*

70. Since its inception in 1984, NED has received money directly from the U.S. Congress. In parallel to its own grants programs, NED also gives grants to NDI, IRI, the AFL-CIO and others. As these NGOs expanded their programs in the former Soviet Union, they began to receive the greater share of the funds for the region from the USAID.

71. Domber, "Evaluating International Influence," 46.

72. Abbas Milani, Michael McFaul, and Larry Diamond, "Playing for the Long Haul in Iran: A Dual Track Strategy for Arms Control and Democratization," *Brown Journal of World Affairs* 12:2 (2006), 259-89.

73. Thomas Carothers, "The End of the Transition Paradigm," *Journal of Democracy* 13:1 (2002), 5-21.

74. In early 2005, Kyrgyzstan's semi-autocratic president Askar Akayev also suffered an ouster at least in part due to the factors described in this essay, but the nature of the events remains too murky—and their implications for democracy too uncertain—to be included in this analysis at this time.

75. For elaboration on these factors, see: Michael McFaul, "Transitions from Post-communism," *Journal of Democracy* 16:3 (2005), 5-19.

76. In addition to Ukrainian poll watchers, the Organization for Security and Cooperation in Europe (OSCE), IRI, NDI, and the U.S.-Ukrainian Foundation deployed international election monitoring teams to observe the Ukrainian election.

77. Michael McFaul, *The Democratic Breakthrough Serbia: Lessons Learned* (Washington: National Endowment for Democracy, 2005). Lincoln Mitchell, *Uncertain Democracy: U.S. Foreign Policy and Georgia's Revolution* (Philadelphia: University of Pennsylvania Press, 2008). Michael McFaul, "Ukraine Imports Democracy: External Influences on the Orange Revolution," *International Security* 32:2 (2007) 45-83.

78. "Declaration by the Presidency of the European Union on Ukraine," November 22, 2004, www.eu2004.nl/default.asp?CMS_ITEM=B2C459EC419347 E59AA019D53CAE787EX1X60623X25.

79. In particular, the Yellow Pora student movement had significant contacts with civic resistance activists from Slovakia, Serbia, and Georgia through the facilitating efforts of Freedom House and the German Marshall Fund. For instance, Freedom House organized and funded a summer camp for Ukrainian youth activists and invited trainers from the Serbian youth movement, Otpor, to attend. Pavol Demes, a leader of the OK 98 movement in Slovakia, traveled to Ukraine several times in the months leading up to the Orange Revolution to train and provide support for Yellow Pora. In their training programs, Znayu also used trainers from Serbia and Georgia. For details, see: McFaul, "Ukraine Imports Democracy."

80. The most common strategy for supporting civil society is direct financial assistance to pay for salaries, equipment (particularly computers, fax machines, and photocopiers), and programs. American organizations also provide training to their NGO partners on such issues as internal governance, fundraising, communications, lobbying, and coalition building. In some countries, American organizations support infrastructure hubs—offices with computers, Internet access, copying machines, and meetings rooms—that can be used by several NGOs.

81. Thomas Carothers, *Aiding Democracy Abroad: The Learning Curve* (Washington: The Brookings Institution, 1999), 212.

82. Steven Finkel, Anibal Perez-Linan, and Mitchel Seligson, "Effects of U.S. Foreign Assistance on Democracy Building: Results of a Cross-National Quantitative Study," Vanderbilt University, November 25, 2005, version 31. Steven Finkel, Anibal Perez-Linan, and Mitchell Seligson, "The Effects of U.S. Foreign Assistance on Democracy Building: 1990-2003," *World Politics* 59 (2007), 404-39.

83. Finkel, Perez-Linan, and Seligson, "The Effects of U.S. Foreign Assistance on Democracy Building," 421. Freedom House scores rate a country's level of democracy. Finkel, Perez-Linan, and Seligson also run models using Polity IV instead of Freedom House and generate the same result.

84. Finkel, Perez-Linan, and Seligson, "The Effects of U.S. Foreign Assistance on Democracy Building," 424. Finkel, Perez-Linan, and Seligson also discovered some sub-sectoral correlations between assistance and outcomes, finding that a positive relationship exists between AID spending on elections, civil society, and governance on the one hand and these sectors in developing democracies on the other, but a negative relationship exists between AID spending on human rights and democratic development. Finally, Finkel, Perez-Linan, and Seligson find a lag time: "The results indicate that if DG obligations were to increase on average by 10 million dollars over a three-year period, then the total impact on democratic growth would be more than one-third of a unit on the Freedom House scale, as opposed to the one-quarter unit estimated in the baseline model. The lag effect itself suggests that democracy programs may take several years to mature; and the fact that both lagged and contemporaneous effects are significant suggests that the effects of DG assistance are to some degree cumulative, with effects in one year augmenting effects in the next."

85. See: Eric Bjornlund, *Beyond Free and Fair: Monitoring Elections and Building Democracy* (Baltimore: John Hopkins University Press, 2004).

86. When NGOs rely on locals for financial support, they must constantly recalibrate their work to meet the demands of their constituencies. Foreign donors can undermine this link. When American donors define goals that contradict local needs, local NGO leaders often adjust their activities to placate American interests, frequently at the expense of working effectively and organically within their own societies. In her research in Russia, Lisa McIntosh Sundstrom found that Western assistance to Russian NGOs was effective when aimed at realizing a universal norm of preventing bodily harm (such as domestic violence against women or conscription) but unsuccessful when the norm promoted by the West did not resonate inside Russia (i.e., gender equality at the workplace). See: Lisa McIntosh Sundstrom, *Funding Civil Society: Foreign Assistance and NGO Development in Russia* (Stanford: Stanford University Press, 2006).

87. Carothers, *Aiding Democracy Abroad*, 221.

88. Seymour Martin Lipset, "The Indispensability of Political Parties," *Journal of Democracy* 11:1 (2000), 48-55.

89. Thomas Carothers, *Confronting the Weakest Link: Aiding Political Parties in New Democracies* (Washington: Carnegie Endowment for International Peace, 2006), 4.

90. The definitive, most well-balanced evaluation of American and European political party assistance is Carothers, *Confronting the Weakest Link*.

91. Thomas Carothers, "The Problem of Knowledge," in *Promoting the Rule of Law Abroad: In Search of Knowledge*, eds. Thomas Carothers and Erik Jensen (Washing-

ton: Carnegie Endowment for International Peace, 2006), 15, 21. The very title of Carothers book underscores the low level of understanding we have about how rule of law emerges or can be nurtured.

92. Thomas Heller, "An Immodest Postscript," in *Beyond Common Knowledge*, eds. Jensen and Thomas Heller (Stanford: Stanford University Press, 2003), 393. In such contexts, state leaders can easily abuse the rights of private citizens, dominate poor and understaffed courts, and quickly learn that maintaining loyalty of coercive elements of the state—the police, army, and intelligence services—is a more important condition for staying in power than providing rule of law to citizens. Rather that attempt the dangerous reform of redirecting these ministries to advance the rule of law, new political leaders instead cut deals with coercive agents, allowing corruption in exchange for loyalty.

93. Francis Fukuyama, *State-Building: Governance and World Order in the 21st Century* (Ithaca: Cornell University Press, 2004), 59. Fukuyama in particular highlights the difficulties in monitoring legal systems because they have such high transaction volumes. Frank Upham emphasizes a similar point in "Mythmaking in the Rule-of-Law Orthodoxy," *Promoting the Rule of Law Abroad*, ed. Carothers, 100-01.

94. In addition to Carothers' *Promoting the Rule of Law Abroad, Jensen and Heller's Beyond Common Knowledge*, and Rachel Kleinfeld's *Lawyers as Soldiers, Judges as Missionaries: US and EU Strategies to Build the Rule of Law from 1990-2006*, D. Phil dissertation (Oxford: Oxford University, 2009), other important studies include: Linn Hammergren, *The Politics of Justice Reform in Latin America: The Peruvian Case in Comparative Perspective* (Boulder: Westview Press, 1998). Rachel Sieder, *Rule of Law in Latin America: The International Promotion of Judicial Reform* (London: Institute of Latin American Studies, 2001).

95. As Linn Hammergren, one of the world's leading experts in the field, observes, "USAID arguably has produced the greatest number of assessments, studies, and evaluations, but it has done a poor job of organizing and disseminating the results, even for internal consumption." Linn Hammergren, "International Assistance to Latin American Justice Programs: Toward an Agenda of Reforming the Reformers," in *Beyond Common Knowledge*, eds. Jensen and Heller, 291.

96. On the U.S. positive intervention on the writing of the Russian legal code, see: Matt Spence, "The Complexity of Success in Russia," in *Promoting the Rule of Law Abroad*, ed. Carothers, 217-49.

97. Again, democratic transition is the big engine of change for decreases in human rights violations. In several countries in the region, democratic transition was a necessary condition for better human rights practices.

98. AID implementers started this program in the early 1990s, even though Russian experts warned that such a foreign practice would never work. For years, the pilot program in nine regions stagnated, but a 2001 amendment to the constitution mandated the expansion of jury trials to the entire country. Opinion polls

suggest that trust in juries among Russians is growing, and Russia's experiment with jury trials has produced some unexpected outcomes in which the will of ordinary citizens trumped the preferences of the state. Seth Mydans, "Rare Russian Jury Acquits Scientist in Spy Case," *The New York Times*, December 30, 2003, A7.

99. Writing on efforts to replicate American formal legal institutions and laws, Carothers—the editor of one of the most comprehensive studies of rule of law promotion published to date—offers the following grim assessment: ". . . it has become painfully clear on countless occasions that trying to promote the rule of law by simply rewriting another country's law on the basis of Western models achieves very little, given problems with laws not adapted to the local environment, the lack of capacity to implement or enforce the laws, and the lack of public understanding of them." As for training and exchange programs, Carothers laments that this method for promoting rule of law "is usually rife with shortcomings and rarely does much good." See: Carothers, "The Problem of Knowledge," 25. The most comprehensive assessment of American rule of law programs in Latin America found limited results, as did a similar study of these programs in the former communist world. See: U.S. General Accounting Office (GAO), *Foreign Assistance: Promoting Judicial Reform to Strengthen Democracies* (Washington: GAO, 1993). GAO, *Former Soviet Union: U.S. Rule of Law Assistance Has Had Limited Impact* (Washington: GAO, 2001).

100. Rachel Kleinfeld, "Competing Definitions of the Rule of Law," in *Promoting the Rule of Law Abroad*, eds. Carothers and Jensen, 51.

101. Upham, "Myth-making in the Rule of Law Orthodoxy," 76.

102. GAO, Foreign Assistance: Promoting Judicial Reform, 4.

103. Monroe E. Price, Bethany Davis Noll, and Daniel De Luce, "Mapping Media Assistance," *The Programme in Comparative Media Law, and Policy* (Oxford: University of Oxford, 2002).

104. Carothers, *Aiding Democracy Abroad*, 241. In 1991, for instance, NED agreed to purchase a printing press for the Russian opposition movement, Democratic Russia. By the time the press started to operate, however, Democratic Russia had dissolved into several factions that then fought over control of the press.

105. Some recent progress has been made. For a bibliography of this emerging literature as well as several original case studies examining the role of external actors in fostering and impeding democratic transitions, go to: http://cddrl.stanford.edu/.

106. Philippe Schmitter and Imco Brouwer, *Conceptualizing, Researching and Evaluating Democracy Promotion and Protection, European University of Florence EUI* Working Paper SPS 99:9 (1999), 11.

107. Larry Diamond, *The Spirit of Democracy: The Struggle to Build Free Societies throughout the World* (New York: Times Book, 2008), 323.

108. For elaboration, see: Diamond, *Spirit of Democracy*, 325, especially footnote 26.

109. General John Abizaid used these percentages several years ago. For more recent

comments in a similar spirit, see: Peter Spiegel, "Defense Chief Gates Wants to Spend More on U.S. Diplomacy," *Los Angeles Times*, July 16, 2008. Secretary of Defense Robert Gates, "Dean Acheson Lecture," United States Institute of Peace, October 15, 2008, www.usip.org/events/acheson/gates.html.

110. Pat Towell, Stephen Daggett, and Amy Belasco, "Defense: FY 2008 Authorization and Appropriations," Congressional Research Service, January 23, 2008, http://www.fas.org/sgp/crs/natsec/RL33999.pdf.

111. Susan Epstein, Nina Serafino, and Francis Miko, "Democracy Promotion: Cornerstone of U.S. Foreign Policy?" Congressional Research Service, December 26, 2007, http://www.fas.org/sgp/crs/row/ RL34296.pdf.

112. Randall Tobias, "Testimony on FY 2008 Foreign Assistance Budget," U.S. Department of State, March 28, 2007, http://www.state.gov/f/releases/remarks2007/82423.htm.

113. U.S. Ambassador Susan McCaw, Marshall Plan 60th Anniversary, June 5, 2007, http://www.usembassy.at/en/embassy/speeches/060507a.htm.

114. Howard Berman, "Opening Remarks by Chairman Berman at hearing, 'Foreign Assistance Reform in the New Administration: Challenges and Solutions,'" United States House of Representatives, House Committee on Foreign Affairs, Committee Press, April 23, 2008, http://www.internationalrelations.house.gov/press_display.asp?id=507.

115. To formalize the rank would require Congressional legislation that has not yet been requested, let alone secured.

116. Secretary of State Condoleezza Rice, "Transformational Diplomacy," January 18, 2006, http://www.state.gov/secretary/rm/2006/59306.htm.

117. For negative assessments of this reform, see: Dennis Shin, Charles Uphaus, Todd Shelton, and Evan Elliot, "Why the 'F' Process Deserves That Grade," *Foreign Service Journal* (2008), 51-55. Gerald Hyman, "Assessing Secretary of State Rice's Reform of U.S. Foreign Assistance," *Carnegie Paper*, February 2008, http://www.carnegieendowment.org/publications/index.cfm?fa=view&id=19906&prog=zgp&proj=zdrl.

118. Thomas Carothers, "A League of their Own," *Foreign Policy* 167 (2008), 43.

Chapter 6

1. Jon Pevehouse, *Democracy from Above: Regional Organizations and Democratization* (Cambridge, UK: Cambridge University Press, 2005).

2. Some human rights advocates prefer to distinguish the focus on human rights from democracy. Historically, however, the two are closely intertwined. Freedom House's scores for "civil liberties" and "political liberties" are highly correlated.

3. See: Kofi Annan, "Why Democracy is an International Issue," Cyril Foster Lecture, Oxford University, June 19, 2001.

4. For details, see: Edward Newman and Roland Rich, eds., *The UN Role in Promoting Democracy: Between Ideals and Reality* (NewYork: United Nations Press, 2004).
5. Kofi Annan, "In Larger Freedom: Toward Development, Security, and Human Rights for All," *Report of the Secretary-General to the 59th Session of the General Assembly*, March 21, 2005, 38.
6. See: James Dobbins et al., *The UN's Role in Nation-Building* (Santa Monica: RAND Corporation, 2005).
7. Pevehouse, *Democracy from Above*, 25.
8. Anthony Lake, "From Containment to Enlargement," Department of States Dispatch 4:39 (1993), 3.
9. Ronald Asmus, *Opening NATO's Door: How the Alliance Remade Itself for a New Era* (NewYork: Columbia University Press, 2002).
10. John Ikenberry, *After Victory: Institutions, Strategic Restraint, and the Rebuilding of Order after MajorWars* (Princeton: Princeton University Press, 2001), chapter 6.
11. Adam Przeworski et al., *Democracy and Development: Political Institutions and theWell-Being in theWorld, 1950-1990* (Cambridge, UK: Cambridge University Press, 2000).
12. Daniel Thomas, *The Helsinki Effect: International Norms, Human Rights and the Demise of Communism* (Princeton: Princeton University Press, 2001). Natan Sharansky, *The Case for Democracy: The Power of Freedom to Overcome Tyranny and Terror* (NewYork: Public Affairs, 2004).
13. OSCE, Office for Democratic Institutions and Human Rights, http://www.osce.org/odihr/13421.html.
14. OSCE observer missions played especially critical roles in overturning fraudulent elections in Georgia in 2003 and Ukraine in 2004. See: Jonathan Wheatley, *Georgia from National Awakening to Rose Revolution: Delayed Transition in the Former Soviet Union* (London: Ashgate Publishing, 2005). Michael McFaul, "Ukraine Imports Democracy: External Influences on the Orange Revolution," *International Security* 32:2 (2007), 45-83.
15. Amichai Magen, "Transformative Engagement Through Law: The Acquis Communautaire as an Instrument of EU External Influence," *European Journal of Law Reform* 9:3 (2007), 361-92. Richard Youngs, *The European Union and the Promotion of Democracy* (Oxford: Oxford University Press, 2001). Michael Emerson, ed., *Democratization in the European Neighbourhood* (CESP: 2005). Frank Schimmelfenning, "The Community Trap: Liberal Norms, Rhetorical Action and the Eastern Enlargement of the EU," *International Organization* 55:1 (2001), 47-80. Heather Grabbe, *The EU's Transformative Power: Europeanization Through Conditionality in Eastern Europe* (NewYork: Palgrave Macmillan, 2006). Geoffrey Pridham, *Designing Democracy: EU Enlargement and Regime Change in Post-Communist Europe* (New York: Palgrave Macmillan, 2005).
16. Beyond the accession process, the EU has launched a series of other mechanisms for promoting democracy, including the European Initiative on Democracy and Human Rights (EIDHR); the Stabilization and Association Process for the Balkan

countries; the Euro-Mediterranean Partnership program, for socio-economic development and governance reform in North Africa and the Eastern Mediterranean;
the European Neighborhood Policy (which offers a stake in the Single Market and
the prospect of enhanced contractual links with the EU in return for progress on
a wide range of domestic governance reforms); as well as political conditionality
embedded in the Cotonou framework governing EU relations with the African
and Pacific group of countries. In July 2008, the EU launched a new regional network called the Mediterranean Union, whose founding charter also devoted substantial attention to furthering democratic development in a region rich with
autocratic regimes. Many of the individual EU states run democracy promotion
programs as well. Juan Mendez, "The Inter-American System of Protection: Its
Contributions to the International Law of Human Rights," in *Realizing Human
Rights: Moving from Inspiration to Impact*, eds. Samantha Power and Graham Allison
(NewYork: St. Martin's Press, 2000), pp. 111-42. Marc Peceny, "The Democratic
Peace and Contemporary U.S. Military Interventions," unpublished manuscript
presented to International Studies Association, March 14-18, 2000, 5.

17. Organization of American States, "Inter-American Democratic Charter," Lima,
September 11, 2001, 3.

18. On the OAS's success in reversing Fujimori's autogolpe, see: Pevehouse, *Democracy from Above*, 129-34.

19. See: Rizal Sukma, "Political Development: A Democracy Agenda for ASEAN," in
Hard Choices: Security, Democracy, and Regionalism in Southeast Asia, ed. Donald Em-
merson (Stanford: Walter H. Shorenstein Asia-Pacific Research Center Books,
2008), 135-50.

20. From Article One of OIC Charter, at http://www.oic-oci.org/oicnew/is11/
english/Charter-en.pdf.

21. Council for a Community of Democracies, http://www.ccd21.org/.

22. Diplomat's Handbook, http://www.diplomatshandbook.org.

23. For recommendations on how to improve the community, see: Theodore Piccone,
"Democracies: In a League of their Own? Lessons Learned from the Community
of Democracies," *Foreign Policy at Brookings*, Policy Paper 8 (2008).

24. Foundation for the Future, http://www.foundationforfuture.org//?q=en/.

25. Address of President George W. Bush, Concert Noble, Brussels, February 21,
2005.

26. OECD, Partnership for Democratic Governance, http://www.oecd.org/
pages/0,3417,en_39406396_ 39407430_1,00.html.

27. Fred Hiatt, "A Few Words between Friends," *The Washington Post*, February 15,
2005, A17, http://www.washingtonpost.com/wp-dyn/articles/A24750-
2005Feb14.html.

28. Joel Brinkley, "Latin Nations Resist Plans for Monitors of Democracy," *NewYork
Times*, June 6, 2005, http://www.nytimes.com/2005/06/06/international/
americas/06oas.html.

29. For reform proposals, see: Stephen Stedman, ed., *A More Secure World: Our Shared Responsibility* (New York: United Nations, 2004). Newt Gingrich and George Mitchell, co-chairs, *American Interests and UN Reform: Report of the Task Force on the United Nations* (Washington: U.S. Institute of Peace, 2005).

30. Harvey Morris, "Conflict intervention push close to the 'outer limit of peace-keeping'," *Financial Times*, July 24, 2008, 5.

31. Program on International Policy Studies (PIPA), Chicago Council on Foreign Relations, and Knowledge Networks, "Americans on Promoting Democracy," September 29, 2005, 10, http://www.pipa.org/OnlineReports/220Am-Role_World/Democratization_Sep05/Democratization_Sep09_rpt_re-vised.pdf.

32. Steven Weisman, "Drive on Corruption Angers Some at World Bank," *New York Times*, September 14, 2006, C1.

33. Jennifer Windsor, "Advancing the Freedom Agenda: Time for a Recalibration?" *The Washington Quarterly* 29:3 (2006), 30.

34. The World Movement held its fifth Congress in April 2008 in Kyiv, Ukraine.

35. This is the "boomerang" effect discussed in: Margaret Keck and Kathryn Sikkink, *Activists Beyond Borders: Advocacy Networks in International Politics* (Ithaca: Cornell University Press, 1998).

36. On the techniques and philosophy of these groups, see: The Centre for Applied Nonviolent Action and Strategies, http://www.canvasopedia.org. Robert Helvey, *On Strategic Nonviolent Conflict: Thinking about the Fundamentals* (Boston: Albert Einstein Institution, 2004). On effectiveness, see: Maria Stephan and Erica Chenoweth, "Why Civil Resistance Works," *International Security* 33:1 (2008), 7-44. Adrian Karatnycky and Peter Ackerman, *How Freedom Is Won: From Civic Resistance to Durable Democracy* (Washington: Freedom House, 2005). Stephen Krasner, *Sovereignty: Organized Hypocrisy* (Princeton: Princeton University Press, 1999).

37. The seminal article in favor of democracy as a human right is: Thomas Frank, "The Emerging Right to Democratic Governance," *American Journal of International Law* 86 (1992), 46-91. See also: Morton Halperin, "Guaranteeing Democracy," *Foreign Policy* 91 (1993), 105-22. Roland Rich, "Bringing Democracy into International Law," *Journal of Democracy* 12:3 (2001), 20-34. Carl Gershman, "Democracy as Policy Goal and Universal Value," *The Whitehead Journal of Diplomacy and International Relations* 6:1 (2005), 19-38. Judith Large and Timothy Sisk, *Democracy, Conflict, and Human Security: Pursuing Peace in the 21st Century* (Stockholm: International Institute for Democracy and Electoral Assistance, 2006). For a compelling opposite view, see: Joshua Cohen, "A Human Right to Democracy?" in *The Egalitarian Conscience*, ed. Christine Sypnowich (Oxford: Oxford University Press, 2006). Gareth Evans and Mohamed Sahnoun, "The Responsibility to Protect," *Foreign Affairs* 81:6 (2002), 99-110.

38. To this list, some might add the U.N.-sanctioned mission to protect the Kurds

after the first Gulf War, and the NATO peacekeeping operation in Bosnia in 1995, although the latter occurred not to stop human rights abuses, but to maintain a peace treaty that had stopped the killing.

39. Martha Finnemore, *The Purpose of Intervention: Changing Beliefs about the Use of Force* (Ithaca: Cornell University Press), 21.

40. Spain's attempt to extradite and try Chilean dictator Augusto Pinochet for human rights crimes committed during his 17-year rule as president decades earlier is perhaps the most dramatic refutation of the sovereignty norm, but the practice now occurs throughout the world. See: Tyche Hendricks, "Ex-Salvadoran officer ruled liable in killing of archbishop in 1980," *San Francisco Chronicle*, September 4, 2004, http://www.sfgate.com/cgibin/article.cgi?file=/chronicle/archive/2004/09/04/ BAG6H8JUL11.DTL.

41. Barney Jopson and Meghan Murphy, "Bashir Charged with Darfur Genocide," *Financial Times*, July 15, 2008, 4.

42. On Darfur, see: The Enough Project, http://www.enoughproject.org; On North Korea. See: U.S. Committee for Human Rights in North Korea and DLA Piper, *Failure to Protect: A Call for the UN Security Council to Act in North Korea* (Washington: October 2006). See: Jack Goldsmith and Stephen Krasner, "The Limits of Idealism," *Daedalus* 132 (2003), 47-63.

43. European Political Cooperation, "Statement by the Twelve on Human Rights," Brussels, July 21, 1986.

44. European Council, "A Secure Europe in a Better World: European Security Strategy," December 12, 2003, http://www.consilium.europa.eu/uedocs/cmsUpload/78367.pdf.

45. "Declaration of Principles for International Election Observation and Code of Conduct for International Election Observers," Commemorated October 27, 2005, at the United Nations, New York, http://www.cartercenter.org/documents/2231.pdf. OSCE/ODIHR, *Guidelines on Freedom of Peaceful Assembly* (Warsaw: OSCE/ODIHR, 2007). International Center for Non-for-Profit Law and the World Movement for Democracy Secretariat at the National Endowment for Democracy, *Defending Civil Society: A Report of the World Movement for Democracy* (Washington: NED, February 2008). National Democratic Institute, *Minimum Standards for Democratic Functioning of Political Parties* (Washington: NDI, 2008).

46. In the case of Haiti, the Security Council directly authorized the intervention (U.N. Security Council Resolution 940, 1994). In the case of Sierra Leone, the Security Council commended ECOWAS's intervention post hoc and endorsed it (U.N. Security Council Resolution 1162, 1998).

47. Peter Ackerman and Michael J. Glennon, "The Right Side of the Law," *The American Interest* 3:1 (2007), http://www.the-american-interest.com/ai2/article.cfm?Id=324&MId=15.

48. For elaboration, see: Charles Sampford and Margaret Palmer, "The Theory of Collective Response," in *Protecting Democracy: International Responses*, eds. Morton

Halperin and Mirna Galic (New York: Lexington Books, 2005), 23-62. Frank, "The Emerging Right to Democratic Governance."

49. To be sure, there will be certain extraordinary instances in which complete transparency would inhibit democratic development rather than foster it. In such cases, both donors and NGOs should follow some norms, rules, and procedures that would help to legitimate these rare cases.

50. Peter Ackerman and Michael J. Glennon, "The Right Side of the Law," *The American Interest*, Vol. 3, No. 1 (September-October 2007), http://www.the-american-interest.com/ai2/article.cfm?Id=324&MId=15 (accessed October 2, 2007).

51. For elaboration, see Charles Sampford and Margaret Palmer, "The Theory of Collective Response," in Morton Halperin and Mirna Galic, eds., *Protecting Democracy: International Responses* (New York: Lexington Books, 2005), pp. 23-62; and Thomas Franck, "The Emerging Right to Democratic Governance," *The American Journal of International Law*, Vol. 86, No. 1 (January 1992), pp. 46-91.

52. To be sure, there will be certain extraordinary instances in which complete transparency would inhibit democratic development rather than foster it. In such cases, both donors and NGOs should follow some norms, rules, and procedures that would help to legitimate these rare cases.

Index